THE ART OF CONFLICT PREVENTION

BRASSEY'S ATLANTIC COMMENTARIES

Series Editor: Eric Grove

Atlantic Commentaries present a series of introductory surveys of important issues affecting the Atlantic Alliance and its future. The booklets are written and edited with the general reader as well as the specialist in mind. Topics include regional security issues, political and economic issues, country studies and future perspectives for international stability in the changing political environment of the 1990s.

Brassey's Atlantic Commentaries are produced in association with the NATO Office of Information and Press and various national Atlantic Committees or other associations and Institutions concerned with different aspects of security. The opinions expressed are the responsibility of the editors and the contributors and do not necessarily represent the official views of NATO or of individual governments.

Brassey's Atlantic Commentaries

NATO's Defence of the North
ERIC GROVE

The Western European Union and NATO
ALFRED CAHEN

NATO 2000
JAMIE SHEA

From Detente to Entente
MARK EYSKENS

Global Security
ERIC GROVE

NATO's Reserve Forces
SJOUKE DE JONG

BRASSEY'S ATLANTIC COMMENTARIES No. 7

THE ART OF CONFLICT PREVENTION

Compiled and edited by Werner Bauwens and Luc Reychler
with contributions by Luise Drüke, Heinz Vetschera,
John Barrett, Stephan Keukeleire and Eric Remacle

Associate Editors:
Bryan Watkins and Nicholas Sherwen

BRASSEY'S
LONDON · NEW YORK

First English edition 1994.

UK editorial offices: Brassey's, 33 John Street, London WC1N 2AT
orders: Marston Book Services, PO Box 87, Oxford OX2 0DT
USA editorial offices: Brassey's, 8000 Westpark Drive, First Floor, McLean, VA 22102
orders: Macmillan Publishing Company, Front and Brown Streets, Riverside, NJ 08075

Distributed in North America to booksellers and wholesalers by the Macmillan Publishing Company, NY 10022

Library of Congress Cataloging in Publication Data
available

British Library Cataloguing in Publication Data
A catalogue record for this book is
available from the British Library

ISBN 85753 105 1

Photoset in North Wales by
Derek Doyle & Associates, Mold, Clwyd.
Printed in Great Britain by BPC Wheatons Ltd, Exeter

Contents

Acknowledgements

'The Art of Conflict Prevention' is an ambitious project, initiated in June 1992 by Werner Bauwens, which examines the whole field of peacekeeping, peacebuilding, peace-enforcement and the need for early warning of impending conflicts as applicable to the UN, CSCE, NATO, EU, and WEU. It examines the theory and practice of conflict prevention and the organisation at the international level which is the prerequisite for its success.

The Editors are indebted to the individual authors for the high quality of their research and analysis and are confident that the collected articles will be seen to represent a unique and timely contribution to the study of this developing field of multilateral diplomacy and decision-making. They would also like to record their gratitude to the Joint Managing Director and Publishing Director at Brassey's (UK) Ltd, Jenny Shaw, and to the Publishing Editor, Bryan Watkins, for their constant encouragement, professional advice and attention to detail which have played a major role in shaping this book.

About the Contributors

Luc Reychler (PhD Harvard University, 1976) is professor of international relations, peace research and strategic studies at the University of Leuven. He is the author of several books on diplomatic thinking, European security and the dynamics of international conflict. His most recent book is *Een onvoltooid belied: De Belgische buitenlandse en defensiepolitiek 1830–2015* (1993). From 1989 to 1992 he served as advisor to the Belgian Minister of Foreign Affairs.

Luise Drüke is Senior European Affairs Officer in the Regional Office of the UN High Commissioner for Refugees (UNHCR) to the European Institutions, Brussels. She has degrees in German Philology, Political Sciences, Economics, Finance and Management, and Public Administration from the Universities of Paris VIII, Hannover, Webster and Harvard and a PhD in Political Sciences from the University of Hannover. A Programme and Management Officer and Deputy Regional Representative in various positions in the UNHCR since 1977, she has lectured widely and is author of numerous books and articles on refugee policy, conflict prevention and humanitarian issues.

Heinz Vetschera (LLD Vienna University 1971; PhD Vienna University, 1974) is researcher and analyst for international law and security policy affairs with the Austrian Ministry of Defence and lecturer on international relations with the University of Vienna, currently serving with the CSCE Conflict Prevention Centre. He has published books and articles on arms control, European security and international law. His most recent publication is *Die Rolle der KSZE als Enrichtung kooperativer Sicherheitspolitik im Rahmen des Interlocking Institutions – Konzepts (1993)*.

John Barrett is Head of Policy Planning in the Political Affairs Division of NATO. A graduate of the University of Toronto (MA) and the London School of Economics (PhD in International Relations). He undertook further research at the University of Tübingen and the Institute of International Relations, at the University of British Columbia, Vancouver. He was formerly Deputy Director of the Centre for Arms Control and Disarmament, Ottawa and Policy Officer for Arms Control and International Security Affairs in the Department of External Affairs of the Canadian Government.

Stephan Keukeleire is a lecturer at EHSAL (Brussels) and researcher at the International Relations Section of the Politics Department of the University of Leuven. His publications include *Time and Tide Wait for No Man: The Changing European Geopolitical Landscape* (Praeger, 1991), *The European Security Architecture: The Role of the EC* (Studia Diplomatica 1991/6), *Franco-German Security Cooperation* in E Kirchner & J C Sperling (ed), *The FRG and NATO* (Macmillan, 1992).

Eric Remacle is Lecturer in Political Science at the Free University of Brussels (ULB) where he collaborates with the Centre for the Study of International and Strategic Relations (CERIS) and the Institute for European Studies. He has a masters degree in International Politics and is preparing a PhD in Political Science on the WEU and European defence. He has published *inter alia* the essay *Esquisse pour un nouveau paysage européen* (UNIDIR, New York, 1990).

Werner Bauwens (LLM Leuven University 1979, SAIS Bologna Centre 1980) joined NATO's International Staff in 1991. From 1981 till 1991 he worked at the Political Affairs Directorate of the Belgian Ministry of Foreign Affairs, dealing in particular with the Conference on Security and Cooperation in Europe and with European Political Cooperation. He has headed Belgian missions to CSCE Meetings (i.e. Peaceful Settlement of Disputes, Human Rights) and has contributed articles on CSCE to several magazines.

Nicholas Sherwen is Head of Publications in NATO's Office of Information and Press. He has a Joint Honours degree in Modern Languages (University of Bradford) and has been a teacher and lecturer in languages, international institutions and security issues. A member of the International Staff of NATO from 1973, he has edited and published many reference books, articles and discussion papers on NATO and related issues. Publications include *The North Atlantic Treaty Organisation Facts and Figures* (editions of 1981, 1984 and 1989); *The NATO Handbook* (successive editions); *NATO's Anxious Birth* (1985); *From Detente to Entente, NATO 2000*, and other Atlantic Commentaries; and *NATO: A Model for International Cooperation*.

Bryan Watkins has been the House Editor at Brassey's since 1986, having previously been Editor of the British Army Review for 12 years. A career officer in the British Army, he has published articles in a number of leading military journals since the 1950s. A former Instructor at the British Army Staff College, he is a graduate of the Imperial Defence College and a past Council Member of the Royal United Services Institute for Defence Studies, where he chaired the Studies and Publications Advisory Committee.

Glossary

ACC	Administrative Coordinating Committee (UN)
ACE	Allied Command Europe (NATO)
ASEAN	Association of South East Asian States
AWACS	Advanced Warning and Control System (aircraft)
CBM	Confidence-Building Measures (CSCE)
CC	Consultative Committee (CSCE)
CFE	Conventional Armed Forces in Europe (Treaty)
CFSP	Common Foreign and Security Policy (EC)
CIG	Current Intelligence Group (NAC)
CINCHAN	Commander-in-Chief Channel (NATO)
CIS	Commonwealth of Independent States
COEC	Council Operations and Exercise Committee (NATO)
COMUN-PROFOR	Commander United Nations Protection Force (former Yugoslavia)
COREPER	Committee of Permanent Representatives (EC)
COREU	Correspendence Européenne (EC)
CP	Conflict Prevention
CPC	Conflict Prevention Centre (CSCE)
CSBM	Confidence and Security-Building Measures (CSCE)
CSCE	Conference on Security and Cooperation in Europe
CSO	Committee of Senior Officials (CSCE)
DEISA	Department of Economic and International Affairs (UN)
DPC	Defence Planning Committee (NAC)

EC	European Community
ECOWAS	Peacekeeping and Enforcement in West Africa
ECSC	European Steel and Coal Community
EEC	European Economic Community
EP	European Parliament
EPC	European Political Cooperation
EUMIL-SATCO	European Military Satellite Communications
FAO	Food and Agricultural Organisation
GDR	German Democratic Republic (former)
GIEW	Global Information and Early Warning Service
IGC	Intergovernmental Conference (EC)
IGO	International Governmental Organisation
INF	Intermediate Range Nuclear Forces (Treaty)
INGO	International Non-Government Organisation
JIU	Joint Inspection Unit (UN)
MBFR	Mutual Balanced Forces Reductions
MEP	Member of the European Parliament
MINURSOR	UN Mission for the Referendum in Western Sahara
N & NA	Neutral and Non-Aligned (States)
NAC	North Atlantic Council
NACC	North Atlantic Cooperation Council
NAEWS	NATO Airborne Early Warning System
NATO	North Atlantic Treaty Organisation
NICS	NATO Integrated Communications System
NORTHAG	Northern Army Group (NATO)
OAS	Organisation of American States
OAU	Organisation of African Unity
ODIHR	Office for Democratic Institutions and Human Rights (CSCE)

OFE	Office for Free Elections (CSCE)
ONUCA	UN Observer Group in Central America
ONUSAL	UN Observer Mission in El Salvador
ORCI	Office for the Research and Collection of Information (UN)
PSCA	Department of Political and Security Council Affairs (UN)
SACLANI	Supreme Allied Commander Atlantic (NATO)
SEA	Single European Act
SITCEN	Situation Centre (NATO)
STANAV-FORLANT	Standing Naval Force Atlantic (NATO)
STANAV-FORMED	Standing Naval Force Mediterranean (NATO)
SWAPO	South West African Peoples Organisation
Troika	CSCE body consisting of the Chairman-in-Office, his predecessor and the succeeding Chairman
UMA	Unusual Military Activities
UNAMIC	UN Advanced Mission in Cambodia
UNAVEM	UN Angola Verification Mission
UNDOF	UN Disengagement Observer Force (Syria/Israel Border)
UNFICYP	UN Peacekeeping Force Cyprus
UNHCR	UN High Commissioner for Refugees
UNIFIL	UN Interim Force in Lebanon
UNIKOM	UN Iraq-Kuwait Observer Mission
UNMOGIP	UN Observer Group in India and Pakistan
UNOSOM	UN Peacebuilding Operation Somalia
UNPROFOR	UN Protection Force (former Yugoslavia)
UNSO	UN Statistical Office
UNTAC	UN Transitional Authority Cambodia
UNTAG	UN Transition Assistance Group Namibia
UNTC	UN Training Centre

UNTSO	UN Truce Organisation
WEU	Western European Union
WEUCOM	Western European Union Communication System
WTO	Warsaw Treaty Organisation (former)

1

The Art of Conflict Prevention: Theory and Practice

Luc Reychler

At different international organizations, such as the UN, the CSCE, NATO, and the EC-WEU, efforts are being made to improve their conflict prevention facilities. In academic circles, research data about crisis prevention and management, preventive diplomacy and other studies related to the prevention of unwanted escalation of conflicts are being reviewed and new research projects set up. Conflict prevention (CP) is in again. This proactive approach to conflict has been enhanced by recent positive and negative experiences.

The Gulf War and the Yugoslavian civil war have destroyed the initial peace-euphoria of the Post-Cold War period. Instead, we have found ourselves with an increasing number of conflicts. Many have been unforeseen; they have escalated faster than expected and rapidly became internationalized. Furthermore we have not been equipped to handle them effectively. Euphoria has been replaced by the expectation that large-scale violence will be part of the European scene because internal instability is likely to persist for at least the next generation, in Central and Eastern Europe, and probably even longer (J. Goodby, p. 154 (see Sources)). The *Sarajevo* effect or the fear of becoming entangled in ethnic and nationalist disputes, has rekindled interest in the prevention of destructive conflicts.

Equally important has been the high cost of peacekeeping and peace enforcement after conflicts have escalated. The Gulf War, measured in direct outlays for military expenditure, cost fifty billion dollars. The budget for two days of 'Operation Desert Storm' would have paid for all UN peacekeeping operations worldwide for a year. The former has not been challenged; the latter remains a chronic problem.

Another criticism is that peacekeeping without peacemaking frequently leads to a 'peaceful perpetuation' of disputes. (S Ryan, p. 141; J Boulden, p. 12–14). The presence of the Blue Helmets and the resulting diffusion of the crisis may ease the sense of urgency felt by the parties to resolve the dispute. They may find it in their interests to perpetuate the peacekeeping presence. Finally, there is a growing awareness of the fact that the management of conflicts after they have escalated is much more difficult. Feelings of hatred and frustration tend to protract them and require increased effort to bring them to a satisfactory conclusion (E Azar).

The discussion of conflict prevention is part of a search for a more cost-effective security organisation. A major lesson of recent experience is that 'one ounce of prevention is far better than a ton of delayed intervention'. Another lesson, following from the great transformation of 1989–1990, is that preventive conflict management has become a feasible option.

A SENSIBLE CONCEPT IN POST-COLD WAR DIPLOMACY

Conflict prevention has become a key concept in the discussion of Europe's new security and peace organization. The semi-permanent battleground of Yugoslavia has taught us that Europe and the United States should be better prepared next time. As long as Central and Eastern Europe remain relatively unstable, incidents may occur that will become threats to European peace and security (J Goodby, p. 155). Despite the prevailing view that there is an urgent need for better conflict prevention the concept remains a sensitive one and has not been spared from criticism. The reservations expressed, are not addressed to the aims, but to the ways and means of implementation.

One source of criticism is those people who tend to associate conflict prevention with the creation of a *collective security system*. They are concerned not only with its feasibility but also its desirability. There is the fear of being dragged into war whenever and wherever aggression occurs. There is also a concern about the loss of national sovereignty. The latter, however, could be alleviated by a looser collective security system in which no automatic and binding commitments would be made, and cooperation would be judged on a case by case basis (see Chapter 5: The NATO Approach). These people also do not expect the preconditions to be realized that must be present if a collective security organization is to take shape and function effectively. They believe that whilst the international moral-political climate has improved, it is as yet far from being sufficiently developed for a collective security system to function successfully. National self-interests are still far from being equated with the concept of the welfare and stability of the international community.

A second source of cricitism lies in those who associate conflict prevention with *domestic interference and intervention*, including military intervention for humanitarian or security reasons. These people protest at the undermining of the principles of non-intervention and sovereignty. Many regimes from Third World countries, for example, believe that they are most vulnerable to collective sanctions and fear that the major powers would misuse intervention to further their own selfish interests (B Buzan). The last source of criticism is those people who associate the concept of conflict prevention with the possible *use of military force* to keep or restore peace. They fear a military interpretation of the idea of conflict prevention.

All these reservations and criticisms make it clear that conflict prevention is one of those things that are easier said than done.

A CONCEPTUAL FRAMEWORK OF ANALYSIS

Conflict management and prevention

In confronting the prospect of increased demands for conflict prevention, it is useful to define the terms and to outline a typology of instruments for preventing unwanted escalation. This is necessary, because the field of study is characterised by a great deal of conceptual confusion. Of course one should keep in mind that the following definitions and typologies are intellectual creations to highlight policy issues rather than neat depictions of reality. The term *conflict prevention* refers to a particular kind of conflict management, which can be distinguished from *conflict avoidance* and *conflict resolution* (C Mitchell). Efforts to avoid the development of contentious issues and the incompatibility of goals are called *conflict avoidance*; and measures which contribute to the prevention of undesirable conflict behaviour once some situation involving goal incompatibility has arisen, fall under the heading of *conflict prevention*; and any activated at the stage when a conflict involves incompatible goals, hostile attitudes and disruptive behaviour *conflict settlement* or in special cases *conflict resolution*. The concept of 'conflict prevention' refers to two types of effort; those which prevent behaviour defined within the relevant international system as undesirable, and those which attempt to confine conflict behaviour within clearly defined limits of permissible activity. The concept is not new. Older terms such as preventive diplomacy, crisis-prevention or deterrent diplomacy all refer to similar efforts.

A typology of conflict prevention measures

The development of a typology of conflict prevention measures requires an understanding of the causes of war and peace. These causes can be clustered into three groups of factors, the first related to the conflict itself, the second to opportunity structure and the third to the decision-making process (L Reychler).

Measures dealing with the conflict

To prevent a conflict from escalating, one can deal with the conflict itself and take measures either to avoid the development of contentious issues and goal incompatibilities or after they have arisen. One can take measures to remove the source of the conflict, through some form of settlement or by resolution of the conflict itself. Each type of conflict requires a different remedy. If it is a facts-based conflict or a disagreement over 'what is', it could be solved by an exchange of information, an increase in military transparency and a more effective set of verification agreements. If it is an interest-based conflict or a disagreement over who will get what in the distribution of scarce resources (e.g. power, territory, economic benefits or respect), it could be managed constructively through peacemaking and peacebuilding efforts.

Peacemaking is concerned with the search for a negotiated resolution of the perceived conflicts of interest between the parties. Three groups of peacemaking methods can be distinguished (S Ryan). The first method is to try to impose a solution either through violence or through power. The second method relies on judicial settlement of disputes. The problems with the use of violence and power and the inappropriateness of recourse to the legal instrument, however, have led many to regard negotiation as the best method of conflict settlement or resolution. Negotiation can be subdivided into two broad categories. The first contains the traditional diplomatic instruments such as negotiation, good office, mediation, enquiry, conciliation and arbitration (R Riggs & J Plano, p. 186–7). Criticism of the conventional methods led to the development of a whole series of alternative methods for dispute resolution. These methods focus a great deal of attention on the process of interaction rather than on the content of the negotiated positions. Exemplary in this field is the work of R Fisher, who works with the Harvard Negotiations Project, and the workshop approach of J Burton, further developed by E Azar and H Kelman. These all believe that conflict managers should not wait until a conflict is ripe for negotiation. Instead they hold that a Track Two non-governmental type of diplomacy should be utilised, designed to establish a pre-negotiation stage in which analytical 'breakthroughs' by the conflicting parties themselves are encouraged. E Azar found that this process tended to create conditions enabling the introduction of other components of conflict management such as strategies for economic development and political institution building. This brings us to 'peacebuilding'. This term refers to a strategy which tries to avoid or resolve conflicts through measures of an attitudinal, socio-economic and political nature. Whereas peacekeeping is about building barriers between the armed groups, peacebuilding strategies involve greater inter-party contact. Peacebuilding tries to build bridges between people. It tries to avoid or reduce conflict escalation through contact plus forgiveness, contact plus the pursuit of superordinate goals, contact plus confidence building, and contact plus education for mutual understanding (S Ryan). Peacebuilding also advocates development diplomacy. The latter aims at reducing the socio-economic

dealing with CONFLICT	*peacemaking*	–imposing a solution through coercion	
		–judicial dispute settlement	
		–negotiation	–traditional methods
			–alternative methods
	peacebuilding	–attitudinal	
		–socio-economic measures	
		–political	–monitoring elections
			–strengthening democratisation process
			–human rights
Dealing with OPPORTUNITY STRUCTURE	*measures of a non-military nature*	–political-diplomatic	
		–legal	
		–economic	
		–informative-educational	
		–normative-ideological	
	military measures	–nuclear deterrence	
		–collective security system	
		–collective defense system	
		–arms control	
		–CSBM's	
		–peace enforcement	
		–peacekeeping	
Dealing with DECISION-MAKING	–reducing misperceptions		
	–creating a less cumbersome decision-making system		
	–searching for better CP strategies		

Table 1.1 Typology of Conflict Prevention Measures

deprivation and at building responsive political institutions. It requires an investment in the human rights of individuals and minorities, political democratisation and socio-economic development.

Measures dealing with the opportunity structure

To prevent a conflict from escalating, one can also deal with the power available to the conflicting parties and the factors which constrain or allow its use. A first distinction can be made between military and non-military measures. The latter involve measures of a political-diplomatic, legal, economic, informative-educational and moral-ideological nature. For example, a country or group of countries could threaten to close diplomatic posts, the Security Council could delegitimize certain kinds of behaviour, the International Court of Justice could decide against a party, an economic boycott could be implemented, violations of international law could be exposed to world opinion; a moral authority could promote a liberation theology and thereby disapprove of the neglect of human rights. Among the military measures used to prevent conflicts one can distinguish: nuclear deterrence, balance of power, collective security systems, arms control, Confidence and Security Building Measures (CSBM's), peace enforcement and peacekeeping. With respect to the recent violence in Europe, a great deal of attention has been given to peacekeeping and peace enforcement. *Peacekeeping* forces are used in situations where a cease-fire has been established and when the main parties to the conflict want help in preserving an unstable peace. They carry light arms and their mission can be compared to that of police forces. *Peace enforcement* is used in situations in which violence is still raging. The purpose is to impose peace. For such an operation, well equipped units are necessary and their mission is comparable to that of a military campaign. To cope with the conflict in Yugoslavia, the international community has made use of peacekeeping operations. Peacekeeping forces could be used for different missions: to carry out humanitarian functions, such as organizing shipments of food and medicine under hazardous conditions, to observe a situation that contains some risk of conflict, to patrol borders or other sensitive areas, to establish a buffer zone between adversarial military forces and to protect enclaves of ethnic minorities (J Goodby, p. 166). The preconditions for using peacekeeping are very strict. Brian Urquhart notes that over the years, agreement has been established on the following seven interconnected preconditions for successful peacekeeping missions:

- the consent of the parties involved;
- the continuing and strong support by the mandating authority, the Security Council;
- a clear and practicable mandate;
- maintenance of strict neutrality;
- the non-use of force except in the last resort of self-defence, including resistance to attempts by forceful means to prevent the peacekeepers from carrying out their duties;
- the willingness of troop-contributing countries to provide adequate numbers of capable military personnel and to accept the degree of risk which the mandate and the situation demand;
- the will of the member states, and especially of the permanent members of the Security Council, to make available the necessary financial and logistical support.

The reluctance of some EC nations to authorize the use of peacekeeping forces in Yugoslavia under conditions of an unstable peace considerably inhibits an effective use of peacekeeping. This 'eighth-precondition' allows the most irresponsible forces in the conflict to determine the use or non-use of peacekeeping forces. This seems to be a very irresponsible way of managing post Cold War crises in Europe.

Measures dealing with decision-making

These measures help the decision makers manage conflicts more constructively by:

- Reducing misperceptions. A great deal of research has been done on the role of misperception in conflict behaviour. For example, the studies of decision making under crisis (e.g. D Frei, G Hopple and I Janis) are very useful. The decision makers could use these findings to improve their conflict management skills. Also important is the availability of specialised and realtime information and early warning facilities. Recent history has taught us that we are not very good at forecasting conflict behaviour. To a great extent this can be accounted for by a lack of institutionalized forecasting (Y Laulan) and an inadequate understanding of conflict dynamics. Realistic means should be devised to help governments, with respect to Yugoslavia, for example, to assess the risks of a limited use of force compared to the risks involved either in a major escalation of force or in not using force at all (J Goodby, p. 165).

- Providing them with a less cumbersome decision-making system which makes it possible to respond more effectively. The CSCE 'unanimity minus one' voting rule is an improvement but leaves the organization structurally impaired as a credible crisis manager. Some interesting suggestions to recast the CSCE and to balance the need to reflect power realities with the need to foster consensus have been made by Charles and Clifford Kupchan. Equally interesting are the proposals made by Thomas Boudreau regarding the establishment of an adequate global communication system and regarding the use of satellite diplomacy.
- By searching for better strategies to prevent unwanted conflict behaviour. Conflict managers should be provided with a wider set of options, including assessments of anticipated costs and benefits.
- The need for a comprehensive conflict prevention strategy.

The inter-relationships among the three above mentioned conflict-prevention strategies are very important. All three strategies tend to be essential for effective conflict resolution. Ineffective peacekeeping or enforcement can seriously hamper the peacemaking or peacebuilding process. Any group wishing to sabotage peace efforts will find it easier to provoke armed clashes, increase the number of martyrs for the next generation and provide all the requirements for a conflict to become a protracted one. If peacemaking and peacekeeping efforts are made without adequate peacebuilding, people will be left out of the peace process. If decision makers exceed the limits of people's tolerance they may lose their support and be forced to abandon their peace efforts. Peacekeeping can discourage violence but cannot by itself build the foundations of an enduring peace. Peacekeeping can buy time but it cannot settle or resolve anything (J Blodgett). Conflict prevention requires a comprehensive strategy. Reducing conflict prevention to mere peacekeeping missions or new negotiation efforts will not do. What is needed is a package of conflict prevention measures and a much better coordination between the conflict-managing organizations.

EVALUATION

During the past few years, at various levels, (UNO, CSCE, NATO, EC-WEU), we have noticed serious efforts on the part of these organizations to evaluate and adapt their respective security strategies and organizations to the new strategic environment. These efforts, however, have not been translated into a successful handling of some of the new challenges. The historic opportunity to replace the old bipolar security organization by a Security Community stretching from Vancouver to Vladivostok is slipping through our fingers. Several ethnic and nationalist conflicts have turned into bloody civil wars. Of course, there have also been successes, for example, those scored by the new generation of peacekeeping operations in Central America, Namibia, Cambodia and the Western Sahara. But on the whole much more will have to be done to prevent international conflicts more effectively.

The state of the art of conflict prevention could be rated on a set of scales of factors which are expected either to inhibit or enhance conflict prevention.

Lack of interest or Common interest

The interests of a majority of CSCE countries seem to be limited to containing the Yugoslav conflict within its boundaries and to preventing a possible spill-over into neighbouring regions. For many people the conflict is 'far away from their bed'. For them, the European House does not extend from San Francisco to Vladivostok.

The 'we-ness' feeling of many Western Europeans does not seem to reach far beyond their Little Europe. They do not consider peace to be indivisible beyond these subjective boundaries. The other Europeans have their hands full with their own domestic problems. Detracting attention from this conflict are the chronically overloaded diplomatic agendas. Equally responsible is the weakly developed strategic culture in Europe. The past 40 years, characterised by an unusual stability and dependence on the Superpowers seem to have retarded the development of a European strategic culture. In some small countries this underdevelopment has been reinforced by the existence of 'small power fatalism' and a strong moral-legal approach to international politics. This weak strategic culture embraces several illusions: for example, the illusion that peace has broken out and that the peace dividend can be used for domestic purposes; or the illusion of distance, or the feeling that one should not be too concerned with faraway conflicts; and, finally, the illusion of time, or the belief that important decisions can be postponed to the distant future.

Lack of foresight or Early warning

Many of the recent upheavals in international relations have been political surprises. Think of the 'velvet revolutions' in Eastern Europe, the Persian Gulf War, the rapid escalation of the ethnic conflicts in Yugoslavia, and the growing tensions between nations and states. It is not only the lack of foresight that is problematic, but also the complacency of the professional diplomats, the diplomatic correspondents and the academics about these matters. The model diplomat tends to be more interested in facts than in probabilities. Few State Departments have effective Planning Offices that do anything more than writing speeches for the Minister of Foreign Affairs. Political forecasting and contingency planning is far from being institutionalized. All this is unacceptable for two reasons. First, because the future will inevitably produce less attractive scenarios and confront us with new crises and threats and historical opportunities could also be more easily overlooked. Second, because such an attitude will not enhance the development of preventive diplomacy or more effective conflict prevention. Several explanations could be given for the failure to anticipate major developments in international relations (L Reychler, 1992). The traditional explanations attribute the lack of foresight in international politics to the state of the art of the science of international relations, including conflict dynamics, and to the lack of good intelligence. A comprehensive explanation, however, should also include: the general lack of interest; cognitive biases; societal and epistemic pressures, and a neglect of the power of public opinion. Among the cognitive biases, there is for example the propensity to treat the future as an extension of the past and as a gradual process. This is psychologically more comforting than living with an uncertain future. Under the heading of societal and epistemic pressures, one can distinguish; (1) the existence of myths and taboos; (2) the short-term attention span of democracies, and (3) the disinformation spread by pressure groups. During the Cold War there were myths about 'the irreversibility of communism', the 'domino effect', and the 'convergence between capitalism and communism', etc. One of the major causes of the many surprises in international affairs, however, is the relative neglect of the opinions of the common people. In Eastern Europe, for example, not enough attention was given to the development of the post-totalitarian mind. According to J Goldfarb, the development of these changes in the public opinion preceded the political and institutional changes. To anticipate developments in the Arab world, research should now be undertaken relating to the development of the post-fundamentalist mind. In addition, a better understanding of the revolutionary thresholds of the people would give us better insight into the dynamics of conflict.

Propensity to react or Propensity to proact

International organizations are often reactive institutions. Getting their attention seems to require a certain quantity of blood. This attracts cameras, and then the journalists and researchers wake up, when the media appeal to their 'instant expertise'. In most universities practically no attention is being given to the development of future-oriented thinking. Most national and international governmental organizations seem to suffer from a bureaucratisation of the art of diplomacy. Encountering unfamiliar problems such as the fighting in Yugoslavia, they shrink from taking resolute action. With respect to this slow reactive approach, Winston Churchill made the following commentary: 'We shall see how the counsels of prudence and restraint may become the prime agents of mortal danger; how the middle course adopted from desires for safety and a quiet life may be found to lead directly to the bull's-eye of disaster. We shall see how absolute is the need of a broad path of international action pursued by many states in common across the years, irrespective of the ebb and flow of national politics' (J Goodby, p. 165). Somewhat related to this strong propensity to evade risks is the general inclination to wait for disputes to 'ripen' before attempting a resolution (R Haas). Reactive conflict management is enhanced by the competitive political environment of democratic systems. The use of peacekeeping or peace enforcement creates openings for the opposition factions. Hence, prior to risking the domestic costs of people being killed in peace operations, democratic elites require more than the assumption of a potential future threat. Driven by the will to stay in power, incumbents tend to insist on evidence of a clear and present danger and usually require several provocations. The low cost tolerance of the public also contributes to the political exhaustion and isolationism that often afflict democratic states (R Schweller). 'Europeans, and Americans too, repeatedly made the tactical mistake of advertising their reluctance to engage in military action. Their purpose presumably was to assure the public that no adventures and no heavy costs were in store' (S Rosenfeld).

Traditional diplomacy or New diplomacy

Several characteristics of traditional diplomacy tend to inhibit an effective prevention of the escalation of ethnic and nationalist disputes. First, traditional diplomacy draws a sharp distinction between civil wars, in which no external power is supposed to interfere, and international conflicts which are the concern of all states. Civil war will only pose a threat when it spills over the boundaries or when major powers become involved. For them, the right approach is to isolate or quarantine the warzone. This is the logic of real politik. Related to this is the overriding concern with the principles of sovereignty and non-intervention. There is the insistence on their 'sovereign equality' and on the 'one-state one-vote' principle or the fiction that all states are equal and each state should have one vote. The new diplomatic thinking, on the other hand, is well aware of the complex interaction between internal and external conflict management and considers certain kinds of intervention necessary for realising a stable international peace (A Henrikson). Second, traditional diplomacy tends to reduce conflict prevention to the employment of the familiar methods of peacemaking and/or peacekeeping and enforcement.

In contrast to this reductionism, the new diplomacy stresses the importance of a comprehensive peace strategy, including peacekeeping, peacemaking and peacebuilding measures. Third, the traditionalists are not acquainted with the battery of new conflict management techniques.

Lack of consensus or Strong consensus

The prevention of the nationalist conflicts in Yugoslavia was seriously hampered by a lack of consensus among the major third party powers involved. The negotiation efforts of the European Community were weakened by contradictory signals sent by the member states. In contrast to the other eleven member states, Germany opted for an early recognition of Slovenia and Croatia. The German pledge that unsuccessful negotiations would result in recognition stimulated the parties who wanted independence to ensure failure. The US assumed a very low profile and warned the twelve members of the European Community that premature and selective recognition would damage prospects of peace and lead to greater bloodshed. Russia opposed the expulsion of Yugoslavia from the Conference on Cooperation and Security in Europe.

Cumbersome decision-making or Effective decision-making

The prevention of the Yugoslav conflict was inhibited not only by the overloaded domestic and diplomatic agenda of third parties, but also by the cumbersome methods for reaching decisions within the international organizations involved. The CSCE mechanism for the peaceful settlement of disputes has not so far proved to be fit for its task. Changes in the methods of reaching decisions are needed, probably including a qualified majority vote under clearly defined conditions or the creation of a European security council. The CSCE 'unanimity minus one' principle is still too cumbersome. Only a smaller body which is more genuinely representative of the order of power within the international system can exercise a greater influence on the actions of states. The UN debate on the Yugoslav conflict in November 1991 showed that non-European members are prepared to obstruct peacekeeping operations for reasons having nothing to do with Europe. This is certainly one sound reason for developing a regional peacekeeping machinery in Europe (J Goodby, p. 168). A second problem hindering international organizations from being more effective in fast-moving crisis situations is the element of competition between international organizations and the lack of a clear division of operational responsibilities between them.

Lack of infrastructure or Adequate infrastructure

Effective conflict management is impaired not only by the cumbersome decision-making procedures of the international organizations involved, but also by the near absence of contingency planning. Contingency planning within and between the UN, NATO, EC-WEU, and the CSCE Conflict Prevention Centre should be authorized so that governments have a better grasp of the issues to be decided if they, for example, are ever to authorize military force in crisis situations (J Goodby, p. 166).

Equally important is the availability, on short notice, of adequate peacemaking, peacekeeping and peacebuilding facilities.

An asset for Europe would be the constitution of a permanent Rapid-Response Peace Force that could be used for peacekeeping or peace enforcement. B. Urquhart's suggestion to equip peacekeeping operations or other forms of preventive action with a trip-wire clause is also to be recommended. If the peaceful settlement of dispute measures provided under Chapter VI prove to be of no avail, then under certain circumstances an automatic transition to Chapter VII type action would be allowed. With such a clause, preventive action and deterrence might begin to have more effect (B Urquhart, 1990).

SUGGESTIONS

Scanning the literature, one finds a plethora of conflict prevention suggestions. To improve the state of the art in Europe, measures could be taken to advance:

Common security thinking

A strengthening of 'common security' thinking requires the development of a European strategic culture and an extension of a 'We-ness' feeling throughout the whole of Europe. A better understanding of the impact of the geopolitical trends on Europe's security would serve to strengthen the Pan-European identity (B Buzan). A clear strategic insight would make people understand that the creation of a Pan-European Security Community would provide them, from the military point of view, with the most cost-effective security organization. They would also realize that this kind of security requires serious investments of a military and, even more so, of a non-military nature (L Reychler, 1991).

Early warning

The installation of early warning systems stands high on the agenda of conflict prevention. Many concrete suggestions are also found here. To enable the UN Secretary General to exercise his preventive role effectively, T Boudreau requests the installation of adequate global communications. R Johanson pleads for an international monitoring agency, under the auspices of the UN, to detect violations of arms control agreements. J Jonah stresses a strengthening of the UN Office for Research and the Collection of Information (ORCI). But in any case a successful early warning system will require more 'intelligence sharing'. Efforts will also have to be made to eliminate the factors which impede political forecasting. Commendable would be an institutionalization of forecasting in the foreign policy making process, and a fundamental research of the international conflict dynamics.

Proactive policy-making

Proactive policy-making could be enhanced by the authorization of contingency planning. High powered analysts would plan not only for a single, but also for a range of possible futures (G Starling). They would focus not only on short-term but also on long-term developments and remedies. The education of the democratic public opinion is of great importance. Efforts will need to be undertaken to convince the people that often the price of not looking ahead is at best a surprise and sometimes a catastrophe.

New diplomacy

Conflict prevention would be enhanced by:

- the development of comprehensive conflict prevention strategies, including peace building, peacekeeping and peacemaking;
- the extension of the rule of law to permit international intervention, such as humanitarian, security and environmental intervention (A Henrikson);
- bringing to bear all the conflict management resources available. The skills of non-governmental organisations or unofficial diplomats, largely ignored in diplomacy, could play major roles in peacemaking and peacebuilding (M Berman and J Johnson).

Consensus building

The lack of consensus between the major external parties in Yugoslavia is to be accounted for not only in terms of differences of interests, but also in terms of different assessments of the options considered. Realistic means should be devised to help governments assess the risks of different options under consideration. The availability of a thorough assessment of policy options would help the governments involved to take resolute action and would probably enhance consensus building.

Effective decision-making

To overcome decision-making problems, measures should be taken to cope more effectively with a chronically overloaded diplomatic agenda, to allow swift and effective decisionmaking and to improve cooperation among the international organizations. To cope simultaneously with several conflicts, these conflicts could be assigned to a department or an ad hoc interdepartmental or interagency team. The burden of conflict prevention could be shared or divided among several countries. A country or a group of countries could *adopt a conflict* and assume responsibility for it. The structural impairment of the decisionmaking in international organizations such as the CSCE could be reduced through the introduction of qualified majority voting under clearly defined conditions or by the creation of a European Security Council (C & C Kupchan; M Eyskens). A better cooperation and division of labour among the UNO, CSCE, NATO and the EC-WEU would also help.

An adequate infrastructure

The impact of declaratory conflict prevention, i.e. delineating in advance what actions will not be tolerated by the world community, is to a great extent dependent on the availability of an adequate infrastructure for peacemaking, peacekeeping and peacebuilding. This entails the further development of conciliation and mediation facilities. It necessitates new ways and means for peacebuilding, to strengthen the respect for human rights, the democratisation process and a sustainable socio-economic development. Some concrete proposals include, the creation of an International Court for Human Rights or the more frequent use of election monitoring units. With respect to efforts to prevent or to stop violence, one finds a great many suggestions concerning arms control and confidence building measures. There is also a trend in the direction of developing a new generation of peacekeeping operations, including, for example, naval peacekeeping operations, peacekeeping in support of emergency humanitarian relief, and peacekeeping methods for the control of drugs (P Diehl & C Kumar; T Weiss, J Blodgett). According to Norton and Weiss, there is also an undercurrent of thought for the development of new and more forceful intervention techniques. Urquhart advises that peacekeeping forces could also be used as a tripwire which would set in motion after suitable warnings, preplanned enforcement action under Chapter VII of the UN Charter. To realize those ideas, A Henrikson suggests the creation of a UN 'Peace Force' consisting of (1) a Standing-Reserve Peace Force composed of predesignated national units; (2) a smaller and more tightly organized Rapid-Response Force, and (3) a Permanent Peacekeeping Force.

A truly effective system of conflict prevention will require major investments. Hopefully the new interest in conflict prevention reflects a megatrend in security thinking and a determination to relieve the peoples of the world of unnecessary conflicts, excessive armament and the constant threat of war. Despite the slow pace of the security reforms and the existing reservations *vis à vis* certain measures, an investment in conflict prevention is prudence in the long run.

SOURCES

E Azar, *The Management of Protracted Social Conflict* (Dartmouth Publishing Company, England 1990)

M Berman & J Johnson (eds.), *Unofficial Diplomats*, (Columbia University Press, New York 1977)

J Blodgett, The future of UN peace keeping, in *The Washington Quarterly*, Winter 1991.

J Boulden, Building on the past: future directions for peacekeeping, in *Behind the Headlines*, Summer 1991 (Canadian Institute of International Affairs)

B Buzan, New Patterns of global security in the twenty-first century, in *International Affairs*, 1991, pp. 431–451.

G. Celente, *Trend Tracking*, (Warner Books, New York 1991)

Chang Heng Chee, The UN: from peace keeping to peace making? in *Adelphi paper 265*, Winter 1991–1992, pp. 30–40 (International Institute

of Strategic Studies)
P Diehl and C Kumar, Mutual benefits from international intervention: new roles for United Nations peace keeping forces, in *Bulletin of Peace Proposals*, vol. 22(4): 369–375 (1991).
M Eyskens, *Diplomatie préventive*. (Texte distribué par la Belgique à ses partenaires des CE lors du Conseil à Lisbonne du 17 février 1992)
R Fisher & W Ory, *Yetting to Yes*, (Penguin Books, England 1983)
D Frei (ed.), *Managing International Crises*, (Sage Publications, Beverly Hills 1982)
J Goldfarb, Beyond Glasnost: The Post-Totalitarian Mind, (University of Chicago Press 1989)
J Goodby, Peacekeeping in the New Europe, in *The Washington Quarterly*, Spring 1992, pp. 153–171.
R Haas, *Conflicts Unending*, (Yale University Press, New Haven 1990)
A Henrikson, *Defining a New World Order*. A discussion paper, May 2 and 3, 1991 (The Fletcher School of Law and Diplomacy.)
J Holst, Enhancing peacekeeping operations, in *Survival*, vol. XXXII, n°3, May/June 1990, pp. 264–275 (International Institute for Strategic Studies)
G Hopple, S Andriole, A Freedy (eds.), *National Security Crisis Forecasting and Management*, (Westview Press, Boulder 1989)
B Inman, J Nye, W Perry, R Smith, Lessons from the Gulf War, in *The Washington Quarterly*, Winter 1992, pp. 57–66.
I Janis, *Victims of Groupthink*, (Houghton Mifflin, Boston 1972)
J Joffe, collective security and the future of Europe, in *Survival*, Spring 1992, pp. 36–50. (International Institute for Strategic Studies)
R Johansen, A policy framework for world security, in M Klare & D Thomas, *World Security: Trends and Challenges at Century's End*, (St Martins Press, New York 1991)
J O C Jonah, Office for research and the collection of information (ORCI), in H Chestnut, P Kopacek, T Vamos (eds.), *International Conflict Resolution Using System Engineering*, (Pergamon Press, Oxford 1990)
Y M Laulan, *La Planéte Balkanisée*, (Economica, Paris 1991)
E Luard, *The Globalization of Politics*, (Macmillan, England 1990)
C R Mitchell, *The Structure of International Conflict* (St Martins Press, New York 1981)
R Powaski, United Nations and the future of global peace, *USA Today*, November 1991.
Ch and Cl Kupchan, Concerts, collective security and the future of Europe, in *International security*, Summer 1991, vol. 16, No. 1, pp. 114–160.
L Reychler, Querela Pacis, in J Nobel (ed.), *The Coming of Age of Peace Research*, (Styx, Groningen 1991)
L Reychler, A Pan European Security community: Utopia or realistic perspective, in *Disarmament: a periodic review by the United Nations*, Vol. XIV, No. 1, 1991, pp. 42–52.
L Reychler, The Price is surprise, *Studia Diplomatica*, October 1992.
R Riggs & J Plano, *The United Nations*, (The Dorsey Press, Chicago, 1988)
S Ryan, *Ethnic Conflicts and International Relations* (Dartmouth, USA 1990)
R Schweller, Domestic structure and preventive war, in *World Politics*.
G Starling, *Strategies for Policy Making*, (The Dorsey Press, Chicago 1988)

B Urquhart, Beyond the 'sheriff's posse, in *Survival*, Vol. XXXII, No. 3, May/June 1990, pp. 196–205. (International Institute for Strategic Studies)

B Urquhart, The UN: from peace keeping to a collective system? *Adelphi Paper 265*, Winter 1991–1992, pp. 18–29. (International Institute for Strategic Studies)

T Weiss and K Campbell, Military humanitarianism, in *Survival*, Vol. XXXIII, No 5 September/October 1991, pp. 451–465. (International Institute for Strategic Studies)

2

The United Nations in Conflict Prevention

Luise Drüke

(*The views reflected in this article are those of the author and do not necessarily reflect those of UNHCR or the United Nations.*)

For fifty years the Mandate of the United Nations has essentially remained the same. The nature of conflict prevention, however, has changed, particularly since the end of the Cold War. Contrary to the situation in 1960, when the then Secretary-General (SG) looked for support among Member States for efforts of preventive diplomacy, this year it was the Member States who looked to the Secretary-General on how to strengthen this activity.

EXISTING PROCEDURES AND FUNDING

The main organs of the UN had little room to manoeuver until the end of the 1980's. The Secretaries-General rarely invoked Article 99 of the UN Charter, except in one case explicitly in the Congo in 1960, and a few times implicitly, including for Korea in 1950, Laos in 1961, Pakistan in 1971, Vietnam in 1972, Lebanon in 1976 and 1978 and Iran/Iraq in 1980. Even though the Mandate of the United Nations is of a universal nature and any conflict threatening international peace and security could be placed on the agenda, the way in which conflicts were treated have nevertheless often depended on the interests of the major States of the Permanent Five of the Security Council.

Procedures

Although *declaratory preventions* might have little authority to delineate and communicate in advance that a certain type of behaviour will not be tolerated, they are a term of reference such as the 1948 Universal Declaration on Human Rights. Most recent declarations and documents have potential to contribute to set the stage for new approaches. They include the statement following the Summit of the Security Council of January 1992 (S/23500) and last year's Security Council resolutions 678 and 688 in addition to, the completion of the *Handbook on the Peaceful Settlement of Disputes between States* (see 46/58) as well as the *Declaration on Fact-finding by the UN in the Field of the Maintenance of International Peace and Security* (46/59) of 1991 give UN organs a stronger basis upon which to operate and provide support in their efforts in conflict prevention.

Clear *decision-making procedures* do exist. The UN Charter provides clearly that, according to its Article 34, the Security Council and, through Article 35, any Member State, may bring to the attention of the Security Council any dispute threatening international peace and security. On the basis of Article 11.3, it is the General Assembly, and of Article 99 the SG, the situations which could endanger international peace and security. There have been situations when timely and effective decision-making was weak or lacking altogether, due to differences among Member States in the Cold War period. In such cases a pragmatic approach usually prevailed.

Facilities

The *conflict prevention facilities* of the United Nations have seen significant strengthening since the late 1980's. In 1987, the Secretary-General proceeded with the establishment of an official early warning facility in the form of the Office for Research and the Collection of Information (ORCI), which in itself, would have been unthinkable even a few years before. An inter-agency *early warning* system was set up in 1991 by the UN Administrative Coordinating Committee (ACC) in the humanitarian field. Recommendations arising from this first experience include the establishment of a consultative mechanism to function effectively, comprising a core group of agencies such as FAO, the Department for Political and Humanitarian Affairs (since March 1992 assigned with the ORCI functions) UNHCR, UNICEF, UNDP, WFP, and possibly the Centre for Human Rights, each of which will need to make a serious commitment to make this early warning effort more effective.

Advanced communication technologies are ensuring rapid transmissions by radio, e-mail, satellite between Headquarters in New York and other important UN Offices around the world, allowing speedy information and analysis for the Secretary-General. According to Under Secretary General Marrack Goulding, in charge of *peacekeeping*, there are today two types of operations: The classic one, which is put into effect to 'create the conditions in which negotiations can go on' and the newer type, seen in Namibia, El Salvador or Cambodia, which forms part of a political settlement which has already been negotiated, but requires an impartial third party to oversee its implementation. Mr Goulding sees the process in El Salvador, where the United Nations were involved with peacemaking efforts, as a model. He also sees two major obstacles for effective UN peacekeeping. First, lack of funds and secondly lack of management capacity.

Funding

The 25 peacekeeping operations from 1948–1992 resulted in a total cost of about $8.311 million. For the current 11 operations the UN calculated a rough annual cost for 1991–1992 of more than $2700 million (including costs for UNPROFOR and UNTAC). Troops deployed from 1948 through January 1992 totalled 527,000, some 450,000 of whom came mainly from the Nordic countries, Austria, Canada, and Ireland. Scheduled troop/civilian police deployment in 1992 in all operations is 44,848. The number of military personnel and civil police serving on 31 January 1992 stood at 11,498. The proposed maximum strength and estimated cost to the UN for the UNTAC Cambodia in military/civilian personnel is 19,500 and $1.9 billion and for UNPROFOR in Yugoslavia is 13,870 and $611 million respectively.

International law abounds with instruments for peaceful settlement of conflicts. Practice and results are less impressive. In most cases, *peacemaking* efforts only start once conflicts have arisen. The experience of the United Nations shows that the application of combined methods, such as, for example, good offices, fact-finding, and negotiation have been successful.

In a few cases the Security Council has applied sanctions to enforce peace (Article 41). However, these have proved rather ineffective. Under the UN, *enforcement* measures have been applied twice. The first was during the Congo operation in 1961, when the Security Council authorized the use of force. The second was in 1990 to evict Iraqi forces from Kuwait with the approval of all five Permanent Members of the Security Council. This was only possible because of the end of the Cold War and the willingness of the Council Members to work out a consensus. With this action the Permanent Five established a precedent of cooperation to take collective action. Iraq provided a scenario in which action by consensus was possible.

The Secretary-General himself defined *peacebuilding* as economic and social development and technical assistance to be given to the protagonists of a dispute once peace has been reached. The United Nations' budget for 1992–1993 for international cooperation for development totals some $320 million. This is the largest item in the budget of the UN, after conference services and administration and management (some $422 million).

Some $280 million from the regular budget of about $2.5 billion for this biennium could be estimated for efforts of UN conflict prevention, bearing in mind that activities including policy making, good offices, peacemaking, peacekeeping, political and Security Council affairs, General Assembly and Secretariat matters, special political questions, the International Court of Justice, human rights and the protection of and assistance to refugees are all related directly or indirectly to conflict prevention.

In the light of the increasing demands on the Organisation and the outstanding Member States payments, including some $810 million for the regular budget and about $500 million for peacekeeping, it is imperative that the Member States provide the UN with adequate funding. Otherwise its effectiveness in the field of conflict prevention will be seriously undermined.

Evaluation

An evaluation of the effectiveness of the UN's conflict prevention efforts on the basis of these findings, indicates that much has been achieved, considering the numerous obstacles that exist. The results could undoubtedly have been better. But let us not forget that they could also have been worse. Incoming pressures and events will starkly determine the measures taken by Member States. Collective measures of conflict prevention must be taken by the UN and in some cases on a regional basis, such as has been the case in Western Africa, as they are recognised to be too complex to be handled by only one or a group of Member States.

Suggested new measures

Suggestions for innovative approaches in addition to existing practices include the following:

- *early identification and management* of potential conflict areas by antennas, such as UN ambassadors and/or political officers in UN field posts functioning as UN resident coordinators and or UNCP representatives;
- *operational linkage* between political and humanitarian affairs and peacekeeping operations, early warning at UN Headquarters and through a core group of concerned UN agencies and offices;
- *establishing an inventory* of available military units and their training and equipment and a strengthening of the training provided for military and civilian peacekeeping personnel in New York and on a regional basis worldwide.
- *strengthening of the Security Council's collective leadership* through efforts to include monitoring, and where necessary, applying existing instruments of disarmament, arms control and non-

proliferation through use of warnings and, if necessary, followed by sanctions;

- *reinforcing coordination* between peacemaking and peacekeeping and other efforts within the system and with outside contacts from relevant business, NGOs and other public interest entities, and academia (to bring the 'glue' to the resources of society) to hold negotiated peace and other agreements together;
- *integration of refugee protection and voluntary repatriation* into the framework of political affairs, peacekeeping and peacemaking efforts;
- *establishing a roster of experts for ad-hoc missions* in the field of electoral assistance, public administration and human rights;
- *increasing budgetary resources* in accordance with the expansion of peacekeeping and peacemaking activities by establishing a special peacekeeping reserve fund to enable the Secretary-General to deploy operations as rapidly and as effectively as possible.

UN CONFLICT PREVENTION: EXPERIENCE AND PROSPECTS

Many conflict situations overwhelmed the powers and resources of the Security Council during the Cold War period. Nevertheless, it did prove possible to contain or limit a number of regional conflicts which might otherwise have led to confrontation between the superpowers.[1]

The concept of preventing conflicts has been used for many years. Dag Hammarskjold for the first time in the late 1950s coined the term 'preventive diplomacy'. The UN's peacekeeping experience is the largest in the world and is recognized world wide. The Nobel Peace Prize for Peacekeeping in 1988 was just a testimony in recognition of their accomplishments. Peacemaking, with activities in political and diplomatic reconciliation, mediation and arbitration, good offices and fact-finding have made some progress, especially since there is no longer superpower confrontation. However, its effectiveness is still totally dependent on the political will of the States concerned. Peacebuilding processes, which could either precede or follow conflict prevention efforts have faced serious obstacles.

For 50 years the aim of the UN has remained the same: to

maintain international peace and security. It is the nature of conflict preventing efforts which has changed particularly since 1989. Today, there are no longer models to guide policy and action. The former models no longer apply. This is both a challenge and an opportunity for the UN and its conflict prevention objectives.

The Members of the Security Council and the new Secretary-General, in recognition of the challenges and opportunities ahead, have both given fresh impetus to explore possibilities to strengthen the capacity for preventive diplomacy by the UN. We will examine the basis of the UN's mandate for maintaining peace and security and thus the prevention of conflicts.

References which could be invoked for conflict prevention

Primary instruments containing a mandate applicable for conflict prevention are contained in the UN Charter, (essentially in Articles 1, 11(2), 24, Chapter VI and VIII, Articles 40 and especially 41, as well as in Article 99).

Article 1 stipulates that the Purposes of the United Nations are:

> To maintain international peace and security, and to that end: to take effective collective measures for the prevention and the removal of threats to the peace, and for the suppression of acts of aggression or other breaches of the peace, and to bring about by peaceful means, and in conformity with the principles of justice and international law, adjustments or settlement of international disputes or situations which might lead to a breach of the peace'.

Article 24 specifies the functions and powers of the Security Council to whom the Member States have conferred the primary responsibility for the maintenance of international peace and security. Article 25 provides that 'the Member States of the United Nations agree to carry out the decisions of the Security Council' in accordance with the Charter. Even though some Member States insist that decisions under Article 25 are only mandatory if taken under Chapter VII, there has developed a general agreement that all formal decisions of the Security Council (whether statements, decisions or resolutions) are mandatory.

Chapter VI and VII of the Charter refers to the peaceful settlement of disputes and action with respect to threats to the peace, breaches of the peace, and acts of aggression. These are key elements for UN conflict prevention. For the peaceful settlement of disputes, the Security Council shall, on the basis of Article 33, call upon the parties of any dispute to settle it by such means as negotiation, enquiry, mediation, conciliation, arbitration, judicial settlement, resort to regional agencies or arrangements, or other peaceful means of their own choice.

In accordance with Article 34, Member States agree that the Security Council may investigate any dispute, any situation which might lead to international friction, or which may give rise to a dispute, in order to determine the degree of possible danger to international peace and security.

Continuance of Article 40 of Chapter VII provides that, in order to prevent the aggravation of a situation, the Security Council may call upon the parties concerned to comply with such provisional measures as it deems necessary or desirable. In exceptional circumstances, the Security Council may proceed under Article 41 and decide on such measures as arms embargo and non-military sanctions.

What efforts have been made to delineate and communicate in advance the type of behaviour that will not be tolerated by the United Nations?

Through the statement of the President of the Security Council of 31 January 1992 (S/23500) the members of the Council reiterated their concern about the humanitarian situation of the innocent civilian population in Iraq. With a view to achieving a more effective role for the UN, the Security Council in this statement invited the Secretary-General to prepare his 'analysis and recommendations on ways of strengthening and making the capacity of the UN more effective within the framework of the Charter.[2]

The Report of the Secretary-General on Preventive Diplomacy, Peace-making and Peace-keeping, which was published in mid-1992, provides the relevant details on this analysis.[3]

Front the point of view of declaratory prevention value, Security

Council resolutions 687 and 688 (Omnibus resolutions) have been the most important for many years as they embrace the various aspects of the conflict. Therefore they may be considered legal precedents as they represent first steps of the Security Council to formulate a position concerning an internal situation in a condition of non-war.

Furthermore, in the Report of the Special Committee on the Charter of the United Nations and on the Strengthening of the Role of the United Nations (46/58) of 1991, the General Assembly expresses its appreciation to the Secretary-General for the completion of the Handbook on the Peaceful Settlement of Disputes between States. He is requested to publish and disseminate widely the Handbook in all the official languages of the United Nations.

The Declaration on Fact-finding by the United Nations in the field of the Maintenance of International Peace and Security (46/59) of 1991 gives the UN Organs an important new basis for preventive work. After recalling previous relevant documents,[4] it outlines in detail the purpose, criteria, procedures and competencies related to UN Fact-finding activities. It is the first instrument with such far reaching possibilities and is likely to play a substantial role in conflict prevention efforts in the future.

The Cold War period inhibited the actions of the Secretaries-General since the 1960s. Its end might allow these declaratory principles of prevention to be invoked more effectively than before. Another element is important to add here. The international human rights community, disarmament agreements and regional conflict resolution work over the past some 20 years do provide important additional terms of reference for the UN's work in the area of conflict prevention. One thing seems to be clear, that the intention to act in anticipation of conflict is now a more generally acceptable concept within the United Nations and its Member States. Although declaratory prevention has not, perhaps, been as effective as was desirable in the past, given the more favourable international political environment of today, it is likely to become an integral part of the future work of the UN in the prevention of conflict.

One should not forget here the declarations in the human rights field, especially the Universal Declaration on Human Rights of 1948.

The decision-making procedures of the UN for conflict prevention

On the basis of the UN Charter Article 34, the Security Council may investigate any dispute, or any situation which might lead to international friction or give rise to a dispute, in order to determine whether the continuance of the dispute or situation is likely to endanger the maintenance of international peace and security. The Security Council may initiate an action itself or a Member may request action. In cases of self-initiation, various Members consult with each other to agree in prior consultations as to whether or not a particular conflict is to be put on the agenda. If one Member wishes to bring an item onto the agenda, it addresses a communication to the President of the Security Council to call for a meeting or, in urgent cases, to call for an immediate meeting for considering the matter.

Once prior consultation on the conflict among the Members is completed, and the action to be taken decided upon, a draft text of a resolution, decision, or statement will be prepared and agreed before distribution to the 15 Members, in the six official UN working languages for review prior to the formal Security Council meeting. There the text is officially agreed upon (it becomes a child of 15 parents representing a consensus of all 15 Members unless there is dissent or a veto, especially from a permanent Member).

On the basis of Article 35 of the UN Charter, any Member or non-Member of the United Nations may bring any dispute, or any situation which might lead to international friction or give rise to a dispute, to the attention of the Security Council or the General Assembly. In addition, any Member of the General Assembly may bring an item onto the agenda. The proposal is first addressed to the General Assembly Committee composed of the 23 Vice-presidents of the General Assembly and chaired by the President of the General Assembly, which decides whether to include the item in the preliminary agenda of the General Assembly. The Assembly in its turn approves the agenda at its first meeting of the session. One of the few situations in which the General Assembly Committee of the General Assembly did not approve an item being put on the agenda was the submission of a request by Iraq which stated that a threat to peace existed due to the build up of Western military forces. If the Security Council is dealing with a matter, it will not be dealt with by the General Assembly.[5]

The Secretary-General could be called upon to play the important roles of mediator and adviser of numerous governments for conflict prevention. In the exercise of his function as chief administrator of the United Nations, he takes decisions, which may be qualified as political. Article 99 provides him with powers that go well beyond those previously given to any head of an international organization. He 'may bring to the attention of the Security Council any matter which in his opinion may threaten the maintenance of international peace and security'. These powers require the Secretary-General to exercise the highest qualities of political judgement, tact and integrity. He has the power to judge whether or not he brings a matter to the attention of the Security Council personally, depending on the circumstances of the moment.

The drafters of Article 99 wished to ensure the existence of a capable organ to which Member States could bring a particularly threatening matter of interest before the UN without delay. The Secretary-General must be prudent in the application of Article 99, for it implies a value judgement of a potentially controversial situation and supposes a favourable response by the Security Council. The Secretary-General risks his good name for measures ultimately taken by the Security Council. That was so for Trygve Lie in the case of Korea and for Dag Hammarskjold in the case of the Congo. Trygve Lie committed his prestige and his influence in an operation (essentially handled by the USA) of which he completely lost control. The developments in the Congo appeared to rest totally on the shoulders of Dag Hammarskjold. These two cases demonstrate very clearly the dangers inherent in the tasks that befall the Secretary-General in times of potential crisis and conflict. In fact, Article 99 offers the same prerogatives as those of Article 11(2)[6] and of Article 35[7], except that the Secretary-General has not the same means at his disposal as the General Assembly or Member States.

In his last annual report, the Secretary-General reiterated that the as yet insufficient development of preventive capacity of the Secretariat has always limited recourse to Article 99, particularly in its anticipatory aspect.[8]

Our research shows that Secretaries-General have rarely invoked Article 99, except, for example, explicitly in relation to the Congo, (1960) and several times implicitly, including Korea, 1950; Laos, 1961; Pakistan 1971; Vietnam, 1972; Lebanon, 1976 and 1978; Iran/Iraq, 1980.[9] The nature of the UN mandate for conflict prevention is universal and any situations that could endanger international peace and security could be put on the agenda.

On the basis of Article 11.3 of the UN Charter, the General Assembly may call the attention of the Security Council to situations which are likely to endanger international peace and security.

Decisions regarding conflict management are made *inter alia* as foreseen in Articles 40, 41, 42, 44, 48, 50 of the UN Charter. Both the Secretary-General and the Security Council may take action to:

- review
- intercede
- act

in order to attempt conflict management. The system of conflict management is yet to be further developed and strengthened. The period during the Cold War impeded the implementation of an effective system.

When the need for action has arisen in the past and the means for timely and effective decision-making were weak or lacking altogether, a pragmatic approach has so far prevailed.

Conflict prevention facilities including early warning for conflict management/conflict prevention and for humanitarian matters:

In the late 1950's, without previous discussion, Dag Hammarskjold began to practise preventive diplomacy by means of his various practical innovations, such as 'UN presences' and the dispatch of personal representatives to potentially dangerous areas'.[10]

In other, less politically sensitive areas, the United Nations started to apply early warning and related concepts, while the United

Nations Statistical Office (UNSO) and the Department of International Economic and Social Affairs (DIESA) developed databases for economic forecasting and reporting, identifying social and environmental indicators, and establishing the issuance of projections as a regular practice of their work (as do the World Bank and IMF). In the early 1970s, the United Nations Environmental Programme (UNEP) established the Earthwatch, and the Food and Agricultural Organization (FAO) set up the Global Information and Early Warning System (GIEWS) in the mid 1970s.[11]

Finally, in 1981, Prince Sadruddin Aga Khan recommended an early warning system in the humanitarian field and one year later Perez de Cuellar, the then Secretary-General, in his 1982 Annual Report, promised to develop in the political arena, a wider and more systematic capacity for fact-finding in potential conflict areas. At the request of the Secretary-General, the Department of Political and Security Council Affairs (PSCA), following the 1982 Annual Report, set up a special service to monitor new agencies' daily releases, and to prepare immediate summaries of these and other reports in the international press.

The real breakthrough followed, however, with the UN financial crisis and the increasing refugee emergencies. This led the General Assembly to appoint the so-called Group of 18 to study the efficiency of the United Nations. Its recommendations in 1986 were directed at streamlining, rationalising, and cutting of duplication within the Secretariat.[12] In the same year another initiative, the Group of Governmental Experts to Avert New Refugee Flows, recommended in its final report to the Secretary-General 'to ensure timely and fuller information on potential refugee situations.[13]

The establishment of the Office for Research and Collection of Information (ORCI) in March 1987 is one of the direct results of the two groups' recommendations. The Secretary-General took this first institutional measure to 'provide early warning of developing situations requiring the Secretary-General's attention'.[15] And to centralise several functions from different services in this new office.

ORCI's function was intended to enable the Secretary-General to provide the Security Council with early information, and thereby play a more central and effective role in the prevention of conflicts and the monitoring of factors related to possible refugee flows.

Early warning for conflict management/prevention

After five years of operation and with the arrival of the new Secretary-General in January 1992, the constellation for UN early warning is newly emerging. As of 1 March 1992, ORCI was dissolved and its various components integrated into the newly established Department of Political Affairs and the Department of Humanitarian Affairs. The decision of Mr Boutros Boutros-Ghali for this rearrangement might be explained in two ways: first, he was aware that ORCI has not been able to fulfil its mandate, and second, he wished to use more traditional manners of organising research and analysis for diplomatic decision-making, divided into geographical areas.[15]

Whereas the ORCI structure represented a single channel for information and advice to the Secretary-General, the new system is divided into several channels. There is the news-gathering section that monitors some 15 to 20 news sources and summarises the relevant developments for the Office of the Secretary-General.[16] This section has been separated from the analytical work of the early warning mechanism. It operates under the SG's Spokesman in the Department for Public Information where political core issues are likely to be less focused on than formerly in ORCI. This physical separation might cause some problems in the future.

Some former ORCI staff who had been responsible for the analysis of incoming information for early warning indications have now been split to deal with Africa, the Middle East, Asia, Europe and the Americas, and humanitarian affairs, with different lines of authority. There are likely to be differences of interpretation of emerging conflict situations, and the need and nature of the involvement of the Secretary-General and the Security Council. The conception of the early warning system and the establishment of the computerised database is expected to continue to be used in the new set-up. It is detached, however, from both the news service and the geographical data units. The hope is to eventually arrive at a state-of-the-art instrument for precedent-based analysis and advice on emerging conflicts, both international and internal, as they affect international peace and security.[17]

Specifically, during the first press conference by the Secretary-General on 19 March 1992 in New York, Mr Boutros Boutros-Ghali was asked whether the United Nations was adequately provided with the most sophisticated intelligence to carry out its work, or whether it should improve its access to sophisticated intelligence in a cooperative effort involving all UN Member States. The Secretary-General replied that he believed that the United Nations must have its own intelligence. He underlined that, if the United Nations wants to maintain its independence, receiving information from the different intelligence of the Member States must be avoided. Though he recognized that this will require additional financial capacity, non-existent for the time being, he emphasized that:

> If we want to have preventive diplomacy, we will need to have our own intelligence and a more important presence of the United Nations in the different countries and in the different regions where there will be the possibility of having military confrontations.[18]

This is an ambitious challenge. As officials responsible for this work in the UN pointed out, the relentless pursuit within the UN to build a viable framework for early warning is becoming ever more urgent, because the opportunities are increasing.

Early warning in the humanitarian field

The main problem of early warning in this field and especially in the refugee area has not been a lack of information, but rather the issue of how existing information could be channeled into the UN decision-making process at high levels. This was also one of the findings of the UN Joint Inspection Unit (JIU) which provided a detailed study on the coordination of activities related to early warning of possible refugee flows in July 1990. Since the JIU arrived at the basic conclusion that the UN lacked a system-wide mechanism to deal with the issue of potential mass flows, its recommendations included the following measures:

- Designate a central focal point of the UN system for this task, and
- Establish a working group on early warning of refugee flows consisting of representatives of ORCI, UNHCR, Centre for Human Rights, UNDRO, FAO, as well as those of UNDP, WFP and others, to work out practical measures for modes of co-operation and procedures to develop an effective early warning system for refugees.[19]

This matter was then discussed in the UN Administrative Coordinating Committee (ACC) which led to the establishment of the recommended Working Group by Decision 1991/9. The mandate of the Working Group of the ACC on Early Warning of New Flows of Refugees and Displaced Persons was defined[20] and the Working Group is to present its final report to the ACC in October 1992.

An issue that seems to have transpired in the process of the ACC Working Group is that, for the consultative mechanism to function effectively, a core group of agencies such as FAO, the Departments of Political and Humanitarian Affairs respectively, UNHCR, UNICEF, UNDP, WFP, and possibly the Centre for Human Rights will need to make a serious commitment to carry out specific fundamental activities. These activities will need to include mechanisms, procedures and the provision of senior staff within their own organisations capable of handling this enormous additional task.[21]

In the resolution of the General Assembly 46/182 of 19 December 1991 that provided the basis for establishing the post of UN Emergency Relief Coordinator to head the new Department on Humanitarian Affairs, early warning is underlined as one of the guiding principles. The academic workshop of York University in its session in early February 1992 suggested the functional structure for a humanitarian early warning system to be divided into five distinct but related functional phases:

- Data collection, exchange and dissemination;
- Analysis of data;
- Coordination and synthesis of the various analyses received;
- Formulation on and communication of the early warning; and

- Action on the warning.[22]

This shows that the United Nations' experience with early warning is considerable. Its effectiveness, however, is difficult to measure. Considering the recently ended Cold War, which impeded substantial work on early warning for both conflict prevention and addressing potential crises, the establishment of ORCI in 1987 for early warning, essentially in the political field, and the setting up of the ACC Working Group for early warning in the humanitarian field, are, and will remain, landmarks. Whatever the outcome of the newly emerging early warning constellation and function in the United Nations, it has become an accepted fact that UN organisations must look ahead together.

Of course, early warning has better prospects of success in small conflicts and crises. Human lives saved, and nuclear catastrophes prevented because of early warning and rapid preventive action make it worth the effort. Even the Members of the Security Council recognised in their Summit meeting in January 1992 that there are new favourable international circumstances under which the Security Council has started to fulfil its primary responsibility for maintaining international peace and security more effectively.[23] There seems to have developed a true political will to take action before and not after the conflicts have blown up. For this to be effective, early warning will be essential. It is likely to be more readily obtainable in this new international environment than before.

Conflict management methods: Peacekeeping, Peacemaking, Peace-enforcement.

Peacekeeping as a concept is not specifically stipulated in the UN Charter, but it has evolved over the years as an internationally acceptable way of controlling conflicts and promoting the peaceful settlement of disputes. It introduces to the military sphere the principle of non-violence. Thus, for the first time in history, military forces are used worldwide not to wage war, but to control and end conflict between peoples or communities.

The first such operation was created in the Middle East in 1948 in the form of an observer mission. The first of the United Nations peacekeeping forces was created also in the Middle East, in 1956.[24] On 10 December 1988, the Secretary-General accepted the Nobel Peace Prize in Oslo on behalf of United Nations peacekeepers. With him were seventeen Blue Berets representing United Nations operations in the field.

At the opening session of the Follow-up Meeting of the Conference on Security and Cooperation in Europe (CSCE) in Helsinki on 24 March 1992, the Secretary-General transmitted a message through Mr Sotirios Mousouris, the Assistant Secretary-General for Political Affairs. This message underlined that the CSCE and the UN share similar ideals and face common challenges and priorities and actions regarding peace and security, such as preventive diplomacy, disarmament, economic and social development, human rights and democracy. Mr Boutros-Ghali referred to the division of labour between the UN and the European Community for peacekeeping and peacemaking efforts, respectively. He also referred to a recent dispatch of UN fact-finding missions to Nagorno-Karabakh, which is intended to complement the CSCE in its peacemaking efforts.[25]

A few days before that, on 19 March 1992 in the UN Headquarters in New York, the Secretary-General gave his first press conference. He reiterated one of his priorities: reinforcing regional cooperation mechanisms for conflict management and making a clear division of labour. For example, a division between the European Community and the United Nations for dealing with peacemaking, and with peacekeeping/maintaining the cease-fire, respectively. He sees the UN role as a complementary one: through cooperation with the different regional bodies to promote preventive diplomacy and even a kind of decentralisation in the different peacekeeping operations.

When asked about peace and development, the Secretary-General mentioned two interesting cases, El Salvador and Cambodia, where the role of the UN is not limited to peacekeeping, but where the UN is moving to the second stage, which is the construction of peace through development. In this connection Mr Boutros-Ghali reminded his audience that the great majority of the 77 military conflicts during the past 45 years have taken place in the countries of the Third World. It is essential, therefore, that the UN maintain a close relation between peacekeeping and peacebuilding.

Discussions and practical efforts to invigorate peacekeeping and cooperation between the UN and regional organisations have so far had limited success. Therefore, a new operation is just starting in Somalia to bring military protection and humanitarian aid. Only recently, the General Assembly urged the United Nations:

> to provide such technical assistance as may be appropriate to the Organisation of African Unity should the latter decide to launch a peacekeeping operation.[26]

Peacekeeping

According to Mr Goulding, Under Secretary-General of the UN in charge of peackeeping, there are two kinds of peacekeeping operations. The classic operation is to help 'create the conditions in which negotiations can go on', usually by helping maintain the cease-fire at the end of a war. The newer type, seen in Namibia, Cambodia, Western Sahara and El Salvador, forms part of a political settlement which has already been negotiated but requires an impartial third party to oversee its implementation. He regards the process in El Salvador (where he worked very closely with his peacemaking colleague, Mr Avaro de Soto) as a model; by contrast, Mr Gouldings describes the arrangements in Western Sahara, negotiated in great secrecy by the Secretary-General's special envoy Mr Issa Diallo as a disaster.[27]

Peacekeeping is in great demand these days. There are 12 operations, including the unprecedentedly ambitious task of bringing peace and reconstruction to Cambodia, which involves supervising both the existing administration and the election of a new one. The cost of this Cambodia operation alone is estimated to be $1.9 billion.

i) What are the problems and means to prevent conflicts?

There are two crucially important problems which actually hinder the UN from being as effective as it could if they did not exist:

The first problem is money. Even before the outbreak of war in Yugoslavia, the Secretary-General experienced serious funding problems.

Now there is a head-on clash over the cost of the Yugoslav operation between the Secretariat and the five permanent members of the UN Security Council, who are reluctant to make available the funds required. Insufficient funding can have serious consequences. For example, the Security Council had drastically to reduce the size of the UN force in Namibia which Mr Goulding had asked for (and he blames this for the deaths of 333 people when, in April 1989, SWAPO guerrillas swarmed across the Angolan frontier straight into the guns of the South African Army).[28]

The second problem is the management capacity of the Secretariat itself. This, according to Mr Goulding, is already 'stretched to breaking point'. He adds 'we need more people, better financial and administrative procedures. We must have the money available when we need it. At the moment we have no authority to spend anything. We need reserves'.[29]

If the money and the management problem did not exist and the political will of the permanent members of the Security Council and concerned parties was always consistent, the UN could be more effective in preventing or suppressing violent conflicts on the basis of the Charter and subsequent arrangements.

For the 25 peacekeeping operations (from 1948 to 1992), the total cost amounts to about $8,311 million. For the current 12 peacekeeping operations, at the time of revising this paper (October 1992) the United Nations calculated an approximate annual cost for 1991–1992 of more than $2,700 million, (including UNPROFOR and UNTAC). The current operations are:

1. UNTSO – UN Truce Supervision Organization
   June 1948 – To present
   Rough annual cost to the UN: about $31 million
   Current strength (military personnel): 300
   Fatalities: 28
2. UNMOGIP – UN Military Observer Group in India and Pakistan
   January 1949 – To present
   Rough annual cost to the UN: $5 million

Current strength (military personnel): about 40
Fatalities: 6

3. UNFICYP – UN Peacekeeping Force in Cyprus
   March 1964 – To present
   Rough annual cost to the UN: $31 million
   Current strength (military personnel): about 2,200
   Fatalities: 158
4. UNDOF – UN Disengagement Observer Force (Syria/Israel border)
   June 1974 – To present
   Rough annual cost to the UN: $43 million
   Current strength (military personnel): about 1300
   Fatalities: 30
5. UNIFIL – UN Interim Force in Lebanon
   March – To present
   Rough annual cost to the UN: $157 million
   Current strength (military personnel): about 5,800
   Fatalities: 185
6. UNIKOM – UN Iraq-Kuwait Observation Mission
   April 1991 – To present
   Rough annual cost to the UN: $67 million
   Current strength (military personnel): about 470
7. UNAVEM II – Angola Verification Mission
   June 1991 – To present
   17 month cost to the UN up to October 1992: £128 million
   Current strength (military/police personnel): about 440
8. ONUSAL – UN Observer Mission in El Salvador
   July 1991 – To present
   16 month cost to the UN up to October 1992: $70 million
   Current strength (military/police personnel): about 1,000
9. MINURSO – UN Mission for the referendum in Western Sahara
   September 1991 – To present
   Estimated cost to the UN for 9.5 months: $59 million
   Current strength (military personnel): about 375
10. UNTAC – UN Transitional Authority in Cambodia
   March 1992 – To present
   Estimated cost to the UN for 15 months: $1.9 billion

Projected max. strength (military/police personnel): 19,500

11. UNPROFOR – UN Protection force (Yugoslavia)
    March 1992 – To present
    Estimated cost for 12 months: £611 million
    Projected max. strength (military/police personnel): 13,870
12. UNOSOM – (Somalia).

Of these UN Peacekeeping organisations, two are funded from the UN regular budget (UNTSO and UNIMOGIP), one is funded through voluntary contributions (UNFICYP) and the rest are financed from their own separate accounts on the basis of legally binding assessments on all Member States. Since the mandates of most forces are renewed periodically, starting from different dates, annual cost estimates for comparative purposes are approximate. The figures provided for operational strength, some of which include both military and police personnel, vary slightly from month to month due to rotation.[30]

ii) What kind of forces could be made available?

Four, of the above mentioned operations also involve civilian police personnel. For 13 operations established between 1956 and 1985, the major troop contributors have been the Nordic countries (except Iceland), Austria, Canada, and Ireland. Some of them were non-aligned. All of them maintained a neutral view of the conflicts, making them acceptable to the parties concerned. They made available personnel, equipment and training, with which they had contributed, as of 1987, out of approximately 450,000 men and women in UN peacekeeping operations.[31]

These countries gained considerable experience during the early years, especially from the Congo, Gaza, and Cyprus.[32] Despite that experience, there is still a clear need for strengthening the UN efforts in training and education – along the same lines as UNHCR, UNICEF and other UN organs dealing with emergency management for higher efficiency in cost and benefits. In the face of dramatic changes worldwide, the UN will need to expand its role in planning, implementing, conducting and controlling complex UN field operations. These will increasingly be composed of civilian personnel. There are suggestions to establish regional training centres.

The New York Training Seminar on Peace-keeping, which took place from 23–27 March 1992 had the purpose of developing a working understanding and knowledge of peacekeeping operations as a major instrument of the United Nations for the maintenance of international peace and security. Distinguished speakers, experts in the field, presented and discussed a number of issues related to the subject with the participants, who were mainly from Permanent Missions to the UN and UN Headquarters officials. The Director of the Training Programmes for Peacekeeping and Peacemaking of the UNITAR Office provided a comprehensive handfile for this Seminar that contains a rich source of documents and most recent research results.[33]

As Sweden has made an outstanding contribution to peacekeeping in terms of training and equipment, it is discussed here in more detail as an example. After some discussion, the Parliaments of Sweden, Denmark and Norway decided in 1964 to organise Stand-By Forces, and Finland simultaneously decided to do the same. Thereafter, Sweden gradually developed a system for recruiting, organising, training and serving abroad. Ten years later, in 1974, the Swedish Parliament adopted a bill which provided the constitutional framework for the Swedish-Stand-By Forces, which stipulates the following:

- within the Defence Forces there shall be a military force voluntarily organized as a Stand-By Force,
- the Government is authorised to put this force at the disposal of the United Nations,
- the Force consists of a maximum of two battalions and a special unit of a size not exceeding a third battalion (mil. observers, disaster relief units, etc.),
- the personnel of the Stand-By Forces is employed for this purpose.

Implementing this bill, the Government had instructed the Supreme Commander of the Swedish Defense Forces to recruit, organize and train the Stand-By Force.[34]

Peacekeeping has grown into an international phenomenon with coverage on all continents – the Americas, Asia, the Middle East, Africa, Europe – by forces coming now from the different continents. Training and equipment of Member States has had a varying degree of preparedness and technological advancement. As a distinguished trainer in the UN system put it:

> peacekeeping in its traditional sense is not a military operation but instead a political operation where the military instrument is used as a 'cooling' tool in order to give time for the political considerations.[35]

Future peacekeeping operations will mean new activities, some of which fall outside the traditional field of peacekeeping. Involved will be considerable components of civilians from which will emerge new requirements for training. This development may serve as a catalyst for change; the current ad-hoc establishment of peace-keeping forces may give way to a more systematic approach.

Peacemaking

International law abounds with instruments urging States to submit disputes according to some means of peaceful settlement ever since the 1899 and 1907 Hague Conventions for the Peaceful Settlement of Disputes.[36] In practical politics, States and organizations have set up a variety of mechanisms for settling disputes and making peace.[37] Furthermore, there are numerous bilateral and multilateral treaties that contain some form of settlement of disputes or handling of conflicts.

The usual means or methods of conflict management may be divided essentially into six groups:

1. Negotiation
2. Good Offices
3. Enquiry and fact-finding
4. Mediation and conciliation
5. Arbitration, and
6. Judicial settlement.[38]

Approaches to peacemaking are by no means mutually exclusive. The experience of the United Nations shows that the Organisation has been most successful when coordinated efforts were undertaken at all levels. In recent years, the functions of the Secretary-General's good offices have been increasingly in demand to come to the aid of parties seeking to resolve their differences. Where possible, peacekeeping should move in step with peacemaking, to help create conditions in which peacemaking can prosper and in a combined effort, lead to the peaceful resolution of a conflict. This is sometimes difficult to achieve. To reach agreement over the causes of a conflict is usually much more difficult than it is to maintain a cease-fire. Long-standing peacekeeping operations do not automatically mean failure, but they may be a measure of its success in preventing a recurrence of hostilities despite any intractability of the conflict between the parties.[39]

The Secretary-General and/or his representatives are responsible for peacemaking. There are task forces for different conflict situations. As practitioners, not every top official required might have the time to keep up with the newest conflict prevention techniques and research-findings.

Peace-enforcement

Certain aspects of the mandate under the Charter are enforceable, in principle, as the Member States agree to accept and carry out the decisions of the Security Council Article 25. In order to prevent the aggravation of a conflict, the Security Council may decide what measures other than the use of force are to be employed to give effect to its decisions. Measures to be applied for enforcement may include complete or partial interruption of economic relations and of road, sea, air, postal, telegraphic radio, and other means of communication, and the severance of diplomatic relations (Article 41).

In order to take urgent military action, Members shall hold air-force contingents immediately available for the combined international enforcement action (Article 44). The action required to carry out the decisions of the Security Council shall be taken by all Members of the United Nations or by some of them, as the Security Council may determine (Article 48).

If preventive or enforcement measures are taken by the Security Council, against another State, whether a Member of the United Nations or not, which has difficulties in implementing these measures, this State has the right to consult with the Security Council for a solution (Article 50). Measures taken by Member States in the exercise of the right to self-defence shall not in any way affect the authority and responsibility of the Security Council.

The Security Council shall, where appropriate, utilise regional arrangements or agencies for the enforcement action under its authority. But no enforcement action shall be taken under regional arrangements or agencies without the authorisation of the Security Council.

On the basis of these provisions in the UN Charter, the following comments may be made. The United Nations is a global organisation for peaceful resolution of conflicts, for enforcing peace, when negotiations fail. Ideological divisions prevented agreements for peacemaking for many years during the Cold War period which led to a polarization of the world. The Security Council has on occasion agreed to negotiate peaceful ends of conflicts, and like the League of Nations, it has made use of military force observers to monitor cease-fires or armistices.

In a few cases, the Security Council applied sanctions to enforce peace (Article 41) which generally proved however rather ineffective. Possibly due to the temporary absence of the Soviets from the Security Council meeting, Article 43 was applied in Korea in 1950 for the first time. Incidentally, the Soviets later proclaimed this operation unconstitutional. The Members of the Security Council asked the USA to conduct the military operation and move this question to the General Assembly.

During the Congo operation, the Security Council, on 21 February 1961, authorized ONUC use of force as a last resort to implement its resolution. This was not done under Chapter VII, which later became questionable. The second and latest application of enforcement was in 1990 to evict Iraqi forces from Kuwait with the approval of all five Permanent Members of the Security Council. This was only possible due to the end of the Cold War and the willingness of the Security Council to work out a consensus.

The peace enforcement mechanism on the Gulf went into motion after Iraq's refusal of 12 UN resolutions. Without going into the details of the Security Council's actions here, the list of resolutions (attached in the annex hereto) indicates the process and efforts to give Iraq a way out. The main points of deliberation were:

- A Sanctions-Committee to oversee the matter,
- Non-recognition of any regime established by the invader,
- Declaration that Iraq's annexation was illegal.

Meanwhile, in response to the appeal of Saudi Arabia for protection, US and British forces were dispatched. Iraq was requested to facilitate the departure of foreign nationals. Whereas Iraq made attempts to break the sanctions, Kuwait invoked Article 51 of the Charter and requested assistance. Soon thereafter, US naval units and, later, Western allies, moved into the Gulf region. The final resolution 678 of 29 November 1991 of the Security Council demanded compliance by Iraq by 15 January 1991.

Subsequent to the meeting of the Secretary-General on the implementation of paragraph 5 of Security Council resolution 678, the United Nations Iraq-Kuwait Observation Mission (UNIKOM) was established on 5 April 1991. Thereupon, the Security Council authorized the destruction of Iraqi weapons of mass destruction (18 April 1991), and approved humanitarian operations and the setting up of Civilian Guards.

Analysis of the Role of the Security Council:

Despite an apparent agreement for joint action, there were differences on a number of questions including:

- Should sanctions have been given more time?
- Should the Soviet peace initiative have been given more time?
- Should the ground war have been launched differently?
- Should there have been any sanctuaries?
- Should the Coalition forces have continued to attack after Iraq had declared that it was withdrawing?

- Should the Security Council have the right to decide on the Kuwait-Iraq border?
- Should the UN really have a right to decide to destroy Iraqi weapons of mass destruction?

The Security Council authorisation of peace enforcement under Chapter VII, first with sanctions and later with the use of force under Article 51 was a result of special circumstances which are unlikely to be repeated. Over the past four years, the Permanent Five members established a precedent of cooperation to take collective action. Iraq provided a scenario where they could act by consensus. The USA had very special relations with Saudi Arabia and had provided naval escort to Kuwaiti ships during the Iraq-Iran war. The United Kingdom also had special relations with the Gulf States, and France had special interest in questions including oil. Similarly, Japan and Germany (non-troop contributors) rely on oil from that region. Iraq had been one of the major friends of the Soviet Union.

The provision of humanitarian assistance to the Kurds became a special feature, which however, left out the Shias in the South of Iraq. In addition, the developing United Nations system for the monitoring, collection and destruction of weapons of mass destruction was a new process, providing food for thought for the future. As the Security Council, especially the Non-Aligned Movement was unprepared to authorize traditional peace-keeping under Chapter VII, the consensus remained very basic. It is therefore likely that dealing with the internal conflict in Iraq, the Security Council will seek a broad consensual agreement of the parties concerned.[40]

Peacebuilding:

In his press conference on 19 March 1992 in New York, the Secretary-General defined peacebuilding as economic and social development and technical assistance to be given to protagonists of a dispute once peace had been attained.[41]

Funding

How much is spent on conflict prevention?

Considering the purpose of the United Nations, to maintain peace and security, the whole budget does contribute either directly or indirectly to conflict prevention.[42] The General Assembly's budget appropriations for the two years 1992–1993 amount to $2.5 billion, of which the following rounded allocations might be considered directly related to conflict prevention efforts:

1. Overall policy-making, direction and coordination	$ 36 million
2. Good offices and peacemaking; peacekeeping; Research/collection of information	$100 million
3. Political and Security Council Affairs	$ 16 million
4. Political/General Assembly/Secretariat	$ 13 million
5. Special political questions, regional cooperation trusteeship and decolonization	$ 9 million
6. International Court of Justice	$ 18 million
7. Human rights	$ 23 million
8. Protection of and assistance to refugees	$ 61 million
Total for 2 years[43]	$276 million

The main source of funds for the regular budget is contributions from Member States to be paid according to a scale specified by the General Assembly. The main criterion on which scale of assessments is based is the capacity of member States to pay.[44] (However, the financial situation of the United Nations is serious. In recent years Member States have requested the Secretary-General to establish 12 peacekeeping/observer operations as compared to a total of 25 since the beginning in 1948. Only one of these twelve operations was financed from the regular budget[45] and the other eleven were established on the basis of a special account through the Security Council.[46]

The special account operations are financed by assessed contributions from all Member States on the basis of a special scale of

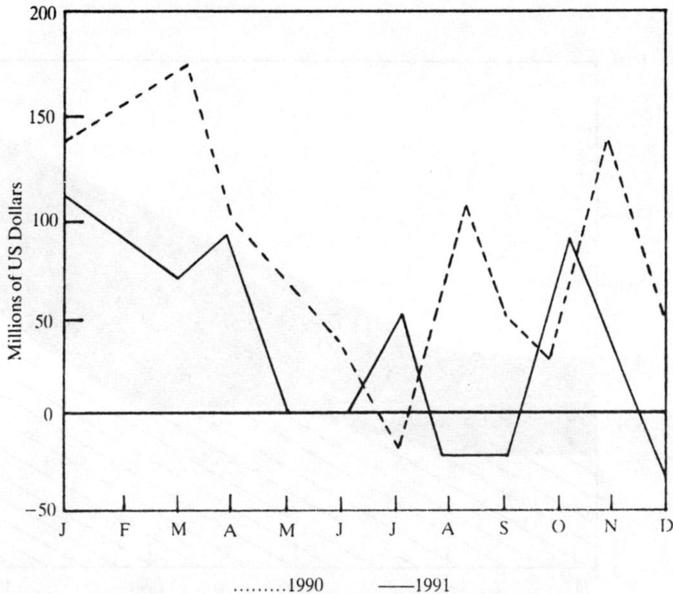

Note: Figures for November and December 1991 are estimated.
(Source: General Assy. Doc. No. A/46/600/Add.1 (19 Nov 91)

Fig. 2.1 United Nations General Funds
Available cash balances 1990 and 1991

assessments, which places a heavier burden on the permanent Members of the Security Council and some wealthier Member States, and reduces that of the least developed countries. This method is generally accepted by the Member States and will probably be applied to future operations without problems.[47]

In his annual report for 1991, the Secretary-General mentioned that the increasingly ambitious and costly operations have led to a serious financial shortfall. At the date of that report some $810 million of the regular budget and $500 million for peacekeeping were outstanding.[48] In view of the 25 per cent scale of assessment applicable to the USA, this country's outstanding payment is by far the highest.

But, even as US financial pressure has been driving the United

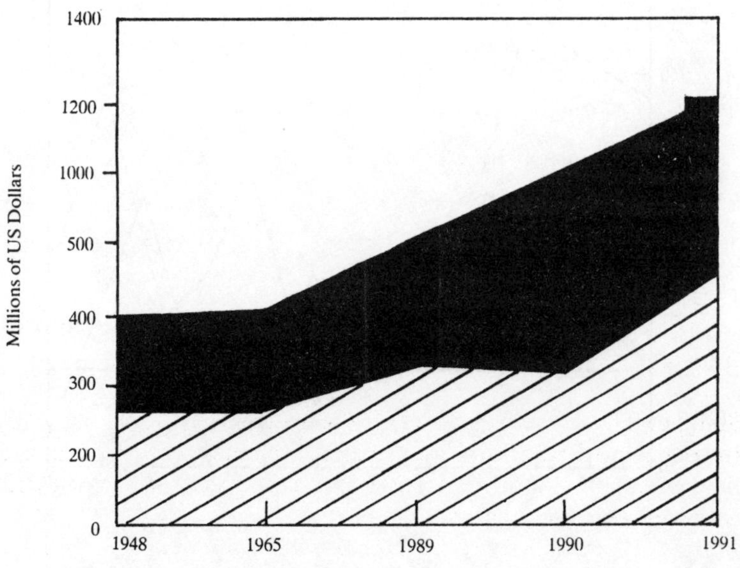

Regular Budget

Peacekeeping

All balances are as at 30 September 1991
(Source: General Assy.Doc. No. A/46/600/Add.1 (19 Nov 91)

Fig. 2.2 Unpaid Assessed Contributions
(Regular budget and Peacekeeping activities combined.)

Nations to the brink of insolvency, the organisation began unexpectedly to demonstrate how it could be made to work best. Namely by providing a reliable instrument for impartial third-party management of international, especially regional conflict situations by way of peacekeeping and peacemaking.[49]

Therefore, the UN needed to draw upon cash reserves (i.e. Working Capital Fund and the Special Account, totalling about $236 million), to meet current operations. Reporting on the financial situation of the organisation, the Secretary-General pleaded that the outstanding contributions to the regular budget and the peacekeeping operations should be paid in substantial amounts.[50]

In order to provide Member States with the necessary elements to address the financial crises, Secretary-General Perez de Cuellar offered the following three proposals in November 1991:

- Establish measures to deal with cash flow problems
- Establish a Humanitarian Revolving Fund
- Establish a UN Peace Endowment Fund ($1 billion).[51]

Brian Urquhart recently advanced some innovative suggestions to address funding problems. They are:

- Shift peacekeeping costs to defence budgets
- Introduce a sort of 'levy' on private companies, especially in the field of shipping or air transport, since they are clearly benefitting from peacekeeping activities, and
- Impose a 1 per cent tax on all international arms transactions.[52]

In fact the Italian Government has already introduced a new mechanism in this regard. By law 180 (6 February 1992), it has established that in order to finance Italy's participation in peace and humanitarian initiatives in the international field it is possible to deploy not only funds appropriated *ad hoc*, but also up to 1 per cent of the funds allotted for development assistance (if such initiative relate to developing countries).[53]

On 13 May 1992, Secretary-General Boutros Boutros-Ghali delivered a lecture in Washington where he also addressed the funding problem of peacekeeping. He stated, given the political will, that funding problems could be easily resolved and suggested the following four steps:

1. A revolving capital fund would be established to finance the start-up cost of peacekeeping operations;
2. As soon as the Security Council decided to set up a new operation, the Member States would be asked to pay

immediately one third of the established cost of its first year and the Secretary-General would automatically be given the authority to commit up to this sum;

3. A reserve stock of basic peacekeeping equipment would be established so that some of the most needed items would always be available;
4. Member States would pay their assessments, both for the initial one third and for the full budget, fully and on time.

On this occasion, Mr Boutros Boutros-Ghali, looking at the costs of peacekeeping, reiterated his belief, that even the UN calculated estimate of $2.7 billion for this exceptional year is not high in relation to the costs of the alternative, namely, continued conflict. On the same occasion, he said that one only needs to recall the astonishing sums of money that were spent to 'win' the Cold War – in the 1980s, global expenditures on arms approached $1 trillion per year, or $2 million per minute – to recognize that peacekeeping is an inexpensive way to help maintain stability in the post-Cold War era.

Aware that the current volume of peacekeeping expenses is creating real problems for Member States, the Secretary-General has started to review existing operations to identify possible areas of saving without affecting their effectiveness.

In considering costs and effectiveness, it is also encouraging to see that of the 13 operations established since 1988, six have already completed their mandate. These include two in Africa, in Namibia (UNTAG), where 46,000 refugees could start to live afresh through UNHCR's support, and where free and fair elections were successfully carried out in November 1989 under UN supervision; and in Angola (UNAVEM I), where from 1989 to 1991, the UN military observers monitored and verified the withdrawal of Cuban troops. In the Middle East, the Military Observer Group (UNIIMOG) that monitored the implementation of the cease-fire between Iran and Iraq, following their eight-year war, withdrew with the agreement of both parties in 1991. In Central America (ONUCA), observers monitoring the cease-fire in Nicaragua helped to verify the cessation of aid to irregular forces in the region; and assisted in the voluntary demobilisation of the Nicaraguan resistance.

They were withdrawn in January 1992. In Cambodia, following the signing of the Paris peace accords in October 1991, an advance mission of military observers (UNAMIC) paved the way for the arrival of UNTAC, which started operating last March.[54]

The agenda of the Secretary-General, mentioned above, addressed the questions of financing and suggested measures for peace and preventive diplomacy.

In concluding this chapter on peacekeeping and peacemaking, on peace-enforcement and peacebuilding, and considering the significant problems that existed, peacekeeping has been, overall, a significant success for the United Nations. The success, however, has not been uniform, especially when peacemaking has not kept the pace with peacekeeping. In addition, there was a human cost. It should never be forgotten that 812 men and women, from 43 countries, have died while in the service of the UN peacekeeping forces.[55]

Looking into the future, the Secretary-General said that others might also be able to undertake peacekeeping operations. In fact, regional organisations have carried out some operations in the 1960s and the 1970s, of which the most successful was an Arab League force deployed between Iraq and Kuwait from 1961 to 1963. On the basis of a resolution adopted by the Organisation of American States (OAS), an Inter-American Peace Force operated in the Dominican Republic from 1965 to 1966. In 1979, Egypt, in cooperation with the USA, organised a Multilateral Force and Observers in the Sinai to help implement the peace treaty with Israel. It is interesting to note that this latter force was established only after a request for a UN peacekeeping operation was rejected (by the Soviets, on behalf of the Arab Member States).[56]

The UN is no doubt the most experienced peacekeeper. The demands have, however, grown to such an extent that time seems to have come to share this responsibility. The decentralization of peacekeeping and peacemaking would be in tune with the radically new international environment of a multi-polar world that should be led by a multiplicity of institutions. Therefore, the regional organisations are obvious candidates for assuming larger responsibilities.

Chapter VIII of the Charter, specifically provides for regional organisations to 'make every effort to achieve pacific settlement of local disputes ... before referring them to the Security Council.

The problem is, however, that regional organisations have almost no experience and lack the necessary structure and procedures, and more importantly, most of them are in an even worse financial situation than the United Nations.

In his address on peacekeeping on 13 May 1992 in Washington, the Secretary-General expressed his belief that regional organisations must help to carry a larger share in this task. He insisted on a clear division of labour in Yugoslavia, between the European Community, which has for some time been engaged there both in peacemaking and peacekeeping, and the United Nations, which is responsible only for peacekeeping in certain areas. He also offered to help the CSCE to obtain some technical advice with regard to its own peacekeeping efforts in the dispute between Azerbaijan and Armenia over Nagorno-Karabakh.

In addition, in setting up the most recent efforts in Somalia, the Secretary-General associated the Organisation of African Unity (OAU), the Arab League and the Organisation of the Islamic Conference. In this most recent operation there is an interesting innovation. In recognition of the important role non-governmental organisations can play in new and broader peacekeeping operations, and after having been involved for many years in their humanitarian aspects, the latest Security Council resolution on Somalia acknowledges that much of the relief work to be protected by the UN military personnel, will be carried out by non-governmental organisations.[57]

The Secretary-General's 1992 *Agenda for Peace* places its policy recommendations in the changing international context and outlines plans and actions after an intensive consultative process both within the UN Secretariat's special task force for this purpose and outside, namely interested governments and organisations. Considerations and suggestions include measures to build confidence, fact-finding, early warning, preventive deployment, demilitarised zones. In the area of peacemaking the Agenda proposes that states should accept jurisdiction of the International Court of Justice, amelioration through assistance, sanction in special economic problems, use of military force and Peace-Enforcement-Units. In the area of peacekeeping, the Agenda looked at the increasing demands, considered new departures in peacekeeping, personnel and logistics. For post-conflict peacebuilding, it examined cooperation with regional organisations and arrangements, safety of personnel and financing. This document gives a fresh basis to embark on a new course for preventive diplomacy and conflict prevention.

A new Under Secretary-General for Humanitarian Affairs (DHA):

Major humanitarian emergencies in the last thirty years have called for new approaches. Resolution 2816 (XXVI), which in 1971 called for the appointment by the Secretary-General of a Disaster Relief Coordinator (and resulted in the establishment of the UN Disaster Relief Coordinator, UNDRO), addressed 'natural disasters and other disaster situations'. Ten years later, resolution 36/225, called for the Secretary-General to designate a lead entity from within the UN system to deal with 'Complex disasters and emergencies of exceptional magnitude.' At that time there appeared to be a consensus that UN emergency responses were not adequate.

Looking back on such experiences as Biafra in the late 1960's, Pakistan early 1970's, the Indochinese outflows, the Horn of Africa, strife and displacement in Central America, operation Lifeline in Sudan and several others in the eighties, all provide lessons and insights for improvement. Both the UN and other organisations, including many non-government agencies, have made significant contributions to bring relief in humanitarian emergencies. UNICEF, for example, acted in the capacity of 'troubleshooter' in several places to mediate for an unblocking of the situation, with or without coordination with other UN agencies.[58] Many of these experiences contributed to discussion on the need to create the post of Under Secretary-General for Humanitarian Affairs to oversee the coordination of operations in humanitarian emergencies.

This new Under Secretary-General would be able to act as a 'trouble shooter' on behalf of those in charge of field operations by interceding at the highest level of the UN's agencies and programmes, with the governments of the countries suffering from emergencies and with the key donors of aid and support. In this way, the authority of the Secretary-General could be brought directly to bear where it was most needed and a proper system of UN priorities could be established in conjunction with all those agencies.[59]

Preceding the finalisation of the basis for setting up a humanitarian office in the Secretariat in New York, Brian Urquhart and Erskine Childers presented a thorough study, which provided practical suggestions on dealing with humanitarian emergencies, with prevention and mitigation and with improving the international response. The authors also offered a description of the responsibilities of the Under Secretary-General, a standing high-level United Nations Board for Humanitarian, Disaster and Migration Affairs.

Finally, after about six months intensive negotiations, the General Assembly adopted Resolution 46/182 to set up the Department for Humanitarian Affairs.[60] Under the chapter of coordination, cooperation and leadership, the leadership of this resolution of the Secretary-General was recognized as critical for coherent response to natural disasters and other emergencies. As Urquhart/Childers had recommended, the General Assembly decided that an Inter-Agency Standing Committee serviced by a strengthened Office of the United Nations Disaster Relief Coordinator should be established under the chairmanship of the high-level official with the participation of all operational organisation and with a standing invitation to the International Committee of the Red Cross, the League of Red Cross Societies, and the International Organization for Migration. Relevant non-governmental organisations can be invited to participate on an ad-hoc basis.[61]

Jan Eliasson, appointed Under Secretary-General for Humanitarian Affairs in March 1992, makes the following comments on a first, albeit initial, evaluation of his office:

> First, while humanitarian assistance must be provided regardless of whether there is an immediate solution at hand, the United Nations has been increasingly called upon to address simultaneously both the humanitarian and the political dimensions of conflict situations. Somalia, Yugoslavia, and Mozambique are cases in point where Humanitarian assistance, delivered impartially, can have a positive impact on

> peacemaking effort. Corridors of peace and zones of tranquility can reinforce peacemaking initiatives.
>
> Secondly, the United Nations is required in an increasing number of emergencies to negotiate not only access, but also arrangements to ensure the safety of personnel and relief supplies. The situations in Somalia, the former Yugoslavia and Iraq are tragic reminders of this dilemma.
>
> Thirdly, the serious problem of land mines, millions of which remain scattered in current and former combat zones, must be urgently addressed. Relief assistance, repatriation and rehabilitation have been and will continue to be seriously hampered unless demining is pursued vigorously.
>
> Fourthly, cooperation among operational organisations is essential for effective UN response to disasters and emergencies. This cooperation must be all inclusive, applying equally to the relationship among the UN organisations and with the International Committee of the Red Cross, International Federation of the Red Cross, the International Organization of International Migration and the non-governmental organizations. Cooperation must also be extended to and strengthened with the relevant regional organizations.
>
> Lastly, while the UN stands ready to meet growing challenges in response to emergencies of increasing magnitude and complexity, it must be provided with the necessary resources to carry out the tasks entrusted to it. This applies not only to the immediate humanitarian requirements, but also to rehabilitation and development resources which should be mobilised to prevent emergencies from recurring.[62]

This initial evaluation still leaves room to pursue the recommendations made in the Secretary-General's Report on the review of the capacity, experience and coordination arrangements in the United Nations system for humanitarian assistance prior to establishing the Department for Humanitarian Affairs. This report foresaw measures, among others, on early warning and prevention. In looking at the responsibilities of the various organisations involved in humanitarian assistance, the office of the UNHCR was examined. It reported on the Working Group on Solutions and Protection, which was convened by the High Commissioner at the request of the Executive Committee to examine the issue of assisting, protecting and resolving the situation of internally displaced persons and refugees fleeing situations of serious internal disturbances and civil war.[63] An analysis of capacities in critical areas for rapid UN responses led the report to state that 'early warning is indispensable for prevention and preparedness activities'. It went on to say that many organisations in the UN already operate early warning.... These include UNHCR (its experimental [Refugee] Emergency Alert System), which aims at providing data on incipient flows of refugees, and its databases in the area of legal protection.[64]

This report, which was a cornerstone towards the establishment of the Department for Humanitarian Affairs, foresees coordinated approach among all UN agencies, in which UNHCR – on the basis of its imminent humanitarian mandate – should play a significant part.

Conclusions

During the Cold War, the United Nations were seriously impeded in carrying out effective preventive actions. As early as the late 1950's the then Secretary-General, Hammarskjold, coined the term 'preventive diplomacy'. Progressively, actions with preventive purpose or content were proposed, discussed, and some of them started in and outside the United Nations. A number of people, in and outside the UN system helped to catalyse forward thinking and conceptualise fresh ideas in this area.

As the analytical discussion of the mandate has shown, there are a number of references that could be invoked for actions designed to prevent conflicts. The efforts to delineate types of behaviour that will not be tolerated by the United Nations are there. The post Cold War era may now offer more opportunities in which declaratory preventive statements could make an impact. Since the end of the Cold War, unprecedented opportunities have developed and almost global cooperation for conflict prevention world wide. In view of the fact that the post Cold War time has led to a renaissance of the United Nations and its different services and agencies, UN conflict prevention endeavours also have new perspectives.

The decision-making process, even though complex has been a reflection of states' willingness to cooperate. If states represented in the United Nations do not cooperate properly, then it is far more the respective governments, which have not adequately used the instruments available in the international organisation, that are to be blamed, rather than the organisation itself. Therefore it would be hypocritical of some states to blame 'the United Nations' for not having acted in one or the other crisis, while having themselves put obstacles in the decision-making by denying their consent, or their political or material support.

The conflict prevention facilities are no doubt the most advanced and experienced of all existing organisations. The effectiveness of early warning and prevention is always difficult to measure as conflicts, if prevented or their impact reduced, are not a matter for publicity but rather for silence. There is broad agreement, however, on the usefulness of United Nations conflict management methods. The heavy demand on peacekeeping, peacemaking and peacebuilding is proof of that. Due to the emerging approach combining humanitarian, political and peacekeeping efforts to deal with existing and potential conflict situations, the United Nations have become *the* magic trouble shooter around the globe. It is an unprecedented expectation and credibility, which in fact places a heavy responsbility on the United Nations.

In view of this heavy demand, the Secretary-General has been calling for decentralization of conflict prevention activities. He wishes to involve regional and other organization more closely in this task and to adapt the cooperative mechanisms to the new international climate, which he also wrote into his *Agenda for Peace*, discussed here. Looking at the funding of peacekeeping situation, the strain currently placed on the United Nations becomes clear. Whereas for the 25 peacekeeping operations, from 1948 through 1992, the total cost amounted to about $8,311 billion, the estimated requirements for the current 12 operations are calculated at some $2,700 billion for 1991–1992.

During the Cold War the two superpowers retained their sphere of influence through containment policies. The political will of states will still remain the crucial ingredient for conflicts and their prevention. The Secretary-General upon a General Assembly resolution at the end of 1991, established a Department for Humanitarian Affairs to also undertake mediation missions, which is expected to have preventive or at least mitigating effects. It is still too early to make an evaluation of the effectiveness of this new office.

The urging for respect for human rights and humanitarian law figures prominently in documents, even in those which would have made no mention of it before. And of course, the Security Council resolutions concerning Iraq, and former Yugoslavia, would have been unthinkable just a few years ago. They did not stop escalation of those conflicts but analysis shows, nevertheless, that without them, conflict and human suffering could have been much worse.

Of course, war is still alive. In former Yugoslavia, in Iraq and in conflicts elsewhere. Conflict prevention, therefore is likely to be more effective in small specific situations rather than in large scale ones. As Emmanuel Kant has already said, there will always be war. What is important is to be on the road to peace. That process seems to be on course, although perhaps invisible to many eyes. Conditions are moving in the direction in which governments, people and the United Nations Organization could join hands, now that almost global cooperation makes peace a more realistic option than conflict.

In conclusion, the United Nations will only be able to continue contributing to conflict prevention efforts if states maintain their support and political will. Not only by the use of the mandate and the decision-making procedure, but also of the conflict prevention facilities and the management methods which they have created in the system. In addition, the United Nations will continue to play its role in international conflict prevention and collective security, subject to states' attitudes in the Security Council, which, now that the Cold War is over, have begun to be effective once more. Despite the existence of potential and actual crises, on an unprecedented scale, an analysis of the facts presented in this chapter shows it to be a reasonable assumption that, together with regional and other organisations and groups of states, the United Nations will remain an important, if not the most important, instrument for conflict prevention world wide.

NOTES

1. See: Brian Urquhart, Mehr als eine Action von Hillssheriffen, in: *Die Bleuhelme, Im Einsatz für Frieden*, (Hrsg. Ernst Koch, 1991 Report Verlag) p. 57.
2. UN. doc. S/23500, 31 January 1992, pp. 3, 4, 5.
3. Boutros Boutros-Ghali, *An Agenda for Peace*, Report of the Secretary-General pursuant to the statement adopted by the Summit Meeting of the Security Council on 31 January 1992. United Nations, New York, 1992.

4. *Declaration on Principles of International Law concerning Friendly Relations and Cooperation among States in accordance with the Charter of the UN*, (2625, XXV); the *Manila Declaration on the Peaceful Settlement of International Disputes* (37/10); the *Declaration on the Enhancement of the Effectiveness of the Principle of Refraining from the Threat or Use of Force in International Relations* (42/22); the *Declaration on the Prevention and Removal of Disputes and Situations Which May Threaten International Peace and Security and on the Role of the United Nations in this Field* (43/51).
5. Interview with a senior official of the UN Secretariat in New York, 2 April 1992.
6. The General Assembly may discuss any questions relating to the maintenance of international peace and security brought before it by any Member of the United Nations, or by the Security Council, or by a state which is not a Member of the United Nations.
7. Any Member of the United Nations may bring any dispute, or any situation that could endanger the maintenance of international peace and security to the attention of the Security Council or the General Assembly.
8. Javier Perez de Cuellar; *Rapport du Secretaire General sur l'Activité de l'Organisation, 1991*, (DPI/1168 – 40924 – September 1991), p. 10.
9. *Congo:* On 13 July 1960, Dag Hammarskjold requested the Security Council by letter for an urgent meeting on the basis of Article 99 (S/4381, 13 July 1960). The resolutions of the Security Council of 14 July (S/4387) and 22 July 1960 (S/4405) were passed on the basis of an initiative under Article 99. (Repertory of Practice of United Nations organs Suppl. 3, Vol. IV, Articles 92–11 of the Charter, United Nations New York, 1973). See also Jean-Pierre Cot and Alain Pellet, La Charte des Nations Unies, Commentaire Article par Article, *Economica*, Bruylant; pp. 1319, 1320.

   Korea: On 24 June 1950, Trygve Lie requested the president of the Security Council for an urgent meeting forwarding a communication by the USA concerning an act of aggression against the Republic of Korea (S/1495). In his mémoires, Trygve Lie stated to have invoked Article 99, this was not used *a la lettre* cf. *Mémoires of Trygve Lie, Au Service de la Paix*, (Gallimard, Paris 1957, pp. 371–373). See also Cot/Pellet, pp. 1319.

   Laos: On 5 September 1961, Dag Hammarskjold, requested the President of the Security Council to convene an urgent meeting outside the framework of Article 99, on Laos. (Repertory of Practice of the UN Organs, Vol. IV, pp. 161–162).

   Pakistan: On 20 July 1971, U Thant submitted a memorandum (S/10410) to the President of the Security Council regarding developments in East Pakistan and the adjacent Indian State and their consequences. With respect to possible consequences of the present situation, not only in the humanitarian sense, but also as a potential threat to peace and security. (Repertory of Practice of the UN Organs, Vol. V, pp. 134).

Vietnam: On 11 May 1971, Kurt Waldheim transmitted a memorandum to the President of the Security Council in which he suggested that the members of the Council consult with each other and examine actively which measures could be taken to put an end to the war. (Cot/Pellet, p. 1321).

Lebanon: On 30 March 1976 and 16 March 1978, Kurt Waldheim drew the attention of the Security Council to the serious situation, while transmitting communications he had received and offering his good offices. (Cot/pellet p. 1321).

Iran/Iraq: On 25 September 1980, Kurt Waldheim directed a letter to the President of the Security Council expressing the opinion that the conflict between Iran and Iraq was undoubtedly a threat to peace and security and that the Security Council should examine it urgently. (Cot/Pellet, pp. 1321, 1322).

10. Brian Urquhart, *Hammarskjold*. Harper & Row, New York, 1972), p. 258.
11. Tapio Kanninen, *The Future of Early Warning and Preventive Action in the United Nations*, (Occasional Papers Series, Number V, The Ralph Bunche Institute of the United Nations, New York, May 1991), pp. 2–3.
12. (UN Doc. 49 (A/41/49), 15 August 1986). *Report of the Group of High-Level Intergovernmental Experts to Review the Efficiency of the Administrative and Financial Functioning of the United Nations, General Assembly Records*; p. 12: Recommendation 18.
13. (UN doc. A/41/324, 13 May 1986). *Note by the Secretary-General. Report of the UN Group of Governmental Experts on International Co-operation to Avert New Flows of Refugees*, p. 18.
14. (UN doc. ST/SGB/225, 1 March 1987): Office for Research and the Collection of Information, p. 1.
15. Jurgen Dedring, 'Early Warning at the United Nations – Revisited', Note for the ISA Convention, Atlanta, Georgia, 1–4 April 1992.
16. The News Distribution of the Spokesman's Office/DPI include 'Political Information Bulletin', see, for example, #3, on News Agencies on Current Political Issues of 1 April 1992.
17. Jurgen Dedring, *Early Warning at the United Nations – Revisited*, p. 3.
18. SG/SM/4718, 19 March 1992, Transcript of Press Conference by the Secretary-General Boutros Boutros-Ghali, held at Headquarters today, 19 March [1992].
19. The Role of the United Nations in Early Warning Regarding Refugees and Displaced Persons: A Background Paper, 20 March 1991.
20. '... to develop an effective early warning system related to new flows of refugees and displaced persons, including measures of cooperation and procedures for gathering, analyzing and disseminating information in a

timely manner to all concerned, and to make recommendations on the need for an interagency consultative mechanism.'

21. Lance Clark, Final Report of the ACC Working Group on Early Warning of New Flows of Refugees and Displaced Persons, Working Document, *Rapporteur* 13 March 1992.
22. 'Towards Practical Early Warning; Capabilities Concerning Refugees and Displaced Persons', Report, (Centre for Refugee Studies, York University, North York, Ontario, 7 February 1992). p. 1, 4.
23. (UN doc. S/23500, 31 January 1992), Note by the President of the Security Council.
24. *The Blue Helmets, A Review of United Nations Peacekeeping*, Second Edition, (United Nations, New York, 1990), p. 13.
25. SG/SM/4723 – DC/2399, 27 March 1992, Secretary-General stresses concerns of UN and CSCE in message to Helsinki Follow-up meeting, DPI UN, New York.
26. (A/RES/46/20, 17 March 1992). *Cooperation between the United Nations and the Organisation of African Unity. Resolution adopted by the General Assembly*.
27. Edward Mortimer. Marrack Goulding, the UN's protector of a fragile peace, *Financial Times*, 29 February–1 March 1992.
28. Edward Mortimer. Financial Times. 29 February–1 March 1992.
29. Ibid.
30. Background Note, United Nations Peacekeeping Operations, Factsheet. Prepared by the Communications and Project Management Division, Department of Public Information, (United Nations PS/DPI/15 – March 1992).
31. Lt. Col. Christian Harleman, *Peacekeepers for a Changing World*. Presentation given to the Special Committee on Peacekeeping Operations, 14 May 1991, pp. 1, 2.
32. *The Blue Helmets. A Review of United Nations Peacekeeping*. Second Edition. (United Nations, New York, 1990).
33. Lt. Col. Christian Harleman. 'Handfile for New York Training Seminar on Peace-keeping, 23–27 March 1992' contains sections on Introduction/Background, Establishment Operation, Management Structure, Developments, Enforcement and Conclusions. UNITAR, 801 United Nations Plaza, New York, NY 10017. Papers contained include Negotiation to Establish a Peacekeeping Operation by C Harleman; Operational Effectiveness of a Peacekeeping Operation by Col. H Purola, Deputy Military Advisor to the Secretary-General; United Nations Peacekeeping Operations: Some Swedish Views and Experiences by Lars-Goran Engfeldt, Deputy Permanent Representative of Sweden to the UN in New York.
34. Lt. Col. Christian Harleman. Education and Training of Swedish UN troops at the United Nations Training Center (UNTC), Almnaes, Sweden, January 20, 1991 (Rev. Mar 3), pp. 1, 2.
35. Lt. Col. Christian Harleman. Education and Training ..., p. 7.
36. *The Conference of 1899 and The Conference of 1907* (ed. James Scott), *The Proceedings of the Hague Peace Conference*, Translation of the

Official Texts (New York, Oxford University Press, 1990) published under the auspices of the Carnegie Endowment for International Peace. The Conventions are still in force among some 60 states. See in: Roy S Lee, A Case for Facilitation in the Settlement of Disputes, *1991 German Yearbook of International Law*, pp. 211–244.

37. See GA Res. 46/58 Report of the Special Committee on the Charter of the United Nations and on the Strengthening of the Role of the Organisation, 9 December 1991, which mentions the completion of the Handbook on the Peaceful Settlement of Disputes between States. It covers i) principles of the peaceful settlement of disputes between States; ii) means of settlement; iii) procedures envisaged in the UN Charter; iv) procedures envisaged in other international instruments.
38. These methods are addressed in the *Handbook on the Peaceful Settlement of Disputes between States*, op.cit. in terms of characteristics, functions, application of the methods, and instrumental and related aspects and outcome. Cf. Roy S Lee, A Case for Facilitation in the Settlement of Disputes, *1991 German Yearbook of International Law*, pp. 211–244.
39. *The Blue Helmets*, op.cit., pp. 7, 8.
40. Cf. to Peace Enforcement by Major General Indar Jit Rikhye, from *Notes for Presentation to UNITAR Seminar on Peacekeeping* on 27 March 1992 in New York.
41. G/SM/4718, 19 March 1992, Transcript of Press Conference by the Secretary-General Boutros Boutros-Ghali. Held at Headquarters, 19 March, 1992.
42. The General Assembly approves the regular programme budget biennially on the presentation by the Secretary-General and the review of Committee for Programme and Coordination and the Advisory Committee on Administrative and Budgetary Questions.
43. (A/RES/46/186, 6 March 1992). Budget Appropriations for the biennium 1992–1993 of the General Assembly, pp. 1, 2, 3.
44. The legal régime governing assessments is Article 17, §2, of the Charter of the UN, which provides: The expenses of the Organisation shall be borne by the Members as apportioned by the General Assembly'. Under the scale which applies to the period of 1989–1990, assessments range from a maximum of 25 per cent for the largest contributor (USA) to a minimum of O.01 per cent (for example, Bangladesh, Haiti, or Liberia). See: *The Financing of the United Nations Peacekeeping Operations, The Need for a Sound Financial Basis*, by Susan R Mills, International Peace Academy, Occasional Paper, No. 3, 1989, p. 5.
45. United Nations Good Offices Mission in Afghanistan and Pakistan (UNGOMAP) Security Council Resolution 622 (1988).
46. UN Iran-Iraq Military Observer Group (UNIIMOG) Sec. Council Res. 619 (1988)
    UN Angola Verification Mission (UNAVEM) Sec. Council Res. 626 (1988)
    UN Transition Assistance Group (UNTAG) Sec. Council Res. 632 (1989) Namibia 435 (1978)
    UN Observer Group in Central America (ONUCA) Sec. Council Res. 644 (1989)

UN Iraq-Kuwait Observer Mission (UNIKOM) (1991)	Sec. Council Res. 689
UN Mission for the Referendum in Western Sahara (MINURSO)	Sec. Council Res. 690 (1991)
UN Observer Mission in El Salvador (ONUSAL)	Sec. Council Res. 693 (1991)
UN Angola Verification Mission (UNAVEM II)	Sec. Council Res. 696 (1991)
UN Advance Mission in Cambodia (UNAMIC)	Sec. Council Res. 717 (1991)
UN Protection Forces (UNPROFOR)	Sec. Council Res. 743 (1992)
UN Transitional Authority in Cambodia (UNTAC)	Sec. Council Res. 745 (1992)

Source: Handfile UNITAR Training Programme, 23–27 March 1992.

47. F T Liu, *United Nations Peacekeeping: Management and Operations*; (International Peace Academy), Occasional Papers on Peacekeeping, p. 31.
48. *Rapport du Secrétaire-Général sur l'Activité de l'Organisation*, 1991, pp. 23, 24.
49. George L Sherry; The United Nations Reborn, Conflict Control in the Post-Cold War World. *Critical Issues 1990.2*, (Council on Foreign Relations, New York) p. 10.
50. (A/46/600, 24 October 1991). *The Financial Situation of the United Nations*. Report of the Secretary-General.
51. (A/46/600/Add.1, 19 November 1991). *The Financial Situation of the United Nations, Proposals to Address the Problems of Today and Tomorrow*. Report of the Secretary-General, p. 2.
52. Speech to the Cosmopolitan Club, New York City, February 1992. In New York Review of Books, April 9, 1992, p. 42. Cited by Roberto Toscano. Address on Peacekeeping in the New International Situation at the International Symposium Prospects of Reform of the United Nations System, Rome, May 1992, p. 23.
53. Law 180 mentions specifically the supply of goods, services and financial contributions to international organisations, foreign countries, Italian and foreign private and public entities having as a goal the maintenance of peace and international security, as well as initiative in the humanitarian field and with the goal of protecting human rights. Given Italy's very substantial effort in the field of development assistance to LDC's, Italian participation in peacekeeping efforts in the Third World is not likely to run the risk of being inadequately funded. It would be an important step if other countries would make such budgetary arrangements to solidify the linkage between peace and development. The meaning of the linkage is twofold: there is no peace without development, but also 'development assistance is useless unless there is peace'. See in Roberto Toscano's address on Peacekeeping in the New International Situation at the International Symposium on Prospects of Reform of the United Nations System, in Rome, April/May 1992, p. 24/25.
54. *Ibid*, p. 8, 9.
55. (SG/SM/4748, 13 May 1992). Secretary-General Delivers Ninth Annual

David M Abshire Lecture, From Peacekeeping to Peacebuilding, p. 5.
56. *Ibid*, p. 5.
57. *Ibid*, p. 6.
58. Source: Discussions with Staffan de Mistura, UNICEF Representative in Dubrovnik, 14 Nov.–20 Dec. 1991 concerning humanitarian corridors.
59. Source: Discussions with Ambassador Jonathan Moore, Deputy Permanent Representative, USA Mission to the UN Headquarters in New York, 2 April 1992.
60. (46/182). Strengthening of the coordination of humanitarian emergency assistance of the United Nations, 19 December 1991.
61. 46/182, paragraph 38.
62. Jan Eliasson, Paper on 'The UN Response to Humanitarian Emergencies' for publication in the ACP/EC *Courier on Humanitarian Action*, forthcoming.
63. (A/46/568, 17 October 1991), p. 10.
64. (A/46/568, 17 October 1991), p. 19.

BIBLIOGRAPHY

The Art of Conflict Prevention: Theory and Practice of the United Nations

Annan, Kofi, *A Case for the Establishment of a United Nations Peace Endowment Fund*, 2 October 1991.

Burton, Jonathan, Libya Sanctions Signal UN Resolve, *The Christian Science Monitor*, 2 April 1992, p. 3.

Center for Refugee Studies, *Towards Practical Early Warning Capabilities Concerning Refugees and Displaced Pesons*, Ontario, 7 February 1992

Childers, Erskine & Brian Urquhart, *Strengthening International Response to Humanitarian Emergencies*, (Dag Hammarskjold Foundation, Uppsala, October 1991).

Clark, Lance, Final Report of the ACC Working Group on the Early Warning of New Flows of Refugees and Displaced Persons (Working Draft), 13 March 1992.

Cot, Jean-Pierre & Alain Pellet, La Charte des Nations Unies – Commentaire article par article.

Dedring, Jeurgen, Early Warning at the United Nations – Revised (Note for the ISA Convention, Atlanta, 1–4 April 1992), 31 March 1992.

Fraser, Colin, *Lifelines*, (Hutchinson Education, London, 1988) pp. 173–187.

Garcia, Francesca, M Garcia, John A Chiappinelli and the Ford Foundation Fellows, *The Evolving Concept on Humanitarian Assistance – Its Definition in International Law and Its Application on the United Nations*, (New York, April 1992).

Harleman, Christian, Peacekeeping and Disarmament in the Peacebuilding Process (Some Ideas for the Future), prepared for publication by *UN Disarmament Quarterly Review*, 1992:3, (New York, March 1992).

——. Negotiation to Establish a Peacekeeping Operation, 13 April 1991.

——. Prospects for Training Within the United Nations, December 1991.

——. Peacekeepers for a Changing World (Presentation given to the Special Committee on Peacekeeping Operations, May 1991).

——. Education and Training of Swedish UN-troops at the United Nations Training Center (UNTC), Almnaes, Sweden, published in *Die Blauhelme*, (Report-Verlag-Frankfurt a.m./Bonn, Germany, 1991).

Holt, Pat M, The Best Military Option: Stronger UN Peacekeeping, *The Christian Science Monitor*, 2 April 1992, p. 18.

International Committee of the Red Cross, Yugoslavia: Dialogue Continues as Plenipotentiaries Meet in Geneva, (Press Communication No. 92/7, 27 March 1992.)

Kanninen, Tapio, *The Future of Early Warning and Preventive Action in the United Nations*, (The Ralph Bunche Institute of the United Nations, New York, May 1991).

Kingue, Michel D, The Secretary General's Report on the Work of the Organization Stresses the Challenges Ahead, *Unitar Newsletter*, No. 2 (1991), pp. 3–11.

Koch, Ernst, (ed.), with contributions including from Peter J Opite, Christian Tomuschat, Horgh Risse, Brian Urquliart.

Lee, Roy S, *A Case for Facilitation in the Settlement of Disputes* (*1991 German Yearbook of International Law*, 30 June 1991), pp. 211–244.

Mistura, Staffan de, Mission (Report) to Albania – 8–16 July 1990.

Mortimer, Edward, Marrack Goulding – The UN's Protector of a Fragile Peace, *The Financial Times*, 29 February – 1 March 1992, p. 16.

Ramcharan, B G, *The International Law and Practice of Early-Warning and Prevention*, (Norwell: Kluwer Academic Publishers, 1991).

United Nations: Repertory of Practice of United Nations Organs – Supplement No. 1, Vol. II, Articles 55–111 of the Charter, New York, 1958.

——: Repertory of Practice of United Nations Organs – Supplement No. 3, Vol. IV, Articles 92–111 of the Charter, New York, 1973.

——: Repertory of Practice of United Nations Organs – Volume V, Articles 92–111 of the Charter, New York, 1955.

——: Role of the United Nations in Early Warning Regarding Refugees and Displaced Persons: A Background Paper, 20 March 1991.

——: 'Together at Last under One Roof – Security Council Summit Examines Future Directions and Priorities', *Secretariat News*, New York: UN Headquarters, February 1992, p 12.

UN doc: A/AC.121/39, 27 March 1992, Comprehensive Review of the Whole Question of Peacekeeping Operations in all their Aspects.

UN doc: A/46/568, 17 October 1991, Special Economic and Disaster Relief

Assistance: Office of the United Nations Disaster Relief Coordinator – Report of the Secretary General on the View of the Capacity, Experience and Coordination Arrangements in the United Nations System for Humanitarian Assistance.

UN doc. A/46/591 – S/23159, 23 October 1991, letter dated 23 October, 1991 from the representatives of Denmark, Finland, Norway, and Sweden to the United Nations addressed to the Secretary-General: Comprehensive Review of the Whole Question of Peacekeeping Operations in all their Aspects, Administrative and Budgetary Aspects of the Financing of the United Nations Peacekeeping Operations (A/AC.121/39, of 27 March 1992).

UN doc. A/46/600, 24 October 1991: The Financial Situation of the United Nations.

UN doc. G A Res. 46/58: on the Report of the Special Committee on the Charter of the UN and on the Strengthening of the Role of the Organization of 9 December 1991 (mentions Handbook on the Peaceful Settlement of Disputes between States – Supplement No. 33 and Corrigendum (A/46/33 and Corr. 1), Annex.)

UN doc. G A Res. 16/59: Declaration on Fact-finding by the UN in the Field of the Maintenance of International Peace and Security, 9 December 1991.

UN doc. S/23457, 22 January 1992: Letter dated 22 January 1992 from the Charge d'Affaires A.I. of the Permanent Mission of Iceland to the UN. Addressed to the Secretary-General.

UN doc. S/23500, 31 January 1992: Note by the President of the Security Council.

UN doc. SG/SM/4722, 26 March 1992: Under-Secretary-General for Humanitarian Affairs to Visit Bangladesh and Myanmar, 30 March–6 April, to Examine Refugee Situation.

UN doc. SG/CONF.5/1, 18 April 1990: Appeal by the Secretary-General (Letter dated 18 April 1990 from the Secretary-General addressed to all Member States).

UN doc. ST/ADM/SER.B/364, 8 January 1992: Status of Contributions as at 31 December 1991.

UN Department of Public Information: Human Rights Committee to Query Yugoslavia on how Current Crisis Affects its Obligations to Respect Rights Recognized in Covenant, (Press Release HR/CT/176, 26 March 1992).

——: Secretary-General Stresses Shared Concerns of UN and CSCE in Message to Helsinki Follow-up Meeting, Press Release SG/SM/4723, 27 March 1992.

——: Background Note – United Nations Peacekeeping Operations Fact Sheet, No. PS/DPI/15, March 1992.

——: Transcript of Press Conference by Secretary-General Boutros Boutros-Ghali Held at Headquarters Today, 19 March, (Press Release No. SG/SM/4718, 19 March 1992).

——: Transcript of Press Conference by Secretary-General Boutros Boutros-Ghali Held at Geneva Today, 10 April, (Press Release No. SG/SM/4727, 10 April 1992).

——: *United Nations Peacekeeping*, (brochure), May 1990.
United Nations High Commissioner for Refugees (UNHCR), The Return of Persons Displaced by the Yugoslav Conflict: Framework of UNHCR Operations (Geneva, 1992).
United Nations Institute for Training and Research (UNITAR), New York Training Seminar on Peacekeeping – 23–27 March 1992 (New York, 1992.)
UNICEF, UNICEF Humanitarian Corridor to Dubrovnik – 13 November–20 December 1991.
Widenfeld, Werner, Cooperation for a New European Epoch (*The International Herald Tribune*, 7 April 1992).

3

European Conflict Prevention: The Role of the CSCE

Heinz Vetschera

In general terms, security means the relative absence of threat. In international relations, security can be identified as the relative absence of the threat of armed conflict, i.e. war.[1] Thus, efforts to enhance European security have, first of all, to aim at reducing the danger of war or any other armed conflict in Europe.

INTRODUCTION

Security rests both on political stability and on military stability. Political stability means that there is no incentive for armed conflict on the political level, be it because no major tensions exist which would induce their military solution, or because the peaceful solution of conflicts has become a regular and accepted pattern of international relations. Military stability means that no state could hope to gain reasonable results by employing military force. If victory is uncertain, or even impossible, (offensive) war has ceased to be an instrument of politics in the Clausewitzian sense. Both political and military stability are complementary to each other.[2] European security will be served best if both political and military stability are high. It will be in severe danger if both political and military stability were low.

'Confrontational' and 'Cooperative' Security Policy

In order to achieve security and to prevent wars, two different approaches can be taken, namely a confrontational, and a cooperative approach. Within the confrontational approach, the first (and one could say: the traditional one) way is individual or collective self-defence, directed against an aggressor coming from outside one's own sphere. It is strictly confrontational, being based either on defence in its traditional sense,[3] or upon deterrence.[4] In most cases, alliances for collective defence have been directed against a more or less defined future opponent.[5] A more sophisticated way is collective security,[6] no longer directed against an identifiable adversary but against any potential aggressor within the system, as for example in the framework of the United Nations.[7] It threatens to use the united force of all participants in the system against the one would-be aggressor,[8] but it normally also aims at the promotion of peaceful relations, including the peaceful settlement of disputes, among its members.[9] International organisations of collective security thus combine elements of confrontational and cooperative security policy.

On the other side of the spectrum, cooperative security policy refrains from the very idea of enforcing stability in a confrontational way. It aims rather at promoting cooperation in order to prevent either the emergence of conflicts in the political sphere, or to reduce the danger of armed confrontation.[10] More specifically, cooperative security policy aims at preventing emerging conflicts from escalating into larger proportions.[11] In this context, emphasis is given to improved predictability by increased openness and transparency. Inasmuch as cooperative security policy is not aimed at enforcement but depends on the cooperation of all, it does not require any special structures for decision-making against one or the other state.[12]

Thus, structures of collective defence or collective security on the one hand and of cooperative security on the other hand differ in several respects in their potential for war-prevention. The first group is primarily aimed at deterring intended aggression via threatening violent reaction. Its preventive effect is thus an indirect one. It is, however, no instrument to prevent 'accidental' wars which do not result out of intended aggression but of misunderstandings, misinterpretations, or miscalculations. In contrast, cooperative security cannot threaten repression, as it requires cooperation by all and would thus be paralyzed by non-cooperation. It is, however, directly preventive in the real sense, with a primary objective in reducing the dangers of 'accidental' war.[13] Collective defence and collective security on the one hand and cooperative security on the other hand thus must not be put on the same footing but have to be seen as basically different, yet complementary instruments of international security policy. Whereas one set has been designed to deter intended aggression but cannot prevent 'accidental' war, the other set has been designed to prevent 'accidental' wars but cannot deter intended aggression.

THE CONFERENCE ON SECURITY AND COOPERATION IN EUROPE (CSCE)[14]

The Conference on Security and Cooperation in Europe (CSCE) has from the very beginning had a broad design, addressing military, economic, and political stability, and a comprehensive participation. Its agenda has stretched across the board of international relations, from basic rules of security and more specific regulations for military conduct (Confidence-Building Measures, CBMs) in the First Basket via economic relations in the Second Basket to the human dimension in the Third Basket.[15] Secondly, it was the only forum explicitly designed for Europe, yet including not only European but also extra-European participants.[16] Finally, it was the only forum encompassing not only those states belonging to both the Eastern and the Western alliances, but also neutral, non-aligned and other countries.[17]

Characteristics of the CSCE

The CSCE differs from other institutions for European security in several respects. The most relevant difference is the fact that, as the name indicates, it has not been created as an international organisation under international law but has always been an undertaking *sui generis*. It stands for a series of conferences and meetings which derived from the original CSCE (the 'Helsinki conference'), and have only recently led to permanent institutions,[18] and these only on a limited scale.[19] Therefore, there is no 'membership' of the CSCE, but states admitted to it are correctly described as 'participating States'.[20]

This factor has led to some characteristics which have been discernible throughout the whole CSCE process of conferences. First and foremost, the function of a multinational conference is to create conditions and to negotiate regulations in a long-term perspective rather than to find ad hoc solutions for short-term problems. Secondly, whereas international organisations frequently adopt the principle of a more or less qualified majority rule in their decision-making,[21] negotiations normally tend to achieve a maximum of agreement among the participants, and therefore in most cases require the consensus rule. Their success rests on the will of the participants to cooperate in finding a solution rather than on the idea to enforce the will of some (or the majority) upon the others. Thirdly, a conference proceeds rather by the initiatives of its participants than by initiatives of its own. A conference is thus not an actor in itself but rather a place to act for participating States.

All these elements are to be found in the CSCE's framework. Because of the need for States to cooperate, the CSCE has since its origins been an archetypal cooperative security structure, practically without elements of an enforcing character.[22] The character of 'cooperative' security has been expressed in the very name of the CSCE, indicating not only that stability in Europe requires both security[23] and cooperation, but also an emphasis on cooperation as a core for security policy. It has found its expression in the security policy instruments within the CSCE, based upon the Declaration on Principles Guiding Relations between Participating States[24] in the political field and the (cooperative) Confidence- and Security-Building Measures (CSBMs) in the military field.

European Security in the CSCE Framework[25]

The Helsinki Final Act does not define 'security' explicitly. The preambles of the chapter on *Questions Relating to Security in Europe* as well as of the two documents on the *Declaration on Principles Guiding Relations between Participating States* and *Document on confidence-building measures and certain aspects of security and disarmament* make it possible, however, to elaborate a concept of European Security, as seen through the CSCE perspective.

The objective of the participating States is to promote 'conditions in which their people can live in true and lasting peace free from any threat to or attempt against their security'.[26] In a similar way, the last paragraph of this preamble links 'peace' and 'security' together, recognising the close link between 'peace and security in Europe and in the world as a whole' and demanding to make contributions to the strengthening of 'world peace and security'. 'Peace and security' are also linked together in several other parts[27] of the same preamble.[28] The meaning of 'security' in the framework of the CSCE appears identical to the meaning it is given in the framework on the UN Charter.[29] In both cases, 'security' is connected to the notion of 'peace', indicating the relative absence of threats to peace by the threat or use of armed force.[30] 'Security' should lead to 'peace'.[31]

The 'Decalogue'

The Declaration on Principles Guiding Relations between Participating States contains, however, additional elements linked to 'peace' and 'security'. One is 'justice'. In a formal way, the issue has been linked to 'peace' and 'security' in the first and third paragraphs of the pertinent preamble.[32] It also derives from the enumeration of principles within the decalogue,[33] which includes not only the 'classical' principles of security[34] but provides also for 'respect for human rights and fundamental freedoms, including the freedom of thought, conscience, religion or belief'[35] as well as 'equal rights and self-determination of peoples'.[36] In the same vein, the principles of 'sovereign equality, respect for the rights inherent in sovereign equality'[37] and 'fulfilment in good faith of obligations under international law'[38] indicate 'justice' as a pillar for security.

The Declaration thus not only provides 'prohibitive' principles of security, but also 'preventive' principles addressing the causes of future threats to security as constituted by injustice. Finally, the Declaration also contains principles providing instruments alternative to the use of force, namely the peaceful settlement of disputes[39] and cooperation among states[40] as instruments to promote peace, security and justice.

'Peace', 'security', 'justice' and the principles of the decalogue are linked together in the following way:[41]

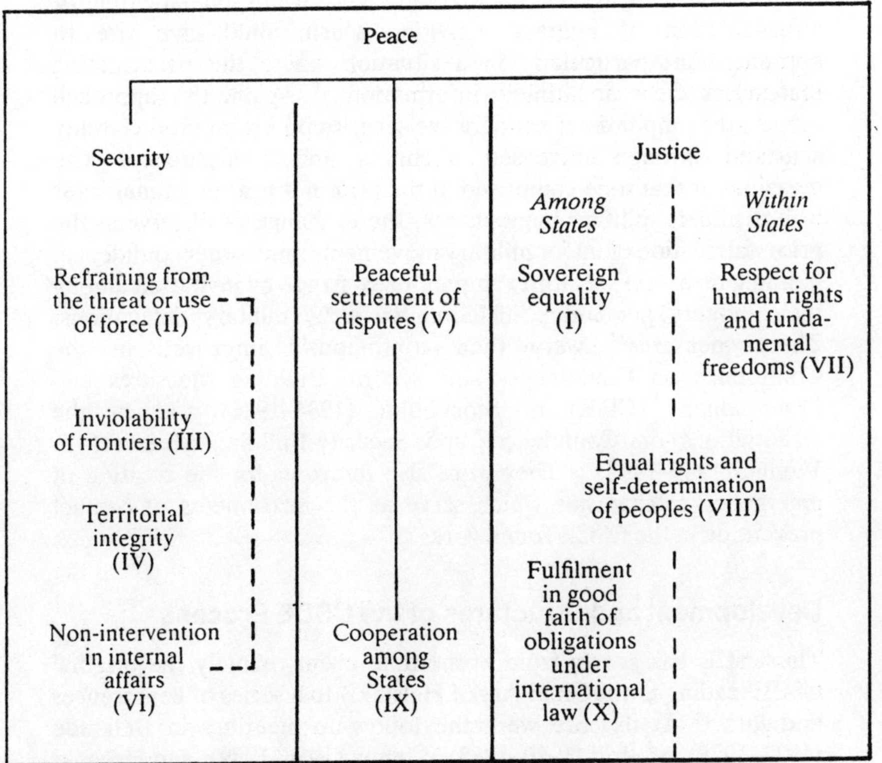

Fig. 3.1 The Principles of the Decalogue

The principles enshrined in the Declaration correspond to the concept of 'declaratory prevention'.[42]

The Operative Side of Security Policy: Confidence- and Security-Building Measures

On the operative side, the first instruments of (preventive) cooperative security policy in the CSCE framework were the Confidence-Building Measures as enshrined in the second Document of the Final Act. They should serve the need 'to contribute to reducing the dangers of armed conflict and of misunderstanding or miscalculation of military activities which could give rise to apprehension, particularly in a situation where the participating States lack clear and timely information'.[43] Again, this approach reflects the emphasis of cooperative security policy on predictability achieved through increased openness and transparency. The measures at that time comprised of the prior notification of major (as well as other) military manoeuvres, the exchange of observers, the prior notification of major military movements, and 'other confidence-building measures', as for example the exchange by invitation among their military personnel, including visits by military delegations. These measures[44] were then continuously improved in the Conference on Confidence- and Security-Building Measures and Disarmament (CDE) in Stockholm (1984–1986) and in the Negotiations on Confidence- and Security-Building Measures in Vienna (1989–1992).[45] They were also the roots for the creation of emergency mechanisms which serve as the instruments of conflict prevention in the CSCE framework.

Development and Structures of the CSCE Process

The CSCE has grown from a one-time event (namely the original CSCE leading to the Final Act of Helsinki) to a series of conferences and fora.[46] At its core were the follow-up meetings in Belgrade (1977–1978), Madrid (1980–1983), Vienna (1986–1989), and Helsinki (1992). Out of these meetings grew several specialized conferences on each of the subjects covered by the broad agenda of the CSCE, most notably (but by no means exclusively) in the field of military security. Here, the follow-up meeting in Madrid gave the mandate[47] to hold a specific Conference on Confidence- and Security Building Measures and Disarmament (CDE). It took place in Stockholm (1984–1986) and led, *inter alia*, to the first breakthrough in the adoption of compulsory on-site inspection,[48] thus paving the way for inclusion of this principle in the INF-Treaty one year later.[49]

The next mandate was given by the follow-up meeting in Vienna which went parallel to the significant changes taking place in the Soviet Union and other then communist countries. The mandate was twofold. On the one hand, the negotiations on Confidence- and Security-Building Measures (CSBMs) were to be continued.[50] On the other hand, however, parallel negotiations were opened on Conventional Forces in Europe,[51] *de facto* replacing the stalled MBFR/MURFAAMCE negotiations.[52] In November 1990, both sets of negotiations led to agreements in the respective fields, namely the (first) Vienna Document 1990 on CSBMs[53] and the CFE Treaty.[54]

At the same time, the CSCE participating States convened in Paris for the 1990 summit which responded to the fundamental changes in Eastern Europe in 1989/1990, and adopted the Paris Charter.[55] Within the Charter and its Supplementary Document[56] they also for the first time created permanent structures (bodies and institutions) in the CSCE framework.[57]

First, the CSCE should have scheduled follow-up meetings of the participating States to be held, as a rule, every two years to allow participating States to take stock of developments, review the implementation of their commitments and consider further steps in the CSCE process.[58] The Heads of participating States will meet on the occasion of subsequent follow-up meetings.[59] Then, the following bodies were created:

- a Council of the participating States' Foreign Ministers, to meet regularly and at least once a year, as the central forum for political consultations within the CSCE process;[60] The Council will consider issues relevant to the CSCE and take appropriate decisions.
- a Committee of Senior Officials (CSO) to prepare the meetings of

the Council and carry out its decisions.[61] The Committee will review current issues and may take appropriate decisions, including recommendations to the Council. Already in the Paris Charter, the 'development of provisions for convening meetings of the CSO in emergency situations' has been mentioned explicitly.[62]

In addition, the following permanent institutions were created:

- a CSCE Secretariat in Prague to provide support for consultations by the Council and the CSO;[63]
- an Office for Free Elections (OFE) in Warsaw to facilitate contacts and the exchange of information on elections within participating States;[64]
- a Conflict Prevention Centre (CPC) in Vienna to assist the Council in reducing the risk conflicts.[65]

Thus, the primary function for reducing the risk of conflict has been entrusted to the CPC. According to the Supplementary Document to the Paris Charter,[66] during its initial stage of operations the Centre's role will consist in giving support to the implementation of CSBMs such as:[67]

- mechanism for consultation and co-operation as regards unusual military activities[66] (UMA);
- annual exchange of military information;[69]
- communications network;[70]
- annual implementation assessment meetings;[71]
- co-operation as regards hazardous incidents of a military nature.[72]

In the latter case, the CPC has to keep the register of (military) points of contact for the pertinent measure of the CSBM-régime.[73] As the Supplementary Document further points out,[74] the Centre may assume other functions and the above tasks are without prejudice to any additional tasks concerning a procedure for the conciliation of disputes as well as broader tasks relating to dispute settlement, which may be assigned to it in the future by the Council of the Foreign Ministers.[75]

The three institutions are subordinated to the Council. They differ, however, not only in their functions but also in their basic structure. Both the CSCE Secretariat and the OFE have no decision-making body of their own but will execute decisions made by one of the mentioned bodies (Council or CSO). Within the CPC, in contrast, there has been established a decision-making body, the Consultative Committee (CC) which until the Helsinki Follow-Up Meeting has, as a rule, been composed of the delegations to the CSMB negotiations[76] in Vienna. The function of the CC[77] is to

- hold the meetings of participating States which may be convened under the mechanism on unusual military activities;
- hold the annual implementation assessment meetings;
- prepare seminars on military doctrine and such other seminars as may be agreed by the participating States;
- supervise the Secretariat of the Centre;
- provide a forum for discussion and clarification, as necessary, of information exchanged under agreed CSBMs;
- have overall responsibility for the communications network within the mandate of the CPC.

The Secretariat of the CPC[78] will carry out the tasks assigned to it by the Consultative Committee to which it is responsible.[79] In particular, it will establish and maintain a data bank, for the use of all participating States, compiled on the basis of exchanged military information under agreed CSBMs and will publish Yearbooks on that basis.[80]

The main task in conflict prevention is, however, the emergency function to hold consultations on unusual military activities. This has been a major element for creating the CPC.

Emergency mechanisms in the CSCE

Within the CSCE framework, emergency mechanisms have been developed on several different tracks and for different emergency situations, namely in the military field and in the field of general political crisis situations.

The military emergency mechanism

The first emergency mechanism has been the mechanism on unusual military activities already mentioned together with ideas for an emergency communications network. The first Western proposal in the NCSBMs[81] contained as Measure 11 the 'development of means of communication' as additional arrangements parallel to the existing diplomatic channels. This idea was elaborated in more detail in the proposal of 9 June 1989,[82] demanding that each participating State should designate a point of contact capable of receiving such information, preferably on a 24-hour basis.

Parallel to the first Western proposal the – then – WTO countries Bulgaria, GDR, CSSR and Hungary tabled a proposal on 8 March 1989,[83] containing the 'development of a special communications system for the mutual clarification of situations giving rise to doubts or apprehensions on any side'.[84] Furthermore, the proposal contained the 'holding on a regular basis of bilateral and multilateral consultations'[85] as well as the 'establishment of a centre for the reduction of the risk of war and prevention of surprise attack in Europe, which should have an informational and consultative character'.[86] The idea of a communications system was also supported in the Romanian proposal[87] of 22 March 1989 'for consultation between the heads of States and Governments and convening high-level meetings in emergency situations',[88] and by the group of neutral and nonaligned (N+NA) States in its proposal of 12 July 1989,[89] demanding a 'system of rapid communications so as to ensure reliability and timeliness of the transmissions'. Furthermore, 'Modern means of communications should be used allowing also for the transmission of maps, diagrams and other graphic information'. Thus, all relevant groups within the CSCE had included the idea of communications into their proposals already at this stage. Furthermore, some had already included ideas of consultation mechanisms, and of creating specific institutions to deal with war/crisis prevention.

In the following stages, the proposals for a communications system and for consultation mechanisms took shape. The Western group proposed an annual implementation assessment meeting[90] in its proposal of 23 February 1990,[91] and in its proposal of 18 May 1990[92] several options for a communications network, including 'a telegram network, direct links between computer terminals, or the use of existing commercial networks exclusively or in part via the international telephone network'.[93] Furthermore, the proposal contained an elaborated 'mechanism for discussion of unusual activities of a military nature'[94] and 'measures reducing the risk of and reporting hazardous incidents'.[95]

The 'mechanism for discussion of unusual activities of a military nature' is of special relevance as it gave the first outline for the following CSCE emergency mechanisms. The proposal envisaged that

> 1. Any participating State which has concerns about an unusual activity of a militarily significant nature, involving conventional forces on the territory of any other participating State in the area of application which are engaged in unscheduled out-of-garrison activities, may request an explanation of such activities from that State. The requested State will answer in writing through official channels at the shortest possible notice, but in any case not later than 48 hours after the request was made.
> 2. The requesting and requested State will immediately provide copies of the communication to all other participating States (e.g. through an eventual CSBM communication network).
> 3. Any participating State which has concerns about an unusual activity, as specified in Paragraph 1, engaged in by any other participating State in the area of application may also request a meeting with the other State to discuss this activity. Such a meeting will be held at the shortest possible notice, but in no case later than 48 hours after the request for such a meeting was made. The State receiving such a request is entitled to ask for the participation of other interested participating States in such a meeting.
> 4. After holding such a meeting the participating States concerned will immediately, jointly or separately, inform all other participating States of the result of this meeting (e.g. through an eventual CSBM communication network).
> 5. Any participating State which has concerns about an unusual activity, as specified in Paragraph 1, engaged in by any other participating State in the area of application may request at the shortest possible notice a meeting of the 35 participating States in order to discuss this unusual activity. The participating States undertake to take part in meetings at which questions concerning them are to be discussed (organisational provisions to be developed).

Another part of the proposal[96] envisaged the establishing of points of contact for hazardous incidents of a military nature.

These ideas were then included in the comprehensive French

proposal for a concluding document,[97] and without major changes found their way into the *Vienna Document* 1990. The *Vienna Document* in its Measure IX (Communications) envisages to establish a network of direct communications between the capitals of all participating States for the transmission of messages relating to agreed measures, complementing the existing diplomatic channels.[98] Each participating State will designate a point of contact capable of transmitting and receiving such messages on a 24-hour-a day-basis.[99] The technical details have been set out in Annex II to the document.[100]

Measure II (Risk Reduction) contains, first of all, the Mechanism for Consultation and Co-operation as regards Unusual Military Activities (UMA). It provides that 'participating States will ... consult and co-operate with each other about any unusual and unscheduled military activities of their military forces outside their normal peacetime locations which are militarily significant ... and about which a participating State expresses its security concern.'[101] The operative provisions then follow the model of the Western proposal: The participating State which has concerns may transmit a request to another participating State where the activity is taking place;[102] the request will state the cause of the concern and, to the extent possible, the type and location of the activity.[103] The reply will be transmitted within not more than 48 hours,[104] and 'will give answers to questions raised, as well as any other relevant information which might help to clarify the activity giving rise to concern'.[105] The requesting State, after considering the reply provided, may then request a meeting to discuss the matter.[106] Request for explanation, reply and request for a meeting will be transmitted to all participating States without delay.[107]

The meeting could be held with the requested State,[108] or as meeting of all participating States[109] and would, in any case, be convened within not more than 48 hours.[110] The two possibilities do not exclude each other, as a State may decide to 'escalate' by requesting a multilateral meeting if the bilateral meeting had been unsuccessful. A bilateral meeting will be held at a venue to be mutually agreed upon by the requesting and the responding State. If there is no agreement, the meeting will be held at the CPC.[111] In the case of a multilateral meeting, the CPC will serve as the forum for such a meeting.[112]

The consultation mechanism has been activated on three occasions during the Yugoslav crisis: The first case concerned multilateral consultations on the military situation in Yugoslavia on 1 July 1991.[113] The second case concerned bilateral consultations between Yugoslavia and a neighbouring State on 1 September 1991. In both cases, the consultations did not achieve a decrease of the scope of violence in (then) Yugoslavia, but led to de-escalation at the borders with neighbouring States, and therefore served their primary purpose. A third case in April 1992 concerned a request by Yugoslavia for an explanation of military activities in a neighbouring State, but did not lead to further steps.

The other mechanism in the area of military risk reduction concerns cooperation as regards hazardous incidents of a military nature. Participating States will 'cooperate by reporting and clarifying hazardous incidents of a military nature ... in order to prevent possible misunderstandings and mitigate the effects of another participating State'.[114] They will designate a point of contact,[115] and in the case of such an incident the participating State whose military forces are involved in the incident should provide the information available to other participating States in an expeditious manner.[116] Communications should preferably be transmitted through the CSBM communications network.[117] The CPC has been given the task to keep available the list of points of contact[118] and to serve as a forum to discuss such incidents, either at the annual implementation assessment meeting, or at additional meetings convened there.[119] There has not yet been any activation of this mechanism by the participating States.

The non-military CSO emergency mechanism

Although the Paris Charter has already explicitly mentioned the 'development of provisions for convening meetings of the CSO in emergency situations', the non-military mechanism of CSO emergency meetings was created only at the Berlin Meeting of the Council in June 1991.[120] It refers to 'a serious emergency situation which may arise from a violation of one of the Principles of the Final Act or as the result of major disruptions endangering peace, security or stability'.[121] If any participating State concludes that an emergency situation, as referred above, is developing, it may seek clarification from the State or States involved. The request will state the cause, or causes, of the concern.[122] The requested State or States will provide within 48 hours all relevant information in order to clarify the situation.[123] Should the situation remain unresolved, any of the States involved in this procedure may address to the Chairman-in-Office of the CSO[124] a request that an emergency meeting of the Committee be held.[125] The request should state the reasons why the matter is urgent and why the emergency mechanism is the most appropriate.[126] As soon as 12 or more participating States have seconded the request within a maximum period of 48 hours by addressing their support to the Chairman, he will immediately notify all participating States of the date and the time of the meeting, which will be held at the earliest 48 hours and at the latest three days after this notification.[127] The meeting will be held at the Seat of the CSCE Secretariat[128] and last no more than two days, unless otherwise agreed.[129] The meeting may agree on recommendations or conclusions to arrive at a solution; It may also decide to convene a meeting at the ministerial level.[130] As the decision state explicitly, this procedure will not be used in place of the mechanism on unusual military activities.[131]

The mechanism has also been activated at the beginning of the Yugoslav crisis in July 1991.[132] It has *inter alia* led to the CSCE's endorsing of the EC monitoring mission and widening its scope by including members from non-EC participating States.[133] Further emergency meetings of the CSO on Yugoslavia were held on the basis of the first meeting, whenever the situation required it. A distinct second emergency meeting was called during the CSO's presence in Helsinki on 6 May 1992, on the situation in Bosnia–Herzegovina.

The humanitarian emergency mechanism

The humanitarian mechanism has been derived from the provisions in the Concluding Document of the Vienna Follow-up Meeting 1986–1989[134] which envisaged that participating States would exchange information and respond to requests for information and to representation made to them by other participating States on questions relating to the human dimension of the CSCE,[135] and would hold bilateral meetings with other participating States that so request, in order to examine questions relating to the human dimension of the CSCE.[136] In order to achieve further progress in this area, the participating States also agreed within the same document to hold a Conference on the Human Dimension of the CSCE, with a first meeting in Paris (30 May to 23 June 1989), a second meeting in Copenhagen (5 to 26 June 1990), and a third meeting in Moscow (10 September to 4 October 1991). The Copenhagen meeting of this Conference transformed the said provisions into an obligatory mechanism with a set procedure, deciding that States should provide, in as short a time as possible, but no later than four weeks, a written response to requests for information and to representation made to them in writing by other participating States under para. 1 of the Vienna Concluding Document,[137] and providing that the bilateral meetings, as contained in para. 2, will take place as soon as possible – as a rule within three weeks of the date of the request.[138] These provisions were amended by the Document of the Moscow meeting to the effect that the written response should be provided no later than ten days after the request for information, and that bilateral meetings would take place, as a rule, within one week of the date of the request.[139] Beyond that, the Moscow document provides to establish a list of experts, from whom an impartial performance may be expected.[140] Participating States may invite the assistance of a CSCE mission, consisting of up to three experts, to address or contribute to the resolution of questions in its territory relating to the human dimension,[141] or may request that the CSCE institution[142] inquire of another participating State where it would agree to invite a mission of experts to address a particular, clearly defined question on its territory relating to the human dimension of the CSCE.[143] If, however, a participating State has either directed an enquiry to another participating State and that State has not established a mission of experts within the given time-frame, or if the State judges that the issue in question has not been resolved as a result of a mission of experts, it may, with the support of at least five other

States, initiate the establishment of a mission of up to three rapporteurs.[144] Rapporteur missions could also be established if a participating State considers that a particularly serious threat to the fulfilment of the provisions of the CSCE human dimension has arisen in another participating State; it may then, with support of at least nine other participating States, trigger such a mission.[145] In a similar way, the CSO, upon the request of a participating State, may decide to establish a mission of experts or of CSCE rapporteurs.[146] The Prague decisions of the second Meeting of the Council in January 1992[147] designated the Office for Democratic Institutions and Human Rights (ODIHR)[148] as the CSCE institution charged with the tasks in connection with expert and rapporteur missions according to the Document of the Moscow Meeting.[149]

The mechanism has been activated once in the context of the Yugoslav crisis in September 1992.

The mechanism for the peaceful settlement of disputes

At the Berlin meeting,[150] the Council also decided upon the mechanism for the peaceful settlement of disputes as elaborated at a CSCE expert meeting at Valletta.[151] The mechanism[152] envisages a third-party function by qualified persons to reconcile differing positions and aims at preventing political disputes from escalating into more severe forms of confrontation.

The mechanism has not been activated so far.

FURTHER DEVELOPMENTS

The Prague Decisions

At its meeting in Prague on 30–31 January 1992 the Council adopted several guidelines for the upcoming Helsinki Follow-up Meeting.[153] They include *inter alia* the role of the CSCE in fostering democratic development and fully integrating participating States into the network of shared CSCE values; the importance of a thorough implementation review, particularly in the area of human rights and individual freedoms; the objective of the CSCE to prevent conflict and consolidate peace through eliminating the root causes of tensions (especially mentioning human rights and rights of national minorities) and by fostering economic and social progress; strengthening the capacity of the CSCE to contribute to a peaceful solution of problems involving national minorities, including possibilities for 'early warning'; further development of the CSCE's capability for conflict prevention, crisis management and the peaceful settlement of disputes.[154]

On the operative level, the meeting decided to strengthen the role of the CSO[155] and make available to its chairman the CSCE communications network;[156] to extend the functions of the hitherto OFE into an Office for Democratic Institutions and Human Rights,[157] with the task, under the general guidance of the CSO, to hold implementation meetings, to serve as an institutional framework for sharing and exchanging information on technical assistance for the new democracies in institution-building and to facilitate contacts as well as cooperation in training and education in pertinent disciplines, to organise meetings and seminars on related subjects,[158] and to cooperate with the Council of Europe and the European Commission for Democracy through Law.[159] Finally, it should also have the tasks connected with expert and rapporteur missions according to the Document of the Moscow Meeting on the conference on the Human Dimension of the CSCE.[160] In this context, the Council also decided that appropriate action may be taken by the Council or the CSO, if necessary, in the absence of the consent of the State concerned,[161] in cases of clear, gross and uncorrected violations of relevant CSCE committments.[162]

In the area of crisis management and conflict prevention,[163] the Council requests the Helsinki Follow-up Meeting to study possibilities for improving the instruments of fact-finding missions, rapporteur missions, good offices, counselling and conciliation and dispute settlement,[164] but also to 'consider carefully' possibilities for CSCE peacekeeping or a CSCE role in peacekeeping.[165] Within the Consultative Committee the CPC has been given the task to serve as a forum for 'comprehensive and regular' consultations on security issues with political–military implications[166] as well as a forum for consultation and co-operation in conflict prevention and for co-operation in the implementation of decisions on crisis management taken by the Council or the CSO acting as its agent;[167] it also has been given authority to initiate, and with the assistance of the CPC Secretariat to execute, fact-finding and monitor missions in connection with the mechanism relating to unusual military activities (UMA).[168] The CPC will, in addition give its existing support to the implementation and verfication of agreements in the field of disarmament and arms control.[169] The decision further underlines the function of the CPC to organise seminars in which other bodies (as for example NATO, the WEU and relevant United Nations bodies) may be invited.[170]

The Ministers in their meeting reaffirmed that the CSCE has a vital role to play in the building and consolidation of a new Europe.[171] It constitutes with its comprehensive mandate and wide participation, a unique forum for security negotiations.[172] They further stressed that 'the CSCE also has a prominent role to play in the evolving European architecture and that the challenges facing Europe call for a multifaceted form of cooperation, and a close relationship among European, transatlantic and other international institutions and organizations, drawing as appropriate upon their respective competence'.[173] They 'requested their representatives at the Helsinki Follow-up Meeting to study further ways and means of fostering such co-operation with a view to enhancing its effectiveness and to avoid duplication'.[174]

The Helsinki Decisions

As agreed in the Concluding Document of the Vienna Meeting 1986, the fourth main Follow-up Meeting commenced in Helsinki on 24 March 1992.[175] At its beginning, the First Additional Meeting of the Council was held on 24 March,[176] and at its end the Heads of States and Governments met for a summit, as envisaged by the Paris Charter,[177] on 9 and 10 July. On 10 July they issued the CSCE *Helsinki Document 1992*.[178] The Document contains two major parts, namely on the one hand the Helsinki Summit Declaration, referring to the new tasks of managing rather than promoting change in Europe, and on the other hand the *Helsinki Decisions* as the result of the Helsinki Follow-up Meeting. The *Helsinki Decisions* build in parts upon the recommendations of the Prague Council Meeting and contain, inter alia, several provisions with regard to the CSCE's role and institutions in conflict prevention.[179]

New Bodies and Institutions in the Helsinki Decisions[180]

In the *Helsinki Decisions*, the participating States 'declare their understanding that the CSCE is a regional arrangement in the sense of Chapter VIII of the Charter of the United Nations',[181] indicating an active regional security policy role. On the organisational side, for the purpose of strengthening CSCE institutions and structures,[182] the *Helsinki Decisions* provide for several bodies to assist the Chairman-in-Office. One is the Troika, consisting of the Chairman-in-Office and the Chairmen;[183] then, *ad hoc* steering groups may be established on a case-by-case basis to assist the Chairman-in-Office, in particular in the field of conflict prevention, crisis management and dispute resolution.[184] The Chairman-in-Office may also designate personal representatives when dealing with a crisis or a conflict.[185] Most of these organisational arrangements have, however, been already followed before in the CSCE. Thus, although the *Helsinki Decisions* refer to them for the first time in a CSCE document, they mostly ratify an existing practice.

Also in the security policy area, the *Helsinki Decisions* create the CSCE Forum for Security Co-operation,[186] with a strengthened Conflict Prevention Centre, as an integral part of the CSCE.[187] The Forum should *inter alia* achieve harmonisation of obligations agreed among participating States under the various existing instruments concerning arms control, disarmament and confidence- and security-building.[188] The arrangements for the Forum will be on the one hand a 'Special Committee', meeting for negotiations on arms control, disarmament and confidence- and security-building, or for consideration of goal-oriented dialogue and, as appropriate, elaboration or negotiation of proposals for security enhancement and co-operation[189] and, on the other hand, the Consultative Committee in respect of the existing and future tasks of the COC.[190] In order to ensure coherence, the representation of the participating States on the Special Committee and the Consultative Committee will in principle be assured by the same delegation.[191] Thus, to a certain degree, the structure of the Forum ratifies the previous practice, based upon the provisions of the Charter of Paris, that the delegations to negotiations and to the CPC are identical, and gives a common framework for two bodies different in their tasks, yet based upon mostly identical delegations in their composition.

The *Helsinki Decisions* established a High Commission on National Minorities[192] to act under the aegis of the CSO as an instrument of conflict prevention at the earliest possible stage in regard to tensions involving national minority issues which have not yet developed beyond an early warning stage but, in his judgement, have the potential to develop into a conflict within the CSCE area, affecting peace, stability, or relations between participating States, requiring the attention of and action by the Council or the CSO.[194] He will be appointed by the Council upon the recommendation of the CSO for a period of three years,[195] and will draw upon the facilities of the ODIHR.[196] He will collect and receive information from various sources,[197] including the media, non-governmental organisations,[198] and the parties involved.[199] The High Commissioner may also request assistance by up to three experts for brief, specialized investigations.[200] If the High Commissioner concludes that there is a *prima facie* risk of potential conflict, he/she may issue an early warning, which will be communicated promptly by the Chairman-in-Office to the CSO.[201] Normally, the early warning would be put on the agenda of the next CSO meeting, but if a State believes that such an early warning merits prompt consultation, it may initiate the CSO Emergency Mechanism.[202] Should the High Commissioner conclude that the situation is escalating into a conflict, or if he deems that the scope for action on his side is exhausted, he shall, through the Chairman-in-Office, so inform the CSO.[203] Should the CSO become involved in a particular issue, the High Commissioner will provide information and, on request, advice to the CSO and any other institution or organisation which the CSO may invite to take action with regard to the tensions or conflict.[204]

The Role of Conflict Prevention in the Helsinki Decisions

Chapter III of the Helsinki Decisions is entirely devoted to 'Early Warning, Conflict Prevention and Crisis Management (including Fact-Finding and Rapporteur Missions and CSCE Peacekeeping), and the Peaceful Settlement of Disputes'.[205] In it, the participating States declare their committment to a more effective role in conflict prevention and resolution, complemented, when necessary, by peacekeeping operations.[206] They will enhance their capability to identify the root causes of tensions through a more rigorous review of implementation to be conducted both through the ODIHR and the CPC, to improve their capability to gather information and to monitor developments[207] and will make intensive use of regular, in depth, political consultations, within the structures and institutions of the CSCE, in order to have early warning of situations within the CSCE area which have the potential to develop into crises, including armed conflicts.[208] The primary responsibility rests with the CSO,[209] but attention may be drawn to the CSO by a State directly involved in a dispute, by a group of 11 States not directly involved, the High Commissioner, by the CC in accordance with para. 33 of the Prague document or following the use of the UMA mechanism, or by the use of the *Human Dimension Mechanisn* or the *Valletta Mechanism.*[210] In the political management of crisis, the CSO may seek independent advice and counsel from relevant experts, institutions and international organisations.[211] The CSO may delegate tasks to the CC of the CPC, or to other CSCE institutions.[212]

The Instruments of Conflict Prevention in the Helsinki Decisions: Fact-finding and Rapporteur Missions, and Peacekeeping

With regard to the instruments of conflict prevention and crisis management, the *Helsinki Decisions* foresee, first, that the CSO or the CC may decide by consensus to establish fact-finding and rapporteur missions[213] 'without prejudice to the provisions of para. 13 of the *Moscow Document in respect of Human Dimension* issues, and para. 29 of the *Prague Document in respect of Unusual Military*

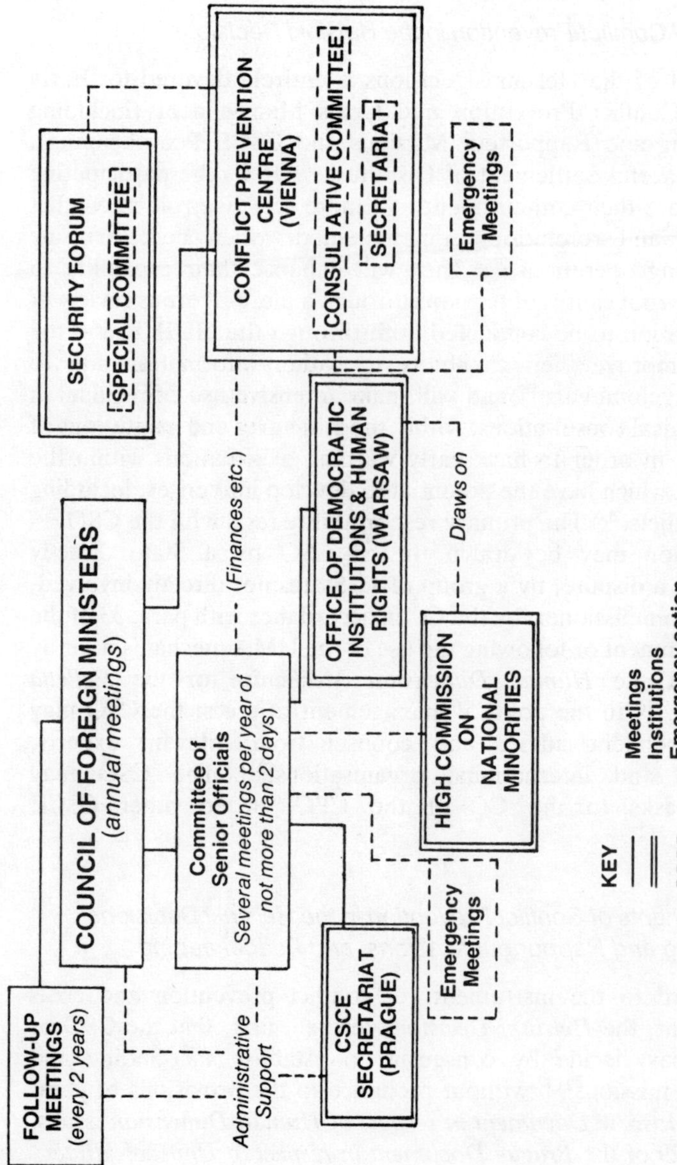

Fig. 3.2 The Organisation and Institutions of CSCE

Activities'. Such decision will in every case contain a clear mandate. The *Helsinki Decisions* also foresee that the participating State(s) will co-operate fully with the mission on its territory in pursuance of the mandate and facilitate its work.[214] The major part of this sub-chapter is, however, devoted to CSCE peacekeeping. The *Helsinki Decisions* emphasize peacekeeping as 'an important operational element of the overall capability of the CSCE for conflict prevention and crisis management intended to complement the political process of dispute resolution. CSCE peacekeeping activities may be undertaken in cases of conflict within or among participating States'.[215] The purpose of peacekeeping activities were, *inter alia*, to supervise and help maintain cease-fires, to monitor troop withdrawals, to support the maintenance of law and order, to provide humanitarian and medical aid and to assist refugees.[216] CSCE peacekeeping operations will be undertaken with due regard to the responsibilities of the United Nations in this field and will at all times be carried out in conformity with the *Purposes and Principles of the Charter of the United Nations*. CSCE peacekeeping will take place in particular within the framework of Chapter VIII of the Charter of the United Nations.[217] The *Helsinki Decisions* contain several principles to be followed within peacekeeping operations, as for example that CSCE peacekeeping operations will not entail enforcement action,[218] that they require the consent of the parties directly concerned,[219] that they will be conducted impartially,[220] and that they cannot be considered a substitute for a negotiated settlement and therefore must be understood to be limited in time.[221] Before the CSCE would dispatch a mission, the following conditions must be fulfilled:

- establishment of an effective and durable cease-fire;
- agreement on the necessary Memoranda of Understanding with the parties concerned, and
- provision of guarantees for the safety at all times of personnel involved.[222]

On the organisational side, the *Helsinki Decisions* foresee that decisions to initiate and dispatch forces for peacekeeping operations will be taken by consensus by the Council or the CSO acting as its agent.[223] They attribute to the CSO 'overall political control and guidance' for peacekeeping operations,[224] but foresee also some role for the CPC. For example, the CSO may request the CC to consider which peacekeeping activities might be most appropriate to the situation and to submit its recommendations to the CSO for decision.[225] The terms of reference of a peacekeeping operation, to define practical modalities and determine requirements for personnel and other resources, should be prepared, as appropriate, by the CC; they will be adopted by the CSO unless it has been agreed otherwise.[226]

In the chain of command, the Council/CSO will assign overall operational guidance of an operation to the Chairman-in-Office, who will be assisted by an ad hoc group established at the CPC. The ad hoc group will, as a rule, consist of representatives of the preceding and the succeeding Chairmen-in-Office, of the participating States providing personnel for the mission and of participating States making other significant practical contributions to the operation.[227] The operational command in the mission area[228] is given to a Head of Mission to be nominated by the Chairman-in-Office for endorsement by the CSO after appropriate consultations.[229] He will be responsible to the Chairman-in-Office, and consult and be guided by the ad hoc group.[230] The ad hoc group will provide operational support for the mission and will act as a 24-hour point of contact for the Head of Mission and assist the Head of Mission as required.[231]

The CC should ensure continuous liaison between the operation and all participating States, through the regular provision of information to it by the ad hoc group.[232] The CC will also be responsible to the CSO for the execution of tasks related to peacekeeping, where the CSO assigns such tasks to the CPC.[233]

A special segment of the *Helsinki Decisions* on peacekeeping is devoted to cooperation by the CSCE with regional and transatlantic organisations,[234] referring explicitly to the EC, NATO, the WEU and the peacekeeping mechanism of the Commonwealth of Independent States (CIS). The CSCE may benefit from resources and possible experience and expertise of such organisations, and could therefore request them to make their resources available in order to support it in carrying out peacekeeping activities.[235] However, contributions by such organisations will not affect the procedures for the establishment or the conduct and command of CSCE peacekeeping operations, nor would they nor would they exclude CSCE participating States who are not members of such an organisation from being eligible to take part in CSCE peacekeeping operations.[236] On the organisational side, the ad hoc group will establish and maintain effective communication with any organisation whose resources may be drawn upon in connection with CSCE peacekeeping activities.[237]

Further Approaches to Conflict Prevention in the Helsinki Decisions

In the context of conflict prevention, the participating States also stress that their commitment to settle disputes among themselves by peaceful means forms a cornerstone of the CSCE process, and that the peaceful settlement of disputes is an essential component of the CSCE's overall ability to manage change effectively and to contribute to the maintenance of international peace and security.[238] Further provisions of the *Helsinki Decisions* refer to the idea of creating a conciliation and arbitration court within the CSCE, so enhancing the Valletta mechanism and establishing a CSCE procedure for conciliation, including directed conciliation, as discussed at the Follow-up meeting.[239]

Within the newly created CSCE Forum for Security Cooperation, States will not only negotiate on arms control, disarmament and confidence- and security-building measures, but also further the process of reducing the risk of conflict.[240] The *Helsinki Decisions* explicitly refer to the Forum, with a strengthened CPC, as an integral part of the CSCE.[241] The participating States in the Helsinki Decisions envisage a further enhancement of the capability of the CPC to reduce the risks of such conflicts through relevant conflict prevention techniques.[242] The same issue is also addressed within the annexed 'Programme for Immediate Action', stating that the CC will keep under consideration the need for improvements in the relevant techniques (of conflict prevention and crisis management).[243]

CONCLUSIONS

The *Helsinki Decisions* have confirmed that the CSCE is the most typical institution of cooperative security policy, most notably in establishing the CSCE Forum for Security Cooperation, but also in its operative provisions. In the CSCE's operations, the possibilities as well as the shortcomings of international security policy institutions become clearly visible. International organisations or institutions do not operate independently from their members of participating States but require the coordinated cooperation of the said States to function. If international organisations or institutions do not operate properly, it is thus far more the governments represented in them, which have not adequately used the instruments provided by the international body who are to be blamed, than the international organisation or institution itself.[244]

This is true for every international organisation or institution. Within the CSCE, however, it becomes visible earlier than in other international bodies which claim the role of an independent actor at the international level. It would thus be wrong to advocate for the CSCE the role of a 'full-fledged international organization', as this step by itself would not automatically improve its operability.[245] On the contrary, it appears appropriate for the CSCE to retain as much of its character as a forum and thus of its flexibility as possible, as has been confirmed by establishing the CSCE Forum for Security Cooperation. As the *Helsinki Decisions* indicate, the CSCE's main purpose is to negotiate (rather than execute) rules and standards for the policies of the participating States. Its institutions are to develop into agencies to service the participating States and assist them in fulfilling the obligations which they had agreed upon in the negotiations, without, however, claiming to enforce obligations against the will of participating States. As an instrument of cooperative (rather than collective) security its primary function would consist of providing mechanisms not so much of coercion *against* another participating State but for cooperation *with* another participating State in order to allow States to extricate themselves from situations which would otherwise be likely to escalate into confrontation or even armed conflict. Thus, the measures provided by the *Helsinki Decisions* – fact-finding and rapporteur missions, monitor missions, good offices, counselling and conciliation, dispute settlement, and peacekeeping – and the establishment of the Security Forum, would readily correspond to this function of cooperative security policy.

In this context, peacekeeping operations[246] deserve special attention in the CSCE's functions in cooperative security policy. In contrast with the enforcement actions foreseen in the context of collective security, peacekeeping operations are based upon cooperation and consensus, first within the broad membership of the international body providing the peacekeeping forces, but also among the parties of the (previous or growing) conflict which should be contained by the operation.[247] The CSCE gives an excellent framework for future European peacekeeping efforts,[248] contrary to a frequently heard view that the CSCE would be less experienced than other already existing European security organisations.[249] Whereas it is true that these organisations have more experience than the CSCE in (confrontational) collective defence or security efforts, they have – as organisations – the same level of experience in peacekeeping operations as the CSCE, namely nil. The solution found within the *Helsinki Decisions* takes a realistic approach. It states explicitly that personnel for such operations will be provided by individual participating States,[250] taking into account that some of the alliance members, but also other participating States in the CSCE have indeed a long-standing, broad experience in UN peacekeeping[251] which should be utilised in the CSCE context. On the other hand, the *Helsinki Decisions* explicitly refer to the 'resources and possible experience and expertise of existing organizations' to be made available for CSCE peacekeeping. The term 'resources', would most probably pertain to capabilities in such fields as long-range transportation and communications.[252] Finally, as peacekeeping is not necessarily bound to wait until a conflict has broken out and a cease-fire has been reached, but could in principle also be employed in a preventive way,[253] it clearly corresponds to the concept of preventive cooperative security policy, fitting into the CSCE's profile of conflict prevention.

To sum up, the CSCE will fulfill its pledged function of conflict prevention best if it is taken in its proper dimension. Because of its unique feature of the broadest participation and the broadest agenda within the whole range of European/Europe-related institutions and organisations, its most effective role will be in areas where a maximum of involvement is required. This stems from the CSCE's traditional function as a forum (rather than an organisation) for negotiations designed to create by consensus the rules which should govern the future conduct of the participating States. The CSCE would not only give the guidelines and shape the 'constitution' of the future Europe but would also contribute to peace and stability by making the conduct of States more predictable.

On the other hand, for the specific role in conflict prevention, the CSCE would also rely on its advantage of broad participation. It has already embarked on a two-pronged approach in addressing both the roots of potential conflicts and the handling of actual emergency situations. The first half of the task should offer chances for participating States to identify future conflicts even before they actually could break out, thus nipping them in the bud before other instruments of security policy (collective security or even collective defence) would have to be employed. In this context, the function of 'early warning', which has now been explicitly enshrined in the *Helsinki Decisions*, would warrant further consideration. It could lead, in a further development, to the establishment of a permanent analytical capacity within the pertinent CSCE institutions.[254] Working on a day-to-day basis, this could give the CSCE bodies concerned the required information or data to address any emerging problems properly. It should not be overlooked that a closer scrutiny by an international body of the situation in (then) Yugoslavia before the latest stages of escalation[255] might have led to a more timely addressing of the developing problems and so have prevented[256] the outbreak of armed conflict which followed.

Such an analytical capacity would also be useful for the second half of the task namely the handling of emergency situations which have not been foreseen. It could at least provide the data required for further steps already enshrined in the *Helsinki Decisions*, such as fact-finding, rapporteur or monitoring missions, or for peacekeeping efforts. It could also contribute to a more in-depth performance of measures like good offices or attempts at mediation.

In conclusion, the CSCE will contribute best to European security if it maintains its character as a flexible forum with a broad participation and a broad agenda, aimed at cooperative security. In its substance, the security policy within the CSCE should continue to emphasize the 'cooperative' element, allowing, on the one hand, for predictable conduct (and thus 'dynamic stability') by means of regulation and the highest possible degree of openness and transparency in security policy in order to identify deviating conduct as early as possible, and on the other hand offering preventive 'stabilizing' assistance from third-party side via fact finding and rapporteur mission, good offices and similar measures. The establishment of the CSCE Forum for Security Cooperation by the *Helsinki Decisions* points therefore in the right direction.

It is evident that emphasising cooperative security would still leave some gaps, despite the broad range of the CSCE's security policy role.[257] It may, however, appear more realistic to concentrate the efforts within the CSCE on those areas where it could contribute to European security in a realistic way, than to raise expections which the CSCE (and most likely also any other international institution or organisation) would in all probability not be able to fulfill. There will still be place for other multilateral, bilateral or even individual efforts to prevent conflicts and to preserve European stability and security.

NOTES

1. Heinz Vetschera, International Law and International Security: The Case of Force Control; in: *German Yearbook of International Law*, Vol. XXIX, 1981 (Duncker & Humboldt, Berlin, 1982), pp. 144–165 (146).
2. The situation between Belgium and France, or between Switzerland and NATO, is clearly asymmetric in military terms. Yet, these smaller states would not fear to be attacked by their larger neighbours because political stability between them is at a high level. Conversely, the situation between NATO and the Eastern alliance during the Cold War clearly lacked political stability. Yet, military stability based upon the ability to deter aggression prevented the outbreak of actual war.
3. i.e. denying the opponent the victory in war.
4. i.e. the threat to inflict unacceptable damage to the would-be future aggressor.
5. As, for example, NATO against the Soviet/WTO military threat.
6. On the concepts of collective security in detail: Otto Kimminich, Das Problem der Friedenssicherung im Völkerrecht des 20. Jahrhunderts; in: Georg Picht/Constanze Eisenbart (eds.), *Frieden und Völkerrecht*, (Stuttgart, 1973, 239–400 (327)); Hans-J. Schütz, Zur Rationalität des Zielkatalogs und des Friedenssicherungsinstrumentariums der Schlußakte der Konferenz über Sicherheit und Zusammenarbeit in Europa

(KSZE); in: *Jahrbuch für Internationales Recht*, Vol. 18 (1975), pp. 146–203 (200).

7. Article 1, para. 1 of the Charter of the United Nations.
8. Confrontational/'negative' function, see, for example, 'the suppression of acts of aggression or other breaches of peace'; *Charter of the United Nations*, Art. 1, para. 1.
9. Cooperative/'positive' function; see, for example, Charter of the United Nations, Art. 1, para. 1 ('... to bring about by peaceful means, and in conformity with the principles of justice and international law, adjustment or settlement of international disputes ...').
10. The general term for cooperative measures in the military field has been arms control ('a nation's military force, while opposing the military force of potentially hostile nations, is also bound to collaborate, implicitly if not explicitly, in avoiding the kinds of crises in which withdrawal is intolerable for both sides, in avoiding false alarms and mistaken intentions, and in providing reassurance that restraint on the part of the potential enemies would be matched by restraint on one's own side'; Thomas C Schelling/Morton H Halperin, *Strategy and Arms Control, 1961*, reprint 1985; (Pergamon/Brassey's, McLean, VA), p. 1.
11. i.e. cooperative crisis management; on crisis stability see also Gert Krell, Die Entwicklung des Sicherheitsbegriffs; in: *Beiträge zur Konfliktforschung*, Vol. 10 (1980), no. 3, pp. 33–57.
12. It could therefore live with the consensus principle.
13. '... in the modern era, the purpose of military force is not simply to win wars, but to deter aggression, while avoiding the kind of threat that may provoke desperate, preventive, or irrational military action on the part of other countries'; T Schelling/M Halperin, *ibid*.
14. On the development of the CSCE see:
    - on its initial stages: Heinz Vetschera, *Sicherheit und Truppenabbau – die Konferenzen, Vienna, 1976*; John J Maresca, To Helsinki, The Conference on Security and Cooperation in Europe, 1973–1975; Durham, N.C., 1985;
    - on its following stages: Hermann Volle/Wolfgang Wagner (eds.), *Das Belgrader KSZE-Folgetreffen*; (Bonn, 1978); and Germann Volle/Wolfang Wagner (eds.), *Das Belgrader KSZE-Folgetreffen*; (Bonn, 1984); Stefan Lehne, *The Vienna Meeting of the Conference on Security and Cooperation in Europe, 1986–1989*, (Boulder, CO, 1991); as a comprehensive survey: Victor-Yves Ghebali, *La Diplomatie de la Détente: La CSCE, d' Helsinki à Vienne*; (Bruxelles, 1989).
15. The term 'basket' refers to the agenda of the conference, as established in the Final Recommendations of the Helsinki Consultations of 8 June 1973, preceding the CSCE in its proper sense (agenda item 'questions relating to security in Europe' in paras. 13–24; agenda item 'cooperation in the fields of economics, of science and technology and the environment' in paras. 25–41; agenda item 'cooperation in humanitarian and other fields' in paras. 42–52). A fourth agenda item concerned the follow-up of the conference (para. 53).
16. Namely the USA and Canada.
17. As well as other participants, as for example the Holy See. On the other

hand, Albania at that time rejected participation in the CSCE and joined it only after the changes in Europe in 1991.

18. The CSCE Secretariat; the Conflict Prevention Centre; The Office for Free Elections/Democratic Institutions and Human Rights; see below.
19. Namely by the Paris Charter; 21 November, 1990; see below.
20. See the Helsinki Recommendations, para. 3.
21. As, for example, in the United Nations' Security Council; cf. Charter of the United Nations, Art. 27.
22. The very fact of debating a participating State's conduct and possible violations of CSCE commitments during the follow-up meetings could, however, be seen as a sort of 'sanction' for non-compliance, albeit without a direct enforcement character.
23. In the narrow sense of war prevention, see above.
24. The 'Decalogue' or 'Ten Commandments' of Helsinki; see below.
25. Cf. Heinz Vetschera, Effects of Basket I: Security and Confidence-Building; in: Hanspeter Neuhold (ed.), *CSCE: N+N Perspectives; The Laxenburg Papers*; (Austrian Institute for International Affairs, Vienna, 1987), pp. 101–125.
26. Paragraph 1 of the preamble of the First Main Document.
27. Paragraph 1 of the first document and also in paragraph 3.
28. In paragraph 1 of the preamble to the second document, 'peace and security' are linked together, too, whereas the second paragraph links 'security' to the notion of 'stability'.
29. Cf. Stefan Verosta, Der Begriff 'Internationale Sicherheit' in der Satzung der Vereinten Nationen; in: *Internationale Festschrift für Alfred Verdross*; (Munich, 1971), pp. 533–447 (533).
30. See in detail H Vetschera, *Force Control*, Note 1, pp. 145/146.
31. This view is supported by the reference to the use of force both in the Declaration on Principles (the 'Decalogue'), demanding that the states' should refrain from direct or indirect threats or the use of force, and in the annexed declaration on 'Matters related to giving effect to certain of the above Principles', referring in its paragraphs 2 and 3 to the states' duty 'to refrain from the threat or use of force in their relations with one another', and the 'use of armed forces'.
32. 'Reaffirming their commitment to peace, security and justice'; 'Reaffirming ... their full and active support for the United Nations and for the enhancement of its role and effectiveness in strengthening international peace, security and justice'.
33. The enumeration in the Final Act follows the enumeration laid down in para. 19 of the Helsinki recommendations.
34. Refraining from the threat or use of force (II); Inviolability of frontiers (III); Territorial integrity (IV); Non-intervention in internal affairs (VI).
35. Principle VII.
36. Principle VIII.
37. Principle I.
38. Principle X.
39. Principle V.
40. Principle IX.
41. H Vetschera, *Effects of Basket I* (Note 25); p. 103.

42. i.e. the delineation of the types of behaviour that will be either expected, or not be tolerated, by the participating States.
43. Para. 4 of the preamble.
44. On the practice with the 'first generation' of CBMs see: H Vetschera, The Practice of Confidence-building Measures in Europe: Patterns of Prior Notification of Military Maneuvers; in: *Defence Analysis* (Lancaster), Vol. 4, No. 2, 1988, pp. 175–180.
45. On the conferences see in detail: John Borawski, *From the Atlantic to the Urals; Negotiating Arms Control at the Stockholm conference* (1988); and J Borawski, *Security for a New Europe; The Vienna Negotiations on Confidence- and Security-Building Measures 1989–90* (1992); (both books Brassey's (London/New York)).
46. See Fig. 2.2.
47. The Final Documents of the Follow-up Meetings follow the structure established by the Helsinki Recommendations and the Final Act. Thus, the mandate is found in the chapter dealing with the 'First Basket' (Questions Relating to Security in Europe).
48. Para. 65.
49. Indeed, one could argue that the very fact that the CDE was to be held in a CSCE rather than a mere East–West framework contributed to keeping the arms control dialogue alive: in December 1983, the Soviet Union had locked herself out from East–West negotiations because of an untenable position in the INF talks. The CDE thus created the face-saving opportunity to resume negotiations first on a multilateral basis, and also paved the way to resume East–West negotiations.
50. Chapter on 'Confidence- and Security-Building Measures and Certain Aspects of Security and Disarmament in Europe', part 'New efforts for security and disarmament in Europe', second paragraph.
51. Chapter on 'Confidence- and Security-Building Measures and Certain Aspects of Security and Disarmament in Europe', third paragraph.
52. See Fig. 2.2.
53. Vienna Document 1990 on the Negotiations on Confidence- and Security-Building Measures Convened in Accordance with the Relevant Provisions of the Concluding Document of the Vienna Meeting of the Conference on Security and Co-operation in Europe; The negotiations were then continued and resulted in the conclusion of the (second) Vienna Document 1992 which contained several improvements over the previous documents.
54. Within the CFE framework, negotiations were continued to achieve ceilings for the manpower of national armed forces, and to take into account the redistribution of holdings of armaments and equipment within the former Soviet Union. They led to the Concluding Act of the Negotiation on Personnel Strength of Conventional Armed Forces in Europe (so-called CFE-IA agreement), signed in Helsinki on occasion of the 1992 CSCE Summit on 10 July 1992.
55. Meeting of the Heads of State or Government, Paris, 19–21 November 1990; Charter of Paris for a new Europe.
56. Supplementary Document to give Effect to certain Provisions contained in the Charter of Paris for a new Europe.

57. Paris Charter; Chapter 'New Structures and Institutions of the CSCE Process'; These bodies and institutions reflect a proposal made within the '*London Declaration on a Transformed North Atlantic Alliance*, issued by the Heads of State and Government participating in the meeting of the North Atlantic Council in London on 5th–6th July 1990'. The declaration, in its para. 22 recommended for the Paris summit that the CSCE governments should establish:
    - ... regular consultations among member governments at the Heads of State and Government or Ministerial level, at least once each year, with other periodic meetings of officials to prepare for and follow up on these consultations;
    - a schedule of CSCE review conferences once every two years to assess progress toward a Europe whole and free;
    - a small CSCE secretariat to coordinate these meetings and conferences;
    - a CSCE mechanism to monitor elections in all CSCE countries, on the basis of the Copenhagen Document;
    - a CSCE Centre for the Prevention of Conflicts that might serve as a forum for exchanges of military information, discussion of unusual activities, and the conciliation of disputes involving CSCE member states; and
    - a CSCE parliamentary body, the Assembly of Europe, to be based on the existing parliamentary assembly of the Council of Europe, in Strasbourg, and include representatives of all CSCE member states.

    It should be noted that the declaration implicitly anticipates the transformation of the CSCE into a fully-fledged international organisation by using the term 'member state' rather than the term 'participating State' as established within the CSCE.
58. Paris Charter; Chapter 'New Structures and Institutions of the CSCE Process', para. 2, pt. 9.
59. Paris Charter; Chapter 'New Structures and Institutions of the CSCE Process', para. 2, pt. 1, 2: '... shall meet next time in Helsinki on the occasion of the CSCE follow-up meeting. Thereafter, we will meet on the occasion of subsequent follow-up meetings'. The Paris Charter thus contains a 'mix' of the traditional mandating the concrete following meeting, and of a generalized rule for further meetings.
60. Paris Charter; Chapter 'New Structures and Institutions of the CSCE Process', para. 2, pt. 2.
61. Paris Charter; Chapter 'New Structures and Institutions of the CSCE Process', para. 2, pt. 4.
62. Paris Charter; Chapter 'New Structures and Institutions of the CSCE Process', para. 2, pt. 6 states that 'the Council will examine the development of provisions for convening meetings of the Committee of Senior Officials in emergency situations'.
63. Paris Charter; Chapter 'New Structures and Institutions of the CSCE Process', para. 2, pt. 8, 'to provide support for these consultations' (namely by the above-mentioned bodies, the Council and the CSO).
64. Paris Charter; Chapter 'New Structures and Institutions of the CSCE Process', para. 2, pt. 11; the office was later renamed as 'Office for

Democratic Institutions and Human Rights' (ODIHR), see below.
65. Paris Charter; Chapter 'New Structures and Institutions of the CSCE Process', para. 2, pt. 10.
66. Chapter F. The Conflict Prevention Centre (CPC).
67. Chapter F, para. 2.
68. On the mechanism see Vienna Document 1990, measure II, Risk Reduction, para. 17. The role of the CPC in this context is to serve as a venue for bilateral consultations (para. 17.2.1.4), or as a forum for multilateral consultations (para. 17.2.2.2); see below.
69. Measure I, para. 10–16.
70. Measure IX, para. 143–150.
71. Measure X, para. 151–154.
72. Measure II (Risk Reduction), para. 18.
73. Para. 18.1.
74. Chapter F. para. 3.
75. In its Berlin Meeting 19–20 June 1991, the Council designated the CPC to act as the nominating institution 'in accordance with Section V of the Provisions of the Report of the Valletta 1991 Meeting on Peaceful Settlement of Disputes, containing the Principles for Dispute Settlement and the Provisions for a CSCE Procedure for Peaceful Settlement of Disputes', i.e. to keep the register of qualified candidates to be nominated by the participating States for a third-party function in the settlement of disputes; Berlin Meeting of the CSCE Council, 19–20 June 1991; Summary of Conclusions, Annex 3, para. 1; On the Valletta mechanism see below.
76. Chapter F. para. 4.
77. *Ibid.*
78. The only really permanent structure within the CPC.
79. Chapter F. para. 6.
80. *Ibid.*
81. CSCE/WV/1, 9 March 1989.
82. CSCE/WV/1 amplified.
83. CSCE/WV2.
84. Pt. V/8.
85. V/5.
86. Pt. V/7.
87. CSCE/WV3.
88. Pt. 5.
89. CSCE/WV5.
90. Measure 14.
91. CSCE/WV7.
92. CSCE/WV8.
93. Measure 11.
94. Measure 15.
95. Measure 16.
96. Reducing the risk of and reporting hazardous incidents; Measure 16.
97. CSCE/WV12.
98. Para. 143.
99. Para. 144.

100. Para. 145.
101. Para. 17.
102. Para. 17.1.
103. Para. 17.1.1.
104. Para. 17.1.2.
105. Para. 17.1.3.
106. Para. 17.2.
107. 17.1.4 (request and reply); 17.2.1.2 (request for a meeting).
108. Para. 17.2.1 ('bilateral meeting').
109. Para. 17.2.2 ('multilateral meeting').
110. Para. 17.2.1.1 for bilateral meetings; para. 17.2.2.1 for multilateral meetings.
111. Para. 17.2.1.4.
112. Para. 17.2.2.2.
113. For details see: Heinz Vetschera, Die KSZE-Krisenmechanismen und ihr einsatz in der Jugoslawien-Krise; in *Österreichische Militärische Zeitschrift (ÖMZ/Austrian Military Journal)*, Vol. XXIX (1991), no. 5, pp. 405–411.
114. Para. 18.
115. Para. 18.1.
116. Para. 18.2.
117. Para. 18.3.
118. Para. 18.1.
119. Para. 18.4.
120. Berlin Meeting of the CSCE Council, 19–20 June 1991, Summary of Conclusions, Annex 2; Mechanism for Consultation and Co-operation with Regard to Emergency Situations.
121. Introductory paragraph.
122. Para. 1.
123. Para. 1.1.
124. i.e. the Chairman of the Council when the Council is not in session.
125. Para. 2.
126. Para. 2.2.
127. Para. 2.6.
128. i.e. in Prague.
129. Para. 2.8; For example, during the Follow-up meeting in Helsinki the CSO met rather in Helsinki (where most of the Senior Officials were present anyhow) than in Prague (the 'Seat of the Secretariat').
130. Para. 2.13.
131. Para. 3; Practice has shown, however, that this may be a problematic provision if it were interpreted too widely, as a military emergency situation will most probably correspond to a general political crisis situation. Therefore, it may be indeed required to address the general political as well as the more specific military side of a crisis at the same time.
132. Cf. *Financial Times*, 5 July 1991, p. 2, and *Le Monde*, 5 July 1991, p. 4.
133. However, in this context the term 'observer' was avoided; see: La CSCE décide l'envoi de deux missions; *Le Monde*, 5 July 1991, p. 4.
134. Concluding Document of the Vienna Meeting 1986 of Representatives

of the Participating States of the Conference on Security and Co-operation in Europe, held on the basis of the provisions of the Final Act relating to the Follow-up of the Conference; Vienna, 15 January 1989.

135. Para. 1.
136. Para. 2.
137. Document of the Copenhagen Meeting on the Conference on the Human Dimension of the CSCE, para. 42.1.
138. Document of the Copenhagen Meeting on the Conference on the Human Dimension of the CSCE, para. 42.2.
139. Document of the Moscow Meeting on the Conference on the Human Dimension of the CSCE, Moscow, 3 October, 1991, para. 2.
140. Document of the Moscow Meeting, para. 3.
141. Document of the Moscow Meeting, para. 4.
142. In all likelihood the Office for Democratic Institutions and Human Rights (ODIHR), see below.
143. Document of the Moscow Meeting, para. 8.
144. Document of the Moscow Meeting, para. 9.
145. Document of the Moscow Meeting, para. 12.
146. Document of the Moscow Meeting, para. 13.
147. See below.
148. See below.
149. Chapter III/para. 14.
150. Berlin Meeting of the CSCE Council, 19–20 June 1991, Summary of Conclusions, Annex 3.
151. Report of the CSCE Meeting of Experts on Peaceful Settlement of Disputes; Valletta, 8 February 1991.
152. Report of the CSCE Meeting of Experts on Peaceful Settlement of Disputes; Section V.
153. Second Meeting of the Council; Summary of Conclusions, Chapter III/para. 6.
154. All quoted elements in: Summary of Conclusions, Chapter III/para. 6.
155. Prague Document on Further Development of CSCE Institutions and Structures, Chapter I/para. 2.
156. Chapter II/para. 5.
157. Chapter III/para. 9.
158. All quoted elements in: Chapter III/para. 10.
159. Chapter III/para. 11.
160. Chapter III/para. 14.
161. The so-called 'consensus minus one' rule.
162. Chapter III/para. 16.
163. Chapter VI.
164. Chapter VI/para. 22.
165. Chapter VI/para. 23.
166. Chapter VI/para. 27.
167. Chapter VI/para. 28.
168. Chapter VI/para. 29.
169. Chapter VI/para. 32; The provision foresees, however, these functions only 'if so requested by the parties to those agreements and agreed

upon by the Consultative Consultative Committee'.
170. Chapter VI/para. 39.
171. Summary of Conclusions, Chapter VI/para. 9.
172. *Ibid.*
173. Chapter VI, para. 10.
174. *Ibid.*
175. Concluding Document of the Vienna Meeting 1986 of Representatives of the Participating States of the Conference on Security and Cooperation in Europe, Vienna, 15 January 1989, Chapter entitled 'Follow-up to the Conference'; the Document also mandated a preparatory meeting, commencing on 10 March 1992.
176. On this occasion, the Council admitted Croatia, Georgia and Slovenia as participating States to the CSCE.
177. Paris Charter, chapter 'New Structures and Institutions of the CSCE Process', para. 2, pt. 1.
178. CSCE Helsinki Document 1992, The Challenges of Change.
179. In addition, the Helsinki Decisions contain *inter alia* provisions on relations with international organisations, relations with non-participating States, and the role of non-governmental organisations, a framework for monitoring compliance with CSCE commitments and for promoting co-operation in the Human Dimension; they create within the economic dimension of the CSCE an 'Economic Forum' within the framework of the CSO, and provide a Programme of Co-ordinated Support for Recently Admitted Participating States. For purposes of this paper, however, only the security policy related part of the Helsinki Decisions will be further analysed.
180. See Chart III.
181. Para. IV/2.
182. Chapter I of the Helsinki Decisions.
183. Para. I/15.
184. Para. I/16.
185. Para. I/22.
186. Chapter V of the Helsinki Decisions.
187. Para. V/9.
188. Para. V/11; this vague wording refers in effect to the harmonisation of the CSBM agreements, the CFE Treaty, and the Open Skies Treaty, which had been negotiated and concluded in Vienna parallel to each other.
189. Para. V/30.
190. Para. V/31.
191. Para. V/32.
192. Chapter II.
193. Para. II/2.
194. Para. II/3.
195. Para. V/9.
196. Para. I/23; Para. II/10.
197. Para. II/11a.
198. Except persons or organizations which practise or publicly condone terrorism or violence; Para. II/25.

199. Chapter II/supplement, para. 23.
200. Chapter II/supplement, para. 31.
201. Para. II/13.
202. Chapter II/14; on the emergency mechanism see above.
203. Para. II/20.
204. Para. II/21.
205. Cf. the title of Chapter III.
206. Para. III/1.
207. Para. III/2.
208. Para. III/3.
209. Para. III/4.
210. Para. III/5.
211. Para. III/7.
212. Para. III/9.
213. Para. III/13.
214. Para. III/14.
215. Para. III/17.
216. Para. III/18.
217. Para. III/19.
218. Para. III/22.
219. Para. III/23.
220. Para. III/24.
221. Para. III/25.
222. Para. III/30.
223. Para. III/29.
224. Para. III/28.
225. Para. III/27.
226. Para. III/34.
227. Para. III/39.
228. Para. III/45.
229. Para. III/43.
230. Para. III/44.
231. Para. III/40; In practical terms, this would also require access by the ad hoc group to the CSCE communications network in order to keep the other participating States informed.
232. Para. III/41.
233. Para. III/42.
234. Para. III/52–56.
235. Para. III/52.
236. Para. III/54.
237. Para. III/56.
238. Para. III/57.
239. Para. III/58.
240. Para. V/8.
241. Para. V/9.
242. Para. V/22.
243. Annex/para. 13.
244. In this context, it is close to hypocrisy if some States tend to blame 'the United Nations' or 'the CSCE' for not having acted in one of the other

crisis, while having themselves blocked decision-making by denying their consent, or their political or material support for the international body.

245. One argument in this context is that by overcoming the consensus rule and creating some sort of 'streamlined' Security Council, the CSCE would become more effective in decision-making. This argument ignores reality however. In the case of the Yugoslav crisis, it was not the large number of potentially diverging opinions which blocked unanimous decision-making, but the inability of the major powers to find consensus among themselves because of their profoundly divergent preferences for the outcome of any approach to solve the crisis. The same divergencies would also have existed in any sort of 'streamlined' decision-making structure among the major powers.
246. For a comprehensive survey see: Indar Jit Rikhyre (Maj. Gen., ret.), *The Theory and Practice of Peace-Keeping*, (London, 1984); on the United Nations' practice see: UN Department of Public Information; *The Blue Helmets*; (New York, 1985).
247. Cf. the enumeration of characteristics for peacekeeping operations in: *The Blue Helmets*, p. 4.
248. It should be noted, however, that actions as for example the conclusion of a status of forces agreement would require a personality under international law which the CSCE by itself cannot provide, being no international organisation. However, its institutions, as for example the CPC, could act in this field. The Helsinki Decisions (para. I/25) explicitly refer to the 'relevance of an agreement granting an internationally recognized status to the CSCE Secretariat, the Conflict Prevention Centre and the ODIHR' which would facilitate any such procedure.
249. As for example NATO or the WEU.
250. Para. III/36.
251. Especially smaller States as for example Austria, Denmark, Finland, Ireland, Norway, and Sweden, but also other States as for example France, Italy or the United Kingdom.
252. With 'possible experience and expertise', due to the lack of peacekeeping experience in the said organisations, it would most probably also refer to the areas connected to the 'resources', i.e. long-range transportation, communication, strategic intelligence.
253. As for example to assist the peaceful transition of power, e.g. in the United Nations operations in West Irian (West New Guinea), or in Namibia.
254. As for example the CPC.
255. There were abundant 'signals' for the deterioration of the situation, especially since mid-1990. They were, however, either ignored or misinterpreted by the majority of the Western governments; see in detail: Heinz Vetschera, Faktoren in der Fehleinschätzung entstehender Krisen: Das Beispiel Jugoslawien; in: Wolfgang Krause/Joachim Kaiser/Uwe Nerlich/Jürgen Nötzold/Reinhardt Rummel/Karl-Peter Stratmann (eds.), *Stabilität, Gleichgewicht und die Sicherheitsinteressen des Vereinigten Deutschland; Stiftung Wissenschaft und Politik*, Vol. 2,

pp. 195–314; (Ebenhausen, Germany; 1991).

256. One should not be too over optimistic, either, as the clear divergence of power interests might not have allowed for unanimous action on the side of the major powers even if the early warning could have been taken into account; see above.

257. It should be noticed, however, that the Helsinki Decisions make a vague reference to 'other measures, ... including the possibility of further strengthening the norms of behaviour among them through the elaboration of additional security instruments' (para. V/20) which could be read as an implicit tendency to generate, in a later stage, the framework for an organisation of collective (rather than cooperative) security policy, embracing also the enforcement of the said 'norms of behaviour'. Furthermore, the Helsinki Decisions refer also to a common security policy by the participating States of 'consultation and co-operation in respect to challenges to their security from outside their territory' (para. V/19), keeping the door open for a development as far as a defensive alliance.

4

Conflict Prevention and Crisis Management: The NATO Approach[1]

John Barrett

Over the years, NATO has gained a specific kind of experience in conflict prevention and crisis management. It has had to handle a number of crises of a different kind. But, for Alliance members, these arose and were dealt with within the Cold War context. The Alliance approach to crisis prevention was, as one observer has put it, to create institutional mechanisms that 'made deliberate challenges to the stability of the bipolar system potentially very costly'.[2]

In the nuclear age, crisis prevention has become paramount to crisis management. A lesson taught to all by the Cuban Missile Crisis was that managing actual crises could not fail to be fraught with uncertainties. Saturated by ideological hostility, and reinforced with formidable conventional and nuclear hardware, crisis management took on a daunting complexion. And since the locus of crisis was nearly always in the central European theatre – Berlin (1953 and 1961), Budapest (1956), Prague (1968), Warsaw (1956 and 1981) – NATO had only limited tools at its disposal for responding.

Underpinned by the Alliance's strategy of 'flexible response' (which emerged during the 1960s and is still in a way at the root of NATO's strategic posture), deterrence could be achieved to cover a range of aggressive actions, from low-level provocation to large-scale attack against Western Europe by the armed forces of the Warsaw Pact countries. It was the transition from crisis prevention to crisis management that gave the planners and theorists headaches. To 'manage' a crisis could include diplomatic sabre-rattling, crisis termination through a combination of war-fighting and damage limitation – all of which could quietly acquire a pre-emptive element. It depended on how certain one assumed the uncertainties to be, once the threshold between conflict prevention (deterrence) and crisis management (certain conflict) was crossed.[3]

However, with the world changing as it has in the past few years, and with the emergence of new kinds of risks and challenges facing the Alliance, the earlier approach, while not entirely superseded by any means, has required adjustment and complementation. Alliance mechanisms for crisis management have to accord with the changed international environment if they are to remain both relevant and effective. They will thus still have to cover the whole range of possibilities, from low-level crises through to major confrontation and repelling aggression.

But while there will always be the national territories of Alliance members to defend, what is there still to deter? An attack on national territories – at least by forces possibly superior in major equipment and resource categories operating in a surprise attack mode – is considered very unlikely in the aftermath of the Cold War. Instead, a term that is used by some is 'crisis response' or crisis handling, where, in addition to the traditional defence-through-deterrence role, the Alliance should undertake new roles in the Central and East European (C+EE) region, ranging from preventing and managing civil wars to monitoring arms control and disarmament agreements.[4]

To its credit, the Alliance has reacted to the recent changes in politico-military circumstances. Declarations issued by NATO's Heads of State and Government have endorsed a string of principles, starting with the *Comprehensive Concept of Arms Control and Disarmament* (May 1989); the *London Declaration on a Transformed North Atlantic Alliance* (July 1990); and the new *Strategic Concept* and the *Rome Declaration on Peace and Cooperation* (Rome 1991). Regarding conflict prevention and crisis management, the *Strategic Concept* stated: 'The success of the Alliance's policy of preserving peace and preventing war in the new political and strategic environment in Europe depends even more than in the past on the effectiveness of preventive diplomacy and successful management of crises affecting the security of its members.' This, in turn, would require a coherent approach in choosing and coordinating appropriate political and military crisis management measures.

In this chapter, the structure provided by the editors is followed, although, as with all attempts to organise details and events around certain themes, the applicability of some aspects of the structure to the case of NATO may be, in places, rather more limited than elsewhere.

That said, this chapter, in following the editors' structure, does try to serve as a descriptive and analytical bridge between the Alliance's still robust military capabilities and its attempt to come to grips politically, militarily and institutionally with the changing politico-military environment noted above. The conclusion I reach (as argued in the section on 'evaluation') is that:

- The Alliance's approach to conflict prevention has essentially brought it beyond the core functions of defence and deterrence;
- The limit of Alliance involvement in conflict prevention remains to be defined;
- However this limit is defined, the Alliance will, for the foreseeable future and in view of the ongoing deliberations within the Alliance, be in a *supportive* role vis-a-vis other institutions in its involvement in conflict prevention.[5]

MANDATE/POLICY FRAMEWORK

NATO's approach to preventive diplomacy and crisis management is currently in the conceptual stage. The policy framework governing this approach is composed of: the commitment to a transformation of the North Atlantic Alliance; the new Alliance Strategic Concept; and, the commitment to the concept of interlocking or 'mutually reinforcing' institutions.

The Alliance transformed

The *London Declaration* set in train the process of Alliance transformation which would, *inter alia*, enhance the political component of the Alliance as provided for by Article 2 of the Washington Treaty.[6] Of fundamental importance in bringing this Article to the fore was the recognition in the *London Declaration* that 'in the new Europe, the security of every state is inseparably linked to the security of its neighbours'. The Alliance was now prepared to extend to the former adversaries of the Cold War the 'hand of friendship'. It was here also that the Alliance indicated its intention to change NATO's integrated force structure and strategy by: fielding of smaller and restructured active forces; scaling back the readiness of active units; relying more heavily on force regeneration if and when required; and moving away from the posture of 'forward defence' in Central Europe. Allied foreign ministers also proposed the establishment (later adopted by the CSCE) of a CSCE Centre for the Prevention of Conflict, which would serve as a forum for exchanges of military information, discussion of unusual military activities, and the conciliation of disputes involving CSCE member states.

The Alliance's new *Strategic Concept*

The new *Strategic Concept* has recognized that the Allies' security is inseparably linked to that of all other states in Europe. Further, it characterised possible risks to Allied security as multi-faceted in nature and multi-directional, resulting in the first instance from adverse consequences of instability that may arise from serious economic, social and political difficulties, including ethnic rivalries and territorial disputes.

Mutually Reinforcing Institutions

The dissolution of the bipolar order of the Cold War era led to an increased importance of international organisations. The challenges to be faced in this new Europe in the time ahead (or even now) cannot comprehensively be addressed by one institution alone. With this in mind, the North Atlantic Council, at its meeting in Brussels in December 1990, pledged the Alliance's support for a new European security architecture which would be composed of a framework of mutually reinforcing institutions that complement and support each other. The CSCE, NATO, the EC, the WEU and the Council of Europe would all be part of this architecture.

At the Rome Summit, Alliance leaders also called for the full implementation of the *Helsinki Final Act*, the *Charter of Paris* and other relevant CSCE documents, and thus to permit the CSCE to face its new and increased responsibilities for conflict prevention, crisis management and the peaceful settlement of disputes. They adopted initiatives to reinforce the CSCE emergency mechanism by giving a more permanent role to both the Committee of Senior Officials and the Conflict Prevention Centre.

To this framework the North Atlantic Cooperation Council – the so-called NACC – was added in December 1991. The NACC was seen as having a potential also for crisis management through the dialogue, consultation and cooperation that it offered to the Alliance's former adversaries. Consultation and cooperation in the NACC framework would focus on security and defence-related issues where the Alliance and NATO members could offer their experience and expertise. These activities were designed, *inter alia*, to aid in fostering a sense of security and confidence in the newly emerging democracies of Central and Eastern Europe and to help transform their societies and economies in an irreversible direction towards democratic life. As such, they too could be considered a contribution to conflict prevention.

As a next step in the development of the Alliance's relations with other international institutions, NATO Foreign Ministers agreed in Oslo in June 1992 that the Alliance could make available its resources and expertise in support of CSCE peacekeeping.[7] They also instructed the Council in Permanent Session, with the advice of NATO Military Authorities, to consider practical options and modalities by which such support might be provided.[8]

Subsequently, the Defence Planning Committee in Ministerial Session (December 1992) directed the appropriate bodies of the Alliance to undertake the necessary planning and preparatory work for the integrated military structure – in areas such as force planning, command and control, logistics support, infrastructure, and training and exercises – in order to ensure that the required capabilities would be available for peacekeeping purposes if and when decided by the Alliance. A week later, at the December meeting of the North Atlantic Council, Alliance Foreign Ministers agreed:

- to further strengthen Alliance coordination in peacekeeping and develop practical measures to enhance the Alliance's contribution in this area;
- to share experiences in peacekeeping with the Cooperation Partners and other CSCE participating states and to join them as required in supporting CSCE peacekeeping operations;
- to respond positively to initiatives that the UN Secretary-General might take in seeking Alliance assistance in the implementation of UN Security Council Resolutions.

The next day, at the annual meeting in Brussels of the North Atlantic Cooperation Council (NACC), Foreign Ministers agreed that, within the context of the NACC, there could be a sharing of experience and expertise in the planning of peacekeeping missions, training, and consideration of possible joint peacekeeping exercises. The NACC Ad Hoc Group on Cooperation in Peacekeeping has since been established to examine in detail the areas where practical cooperation might be undertaken.

DECLARATORY PREVENTION

The fundamental declarations of the Alliance concerning the prevention of crisis are contained in the Washington Treaty itself, signed in 1949. Article IV establishes the commitment to consult together when the territorial integrity, political independence or security of any of the Parties is threatened; Article V, the commitment to collective defence in the event of armed attack against one or more of the Parties.

To these fundamental declarations one could add the various declarations, communiqués and statements issued either periodically or as circumstances warrant. Since the end of the Cold War and the dissolution of the Warsaw Treaty Organisation, the most salient of these in the area of crisis prevention/crisis management are: the *Statement on the Core Security Functions of the Alliance* (Copenhagen, June 1991); the *Alliance Strategic Concept* and the *Rome Declaration on Peace and Cooperation* (Rome, November 1991); the establishment of the North Atlantic Cooperation Council (Brussels, December 1991). To these could be added more recent NATO communiqués in which Alliance support of CSCE and/or UN peacekeeping are specifically mentioned (i.e. the Oslo and Brussels Communiqués, June and December 1992, respectively). Regarding conflict prevention, a special meeting of the North Atlantic Council in August 1991 issued a communiqué on the implications for East–West security and stability of the attempted coup in the Soviet Union.

Beyond the communiqués and statements, however, is another level at which declaratory actions could play an important role in conflict prevention and crisis management. Alliance members have recognised that, in the new security environment in Europe and between East–West generally, any major aggression would be much less likely and most probably preceded by significant warning time. As part of the response to this change, a review of existing mechanisms for crisis management has included a revision of the *Inventory of Preventive Measures*.[9] These are diplomatic and economic preventive measures which could be considered selectively in situations of risks and crises that might have a direct effect on the security of the Alliance.

In the public realm there are a number of documents which also have a direct bearing on the Alliance's approach to conflict prevention and crisis management. For example, arms control and disarmament agreements contain a number of provisions which are specifically designed to apply in crisis situations (i.e. the *Vienna Document 1992*, which includes mechanisms for consultation and cooperation as regards unusual military activities) or which could be utilised as preventive measures (i.e. cooperative measures concerning military contacts). Verification measures provided under various arms control and disarmament instruments are also of particular significance in this regard.

As explained in the previous chapter, the CSCE process in particular the new Forum for Security Cooperation (FSC) established by the 1992 CSCE Helsinki Summit Meeting, and the Conflict Prevention Centre (in Vienna) offer specifically designed mechanisms pertinent to conflict prevention and crisis management.

DECISION-MAKING PROCEDURES

A key factor in crisis management is the supremacy of political responsibility. All decisions within the Alliance are taken by and under the political authority of the North Atlantic Council (NAC), composed of the representatives of the government of the sixteen Alliance members. Their consensus is a requirement for reaching Alliance decisions. The Defence Planning Committee (DPC), composed of defence ministers, is responsible for activities of the Alliance's integrated military force structure in responding to crises.

The North Atlantic Council and, when appropriate, the Defence Planning Committee act as fora for consultation wherein member governments express views and harmonise them to achieve consensus. The NAC and the DPC give guidance and direction to Military Authorities and ensure military activities are subordinate at all time to political control. They are supported by a number of specialised committees, such as the Military Committee, the Political Committee, the Alerts Committee (both the name and the terms of reference of the Alerts Committee are currently under review) and the Senior Civil Emergency Planning Committee. In times of crisis or tension, immediate and continuous consultation among the Alliance members would take place at NATO Headquarters through the North Atlantic Council in Permanent Session.

As for the practical arrangements for crisis management and the preparation and conduct of exercises designed to test the system, these are coordinated by a Council Operations and Exercise Committee. The principal responsibilities of this Committee include the development, in close liaison with the NATO Military

Authorities, of the policies governing crisis management arrangements. The Council Operations Directorate provides staff support for the Council Operations and Exercise Committee (COEC) and is responsible for developing and revising operating procedures.[10]

CONFLICT PREVENTION FACILITIES

Early Warning

Early warning of an impending crisis would come from a number of sources. From a strictly NATO perspective, the main sources would be the national intelligence-gathering and assessment systems of individual Allies, whose products are then fed into and exchanged among Allies at the Headquarters in Brussels. Joint staff groups such as the Current Intelligence Groups (CIG) produce daily summaries of current intelligence which are then circulated to capitals, NATO military commands and within the Headquarters itself. The NATO Precautionary System brings into play actions which represent, as it were, the first layer of responses to a crisis which may be threatening the security of the Alliance nations.

Of course, there are other forms of early warning available to Allies on a national basis which might involve the Headquarters because of the ongoing general coordinating functions carried out there. For example, first warning of potentially hostile military actions could come through anomalies reported through inspection and evaluation activities carried out in connection with the CSCE *Vienna Document (VD) 1992* on confidence- and security-building measures. Similarly, anomalies reported through routine as well as challenge on-site inspections under the Treaty on Conventional Force Reduction in Europe – the CFE Treaty – may give cause for alarm.[11] Although such monitoring activities are, for both the VD 92 document and the CFE Treaty, national prerogatives, NATO members have a coordination and consultation mechanism in the form of the Verification Coordination Committee. This Committee would also act as a kind of 'early warning' consultation centre, should evidence arise of a possible abrogation of politically and legally binding arms control and disarmament commitments on a level of military significance that would point towards potential crisis.

Communications

The monitoring of potential crisis developments is carried out by the NATO Situation Centre (SITCEN) with NATO-wide communications, supported by the automatic data processing resources of the NATO Integrated Communications System. The SITCEN is jointly manned on a 24-hour basis by civilian and military staffs; it assembles, collates and disseminates all intelligence and information made available by member nations and the NATO Military Authorities with regard to developing situations. It thus provides, at all times, the technical means for effective and rapid consultation among national representatives, their capitals and the NATO Military Authorities, against a background of common information drawn from a collective data base. Communications – secure voice, telegraph and fax – are all in place on a 24-hour basis. Representatives from SACEUR and SACLANT/CINCCHAN serve in the NATO HQ to facilitate communications with their respective headquarters if military responses are required. Communications systems include the Forward Scatter and Satellite Stations and the NATO Airborne Early Warning Systems (NAEWs).

Conflict Management Methods

In his recent monograph, *An Agenda for Peace*, the UN Secretary General set out several definitions that essentially describe different aspects of conflict management.[12] Each of these aspects could be termed a 'conflict management method'.

The recent involvement of the Alliance in supporting UN efforts to deal with the crisis in the former Yugoslavia reflects its step-by-step transformation into a contributor to a more general kind of conflict management. This evolving role is best described through the actions taken by the Alliance over the past few months. These can be grouped under the three headings of peacekeeping; peacebuilding; and preventive diplomacy.

Peacekeeping

Activities by the Alliance under this heading have to date included: (a) various activities through which support is given to the implementation of UN Security Council Resolutions concerning the conflict in the former Yugoslavia; (b) ongoing doctrinal development for conduct of peacekeeping operations; and (c) conduct of training and education programmes for potential NATO contributors to peacekeeping operations.

Peacebuilding[13]

Measures undertaken by the Alliance have included, *inter alia*: (a) political statements in support of efforts to reach a lasting political settlement of the conflict in the former Yugoslavia; (b) political support of CSCE efforts in the human dimension in the former Yugoslavia and in other areas of conflict; (c) cooperation in verification and implementation of arms control and disarmament measures in Europe; (d) cooperative activities under the aegis of the NACC (as contained in the annual NACC Work Plans); and (e) provision of personnel to provide a command and control element for UN HQ (Bosnia–Hercegovina).

Preventive diplomacy

Measures undertaken by the Alliance have included, *inter alia*: (a) support of CSCE confidence- and security-building measures, including unusual military activities and risk reduction; (b) development of contingency planning in the context of the Yugoslavian conflict (i.e. prevention of spillover); (c) support of CSCE efforts in the area of preventive diplomacy and conflict prevention; (d) preparation of CSBM and verification measures in support of the International Conference on the former Yugoslavia; (e) contribution to humanitarian aid effort to assist newly democratic states of former Soviet Union; and (f) coordination and political-military advisory assistance to other European regional arrangements and organisations, e.g. WEU.

However, the use of any of these methods requires that certain instruments or assets for conflict management be at hand. It is therefore important to examine briefly some of the NATO assets which may be relevant to conflict management and which are commonly owned and/or elements of the Alliance's integrated military structure.

(i) *Infrastructure:*
Alliance infrastructure includes airfields, telecommunications installations, command, control and information systems, military headquarters, fuel pipelines and storage, radar warning and navigational aid installations, port installations, forward storage sites and support facilities for reinforcement forces. Installations of this kind, set up at the request of Major NATO Commanders (MNCs), in close collaboration with national military authorities, may be designated as 'NATO common infrastructure'. Installations and equipment so designated are financed collectively by the governments of participating countries within agreed limits for common funding. They may be used by one or more NATO nations, but the acquisition of the sites themselves and the provision of certain local utilities remain a 'host nation' responsibility.

(ii) *Logistics:*
The movement and maintenance of NATO forces consist of several different logistic functions which could be called on in crisis: firstly, the storage, movement, distribution, maintenance, and disposition of material and equipment; secondly, the movement of personnel and, where necessary, evacuation and hospitalisation; thirdly, facilities for acquisition or construction, maintenance, operation and disposition of installations; and lastly, services, including the essential provision of food and other commodities.

(iii) *Forces:*
As regards the integrated military structure, multinational NATO headquarters have command in peacetime over certain specific multinational capabilities such as NATO Airborne Early Warning aircraft, air defence assets and standing naval forces. Additionally,

Alliance members maintain substantial land, air and maritime forces of various types in differing states of readiness, trained and equipped to NATO standards to maximise interoperability; most of which may be placed under NATO command in times of crisis, according to Alliance political decision. For immediate response to crisis, the Alliance currently maintains, in addition to the capabilities identified above, multinational land and air forces, ready at short notice and consisting of predesignated national units specifically trained, rehearsed and equipped for rapid deployment. This force, the ACE Mobile Force, has a land component capable of deploying up to a brigade of about 5,000 soldiers in units contributed by nations and an air component capable of deploying up to six squadrons of ground attack, reconnaissance and interceptor aircraft also provided by nations.

As a consequence of the adoption of the new *Alliance Strategic Concept*, NATO's forces are being extensively restructured specifically to enhance crisis response capabilities. The Allied Command Europe (ACE) Mobile Force is now being replaced by multinational Immediate Reaction Forces, with naval as well as land and air components. These forces will be maintained at high readiness and available for deployment at short notice. Additionally, the Alliance is forming an Allied Rapid Reaction Corps, also with land, air and naval components, to provide more substantial capabilities to handle crises. It is planned to become fully operational by April 1995.[14]

These, then, give an indication of some of the instruments and assets available to the Alliance for conflict management. Additional contributions could be sought, as required, from individual Allies. Together, either as Alliance or national resources and assets, they can be grouped as follows: (a) *non-materiel resources* (e.g. information, expertise, assistance, techniques, education and training, coordination with other involved agencies and IGOs/NGOs); (b) *materiel resources* (e.g. Alliance infrastructure transportation of civil and military resources to and from the area of operation, telecommunication systems, logistic support and peacekeeping equipment, etc.); and (c) *constituted military forces* (e.g. Alliance collective forces such as the Standing Naval Force

Atlantic (STANAVFORLANT), Standing Naval Force Mediterranean (STANAVFORMED), elements of the Rapid Reaction Force, and the NATO Airborne Early Warning force).

Cooperation with other institutions

Crisis management, preventive diplomacy and early resolution of crises are becoming important aspects of Alliance efforts to preserve peace and prevent war. In addition, relations with other international institutions such as the UN and WEU will also have an impact on the development of NATO's crisis management capability. Given the absence of direct threats to the territory of Alliance members, the Alliance's role in the areas listed above will for the foreseeable future, given ongoing Council discussion, be a *supportive* one which contributes to efforts undertaken by collective security institutions such as the UN and the CSCE.

This supportive role, which would be likely to take place beyond the territories of Alliance member states, is essentially political in character. For example, the process of support in areas of preventing diplomacy and crisis management (including peacekeeping) will have the following *political* elements: (i) the identification of a particular crisis for Alliance consideration and possible involvement; (ii) identification of a possible role; (iii) consultation with other institutions on the specific nature of a supportive role; and (iv) Alliance consultation and decision-making procedures in playing such a role.

At present, the Alliance is at an early stage in the development of its role of supporting other institutions rather than handling crises completely on its own. Crisis handling will be increasingly difficult, if next to impossible, to maintain as an activity entirely separate from the interests and involvement of other institutions. The current involvement of the Alliance in the Yugoslavian crisis through its support of UNPROFOR demonstrates very clearly the political dimension of this involvement. The Alliance has sought to assure the UN that any NATO contribution to UN activities will and must remain securely and demonstrably under the guidance of the UN Secretary-General.

The Alliance's involvement in the former Yugoslavia has, at the time of writing, taken a number of forms.

In response to a request from the CSCE Chairman-in-Office, the North Atlantic Council agreed in September 1992 to share with the UN and the CSCE details of the preliminary contingency planning on protection of humanitarian relief operations and on heavy weapons monitoring undertaken to date by NATO Military Authorities. These were sent by Secretary-General Woerner to the CSCE Chairman-in-Office and the UN Secretary-General. NATO representatives gave a presentation to a meeting of the CSCE Ad Hoc Group on the Monitoring of Heavy Weapons in Vienna the following month.

In addition, the Alliance put at the disposal of the relevant Working Groups in Geneva at the International Conference on the former Yugoslavia (ICFY) its specific experience and proposals in the area of confidence- and security-building measures and in verification activities.

In September 1992, Allied personnel were withdrawn from the Alliance's Northern Army Group (NORTHAG) to contribute to the UNPROFOR II Headquarters in Bosnia–Hercegovina, in support of the latter's establishment under UN Security Council Resolution 776. With the expansion of the UNPROFOR mandate, there was an obvious need for a UN Headquarters in Bosnia–Hercegovina that would be capable of all routine staff functions, such as personnel, administration, intelligence, operations, and logistics, with special elements to handle public information, field security, civil-military cooperation, linguistic support and legal affairs. The NATO framework division headquarters had the distinct advantage of capitalising on existing and staffed organisations, standardised procedures and practicable operational expertise. Most importantly, regardless of the configuration of the NATO command and control arrangement, it could very easily be subordinated to COMUNPROFOR. (This HQ is in direct support of the UNPROFOR Commander's operations in providing protection for humanitarian assistance in Sarajevo and others parts of Bosnia–Hercegovina.)

In conjunction with WEU naval forces, the Alliance has conducted maritime monitoring operations in support of UN Security Council Resolutions 713 and 757, which imposed an arms embargo on all of the republics of the former Yugoslavia and an economic embargo on Serbia and Montenegro.

In October 1992, the UN NATO Advanced Early Warning (AWACS) aircraft began monitoring operations as part of the Alliance contribution in support of UN Security Council Resolution 781, which established a 'no-fly' zone over the region. As a result, NATO AWACS aircraft are now using flight patterns over Hungary and the Adriatic. The data obtained from these AWACS operations is being provided to the appropriate UN authorities on a timely and regular basis.

In late November of the same year, the Alliance began maritime operations in the Adriatic Sea as a contribution to the enforcement of UN embargoes on the former Yugoslavia, (UN Security Council Resolution 787). To date, thousands of ships have been challenged, and suspected embargo-violators have been diverted to Italy and placed in the hands of Italian authorities. Arrangements have now been made with the Albanian authorities to extend the coverage of NATO enforcement operations into Albanian territorial waters.

In addition, the North Atlantic Council has directed the NATO Military Authorities to carry out *contingency planning* in a number of areas related to actual and potential UN activity in the former Yugoslavia. This contingency planning has dealt with:

- the supervision of heavy weapons in Bosnia–Hercegovina, as part of a CSCE examination of how such supervision might be carried out operationally;
- the modalities of airspace monitoring over Bosnia–Hercegovina;
- the protection of UN humanitarian relief operations, involving both land- and air-based options. (Some of these involved delivery of humanitarian relief from the air, some involved use of air assets in support of land convoys, and two options dealt exclusively with the use of troops on the group to protect UN relief convoys.)
- the command and control arrangements for the *enforcement* of a no-fly ban over Bosnia–Hercegovina;
- the protection of UNPROFOR and other UN personnel on the ground in Croatia and Bosnia–Hercegovina;
- the prevention of spillover of the conflict into Kosovo and the former Yugoslav republic of Macedonia; and

- the establishment of relief zones and safe/secure areas in Bosnia–Hercegovina.
- the force requirements and requisite command and control for implementation of the Vance–Stoltenberg peace plan for Bosnia–Hercegovina.

In each case, the Secretary-General has conveyed to the UN Secretary-General, on behalf of the Alliance, various elements of this planning. (The contingency planning relating to the supervision of heavy weapons was conveyed also to the CSCE Chairman-in-Office.) Planning has taken account of the primary authority of the UN and/or the CSCE as well as emphasized the need for coordination with other organisations involved in supporting UN peacekeeping activities in the former Yugoslavia.

Funding

Funding for 'internal' crisis management procedures and operations would be through the financial contribution that each individual Ally makes to the Alliance.[15] In the case of Alliance support of other organisations in conflict prevention and crisis management, one can only make a couple of observations, since this is a new and untried area of activity for the Alliance. The funding of the NATO contribution to UNPROFOR II and other UN activities relating to the crisis in Yugoslavia depends on whether a commonly owned asset (such as the NATO AWACS aircraft) is being used or whether the resources committed to the UN come under the aegis of the individual contributing nations. The UN Secretary-General has made it clear to all contributing nations that they will have to bear the burden of the costs involved in supporting the UN's activities in Yugoslavia. Regarding the CSCE, the *Helsinki Final Document* states that 'costs of CSCE peacekeeping activities, will be borne by all CSCE participating States' (Section III, paragraph 47). Presumably any organisation that supports CSCE peacekeeping would do so on a 'cost-recovery' basis.

EXPERIENCE

The Persian Gulf crisis provided a recent actual example of how NATO can indirectly provide support for an operation, sponsored by another international organisation (in this case, the United Nations). Although NATO was not directly involved in the Gulf, the North Atlantic Council was able to provide political support for the coalition operation under the UN, while its member states provided, of course, substantial components of the coalition force.

During the Gulf Crisis, NATO's concern was: (a) to demonstrate solidarity with Alliance members who were also members of the Coalition; (b) to deter aggression against Turkey, as a member of the Alliance; and (c) to ensure security of the Southern Region of NATO, where there were potential threats. Forces of NATO members deployed with the Coalition were supported, within the NATO area, by NATO infrastructure, communications, transport and medical coordination. NATO deployed AWACS aircraft, the multinational Allied Mobile Force (AIR), air defence assets, additional communications, anti-chemical warfare equipment to counter the specific threat to a member state (Turkey); additional AWACS and maritime patrol aircraft to the Mediterranean by over twenty additional vessels. The civil emergency organisation assisted in coordinating the repatriation from Jordan of Kuwaiti and Iraqi refugees.

It might also be noted that the forces provided to the Coalition by other nations were able to adapt to and use the same procedures as NATO's. The Gulf crisis demonstrated that Alliance arrangements, procedures and measures for this kind of crisis management are flexible and adaptable enough to support other international institutions and accommodate the participation of other nations, while ensuring appropriate political control and oversight. A precedent has therefore been set for Alliance support of the UN under its Chapter VII authority.

EVALUATION

The Alliance's new role in conflict prevention and crisis management is at the present time of writing still under discussion within the Alliance. However, the most likely outcome is that such a role will, for the foreseeable future, be a supportive one. In the Oslo Communiqué of June 1992, the Alliance foreign ministers, while giving their blessing to support of the CSCE in its future peacekeeping activities, also insisted that NATO involvement should not prejudice or preclude the involvement of other, non-NATO CSCE participating states.[16] A basic credo is that other nations will likely work alongside NATO in carrying out CSCE peacekeeping operations. At the same time these political and conceptual aspects were emerging, actual operational involvement of the Alliance in Yugoslavia in support of UN Security Council resolutions in that region was and is still taking place.

Here a problem is touched upon that has not entirely been resolved as yet. For its supportive role to be effective, the Alliance should: (a) communicate to the institutions having the primary role in conflict prevention/crisis management exactly what Alliance 'resources and expertise' are in fact available; and (b) await a request from the primary institution availing itself of whatever it requires from these advertised resources and expertise. While it would seem that these two aspects – i.e. building the inventory of resources and capabilities that could be offered and consulting closely on the political level with international institutions over possible requests and appropriate procedures – would logically be developing hand-in-glove, this complementarity is not proceeding as smoothly as one might have supposed.

There is still the question of a request to provide such support. For example, the CSCE *Helsinki Final Document*, adopted by CSCE Heads of State and Governments on 10th July 1992, does not spell out in detail the exact ways and means by which contact or liaison would be established by the CSCE in the event of a request for Alliance support. The relevant paragraph of the Final Document states, *inter alia*:[17]

> Decisions by the CSCE to seek the support of any such [international] organisation will be made on a case-by-case basis, having allowed for prior consultations with the participating States which belong to the organisation concerned.

Accordingly, the CSCE Chairman-in-Office will presumably undertake consultations regarding prospective participation in a CSCE peacekeeping mission, including consulting with those international organisations such as NATO which may later be requested more formally to provide support to these peacekeeping activities.[18] However, it should be recalled that the CSCE reaches its decisions on crisis management/peacekeeping by consensus. Any single participating State can thus prevent the request to another organisation from being made.[19]

As for the United Nations, the conceptual approach laid out by the UN Secretary-General has accorded a role for regional organisations in support of UN peacekeeping activities. This conceptual work is still at its early stages. Nevertheless, it is the UN Secretary-General's view that 'regional arrangements or agencies in many cases possess a potential that should be utilised in serving the functions covered in this report: preventive diplomacy, peacekeeping, peacemaking and post-conflict peace-building'.[20]

SUGGESTIONS FOR IMPROVEMENT

The Secretary-General of NATO, Manfred Woerner, perhaps said it best in a recent speech at Chatham House:

> Of all existing international organisations, NATO is best equipped, not only with the necessary military means for the defence of its member countries but also with the politico-military instruments for crisis management. But in order to be able to act, it would need both a mandate by the United Nations or the CSCE and a consensus of its 16 member nations.[21]

The clear implication of these remarks is that, if the Alliance is really going to play an effective role in conflict prevention and crisis management, it must be requested by an organisation such as the UN or the CSCE *and* it must free itself from its own self-imposed restrictions on taking on this role. Thus, at the present stage, the main area for improvement has to be the gaining of political consensus, both internally and externally, for the Alliance to act. This starts, in the first instance, in the North Atlantic Council, which alone has the authority to commit the Alliance to any action. But there must also be the political consensus within the UN Security Council and the CSCE for requests to be made to the Alliance for assistance or support of conflict prevention and crisis management. If both these sides of the equation develop harmoniously, then the main hurdle will have been passed and the principles established. Then the chief element of consideration will be the decision, on a case-by-case basis, to undertake action and the identification and deployment of the appropriate resources or capabilities for effective conflict prevention and crisis management.

CONCLUSION

NATO has collective experience in crisis management. Its consultative mechanisms, its military structures, its experience in the political control of military operations, its range of military capabilities, and its transatlantic membership – together these bring a combination of expertise, experience and capability that could be placed at the disposal of either the UN or the CSCE as appropriate, in support of a wide-range of conflict prevention and crisis management activities under the authority of those international organisations. The Alliance has embarked upon a reorganisation and refinement of its own internal crisis management procedures. However, given the 'multifaceted and multidirectional nature' of future risks and challenges facing the Alliance, as recognised in the Alliance's new Strategic Concept, it is not surprising that the Alliance would identify conflict prevention and crisis management as a means for maintaining and improving the security of its members.

Yet the Alliance has also acknowledged that any action in this regard will be tempered by the fact that overall political authority for crisis management in territories *outside* of the Alliance will be vested in either the UN or the CSCE. NATO will therefore have to resolve the potential tension between its own institutional autonomy in decision-making and operational control of its resources and expertise and the new requirement that it be supportive of other bodies. Reconciling these will be one of the chief preoccupations of the Alliance as it seeks to define its new role in the area of conflict prevention and crisis management (including peacekeeping). While this transformation will not happen overnight, nor are all the possible political implications entirely foreseeable, it is clear that the process is nevertheless already underway.

NOTES

1. The views and opinions expressed in this article are solely those of the author and are not attributable to those of the Alliance or its member states.
2. Further: 'Crisis prevention was to be achieved through deterrence of deliberate Soviet aggression. Modifying the environment through a strategy of anticipation came to mean influencing Soviet behaviour through a strategy of deterrence.' See: Phil Williams, Crisis Management in Europe: Old Mechanisms and New Problems, in: Alexander L George (ed.), *Avoiding War: Problems of Crisis Management*. (Oxford: Westview Press, 1991), p. 503.
3. A fuller discussion of the elements of NATO's earlier approach to conflict prevention, including the efficacy of command and control arrangements which would be at the heart of the transition from 'prevention' to 'management', is beyond the scope of this paper.
4. See: David Abshire, James Woolsey and Richard Burt, *The Atlantic Alliance Transformed*. (Centre for Strategic and International Studies, Washington, 1992). The authors also see new roles for the Alliance in the area of conflict prevention, such as: building an East–West defence community to encompass the fledgling democracies of Central and Eastern Europe; verifying and enforcing arms control agreements; and new work on missile defence to protect Europe against the proliferation of ballistic missiles.
5. In other words, will the Alliance go further than the politically supportive statement, the provision of expert assistance (contingency planning, etc.) and/or the supportive military response of 'classical' peacekeeping? Will the *imposed* suppression of conflict and the compellence of dispute settlement become the crisis response to the new civil wars in Europe?
6. Article 2 states: 'The Parties will contribute toward the further development of peaceful and friendly international relations by strengthening their free institutions, by bringing about a better understanding of the principles upon which these institutions are founded, and by promoting conditions of stability and well-being. They will seek to eliminate conflict in their international economic policies and will encourage economic collaboration between any or all of them.'
7. See paragraph 11 of the Oslo Communiqué, 4th June 1992: 'The Alliance has the capacity to contribute to effective actions by the CSCE in line with its new and increased responsibilities for crisis management and the peaceful settlement of disputes. In this regard, we are prepared to support, on a case-by-case basis in accordance with our own procedures,

peacekeeping activities under the responsibility of the CSCE, including by making available Alliance resources and expertise.'

8. The range of possible options and modalities are examined in Section 4(d), below.
9. The Inventory is part of an integrated approach to crisis management arrangements and measures at the disposal of the Alliance. Other measures of a preventive nature are found in, *inter alia*: the *NATO Precautionary System* (MC67/4); *Civil Emergency Preparedness*; and the Military Committee's '*Potential Military Response Options*' (MC/294). These documents, including the *Inventory of Preventive Measures* (C-M(81)7), are not available to the public.
10. The NAC, the DPC and the NATO Military Authorities practise their readiness for their respective roles and responsibilities in a period of tension or crisis by means of exercises at regular intervals, most recently in February 1992.
11. Parties to the CFE Treaty include: the sixteen NATO nations plus Russia, Ukraine, Moldova, Belarus, the Czech Republic, Slovakia, Hungary, Poland, Romania, Bulgaria, Azerbaijan, Armenia, Kazakhstan and Georgia.
12. Boutros Boutros-Ghali, *An Agenda for Peace: Preventive Diplomacy, Peacemaking and Peacekeeping* (New York: United Nations, 1992). *Peacekeeping:* 'the deployment of a United Nations presence in the field, hitherto with the consent of all the parties concerned ...' *Peacemaking:* 'action to bring hostile parties to agreement, essentially through such peaceful means as those foreseen in Chapter VI of the Charter of the United Nations.' (To this could be added *peace-enforcement*, which would be action undertaken to bring a hostile party (parties) into compliance with UN Security Council resolutions under Chapter VII of the UN Charter.) *Preventive diplomacy:* 'action to prevent disputes from arising between parties, to prevent existing disputes from escalating into conflicts and to limit the spread of the latter when they occur'. (To the generic term 'preventive diplomacy' could be added post-conflict *peacebuilding:* i.e. 'action to identify and support structures which will tend to strengthen and solidify peace in order to avoid a relapse into conflict'.) (*Ibid.*, p. 11).
13. For an elaboration of the Alliance role in the conflict management method of 'peace-enforcement', see page 130. The sole example of Alliance involvement in peace enforcement is dealt with there in connection with Alliance support of the United Nations resolutions dealing with the conflict in the Persian Gulf arising from the Iraqi invasion of Kuwait in 1990.
14. Once the reorganisation is complete, NATO forces will comprise: (a) the Immediate Reaction Force (to respond instantly to crisis; (b) the Allied Rapid Reaction Force (on 15 days' notice to move); (c) the Main Defence Forces; and (d) Augmentation Forces (to provide reinforcement). See: *Defense News*, 5 October 1992.
15. The question of 'burden-sharing' within the Alliance and the ramifications of the civil budget and other financial details of the Alliance are beyond the scope of this chapter.
16. See: Oslo Communique, 4th June 1992, paragraph 11.

17. See: *Challenges of Change, CSCE Helsinki Final Document*, Chapter III, paragraph 53.
18. For a detailed, 'behind-the-scenes' description of how the relevant passages of the *Helsinki Document 1992* on peacekeeping were negotiated, see: Gajus Scheltema, CSCE Peacekeeping Operations, in: *Helsinki Monitor* Volume 3, Number 4 (1992), pp. 7–17.
19. At the Second Meeting of the CSCE Council of Ministers in Prague in January 1992, the CSCE adopted a 'consensus-minus-one' principle that would apply in certain circumstances to obviate this inherent veto power. However, this would apply only to issues relating to safeguarding human rights, democracy and the rule of law. According to Section IV, Paragraph 16: '... appropriate action may be taken by the Council or the Committee of Senior Officials, in necessary in the absence of the consent of the State concerned, in cases of clear, gross and uncorrected violations of relevant CSCE commitments. Such actions would consist of political declarations or other political steps to apply outside the territory of the State concerned.'
20. Boutros Boutros-Ghali, *op. cit.*, p. 37.
21. See: Speech delivered by the Secretary-General of NATO, Manfred Woerner, to the Royal Institute of International Affairs, Chatham House, London, October 1, 1992.

5

The European Community and Conflict Management

Stephan Keukeleire

The European integration process can be considered as one of the most successful conflict management operations in 20th century European history. The 1951 European Community for Steel and Coal (ECSC) and the 1957 European Economic Community (EEC) assured lasting peace and cooperation between the hereditary enemies France and Germany. During the last forty years, the European Community (EC) has also proved to be an excellent instrument to prevent the development or escalation of conflicts among the member states. This internal conflict management dimension may become even more important in the future, as the future enlargements of the EC may also lead to an internalisation of what are now external conflicts.

The aim of this chapter is not to examine this 'internal' conflict management dimension but to analyse the 'external' conflict management efforts and capacity. However, it is important to note from the beginning that external conflict management was not at all one of the objectives of the EC. Thus, when creating the EC, its member states did not provide it with an institutional structure and the instruments needed for external conflict management. This was not seen as necessary or even desirable, most conflicts being part of the general East–West conflict which was managed through the Atlantic Alliance under American leadership. Moreover, the failure in 1954 of the plans for a European Defence Community resulted in EC involvement in security and especially military issues becoming a taboo.

Only since the first signs of détente at the end of the 1960s did the EC gradually start to formulate a policy of its own on certain economic and political aspects of security, thus shaping a basis for a limited conflict management capability. This occurred within the new establishment of European Political Cooperation (EPC), which is concerned with intergovernmental cooperation between the EC member states in some fields of external relations. The EPC works independently from the EC. It was only in the 1980s that the strict separation between EC and EPC gradually diminished.

With the end of the East–West confrontation, the rise of new (kinds of) conflict, and the main military organisation (NATO) and leading Western power (the USA) no longer taking the lead automatically, the EC felt compelled to elaborate further its conflict management capabilities. This development was also a by-product of the Community's internal dynamism, which increased the importance of the external dimension.[1] The Yugoslav crisis in particular led to an acceleration of the EC's involvement in conflict management.

However, the question of the development of the EC's conflict management role and capability is still part of the ongoing struggle among the member states about the nature of the Community and about its position in the new European security architecture. This implies that a large degree of ambiguity and doubt exists over the extent of actual developments. Are these to be considered as exceptions or as precedents for the future?

A first important result of this struggle about the transformation of the EC is the *Treaty of European Union* which was accepted by the twelve Heads of State and Government in Maastricht on December 1991 and signed on February 7, 1992. This treaty, which will influence the conflict prevention capacities of the Community, will come into force after being ratified by all member states. It is impossible to predict its real impact in view of the different interpretations being put upon it.

The EC not having been created with any commitment to external conflict management and only recently developing its instruments for external policy action, an evaluation of the EC's conflict management capabilities has to be seen from an evolutionary perspective. In addition to making an evaluation of the EC's past and present achievements and capabilities, it is essential to consider the possible consequences of recent developments and initiatives.

THE MANDATE

An analysis of the documents underlying the European Community shows that (external) conflict management is not an objective of the Community. However, whereas the concept 'conflict management' is never mentioned, the more general concept, 'preservation of peace' appears in one form or another in the four basic texts.

The Preamble of the *Treaty establishing the European Coal and Steel Community* (ECSC, 1951), signed only six years after the end of the Second World War, extensively treats the internal peacebuilding purposes of the creation of the ECSC, which is considered important for world peace.[2] 'Preservation and strengthening of peace' is mentioned only once in the preamble of the *Treaty of Rome establishing the European Economic Community* (EEC, 1957).

The 1986 *Single European Act* (SEA), amending the Treaty of Rome, implicitly refers in its Preamble to (external) conflict management:[3]

> Aware of the responsibility incumbent upon Europe ... to act with consistency and solidarity in order more effectively to protect its common interests and independence, ... *so that together they may make their own contribution to the preservation of international peace and security* in accordance with the undertaking entered into by them within the framework of the UN Charter.

The 1992 *Treaty on European Union* will not give an explicit mandate for conflict prevention. However, Articles J.1(1) and J.4(1) of Title V ('Provisions on a Common Foreign and Security Policy' (CFSP)) point to a stronger implicit mandate:[4]

- 'The Union and its Member States shall define and implement a common foreign and security policy ... *covering all areas of foreign and security policy*'.
- The CFSP shall include all questions related to the security of the Union, including the eventual framing of a common defence policy, which might in time lead to a common defence'.

Article J.1(2) mentions as objectives of the CFSP, *inter alia*, the following two aspects.

- 'to preserve peace and strengthen international security, in accordance with the principles of the UN Charter as well as the principles of the *Helsinki Final Act* and the objectives of the *Paris Charter*';
- 'to develop and consolidate democracy and the rule of law, and respect for human rights and fundamental freedoms'.

The second objective clearly can be considered as a clear mandate for peacebuilding activities. The first objective can be interpreted as an implicit mandate for peacekeeping and enforcement and peacemaking. Important again is the reference to the legitimising basic texts of the UN and the CSCE.

The European Council in Maastricht asked the Ministers of Foreign Affairs to define the basic elements of the CFSP.[5] The resulting report, approved by the European Council in Lisbon on June 27, 1992, provides an explicit mandate for peacebuilding and peacemaking and might give an implicit mandate for peacekeeping and enforcement.[6] The report's subdivision 8 reads as follows:

> ... the CFSP should contribute to ensuring that the Union's external action is less reactive to events in the outside world, and more active in the pursuit of the interests of the Union and in the creation of a more favourable international environment. This will enable the European Union to have an improved capacity to *tackle problems at their roots in order to anticipate the outbreak of crises*. Furthermore, the Union will be able to make clearer to third countries its own aims and interests, and to match more closely those parties' expectations of the Union.

Subdivision 10 gives six examples of the specific objectives which 'the Union should define in order to elect the issues in which joint action may be envisaged'. Four of these objectives are closely related to peacebuilding:

- 'strengthening democratic principles and institutions, and respect for human and minority rights;
- promoting regional political stability and contributing to the creation of political and/or economic frameworks that encourage regional cooperation or moves towards regional or sub-regional integration;
- strengthening existing cooperation in issues of international interest such as the fight against arms proliferation ...;
- promoting and supporting good government'.

The two other objectives seem to give a clear and explicit mandate for peacemaking and at least an implicit mandate for peacekeeping and enforcement:

- 'contributing to a more effective international coordination in dealing with emergency situations'.
- '*contributing to the prevention and settlement of conflicts*'.

Despite the fact that these objectives are not yet formally accepted but only given as examples, the report accepted by the European Council clearly points in the direction of a more active EC interest in all aspects of conflict management.

The four basic texts of the Community do not give details on the type of conflicts that can be put on the agenda. The above mentioned report lists certain factors that should be taken into account when defining the issues and areas for joint action:

- the geographical proximity of a region or country;
- an important interest in the political and economic stability of a region or country;
- the existence of threats to the security interests of the Union.

The report identifies some countries and regions which, 'in a first phase', should be given priority. Those in the first priority are Central and Eastern Europe, the Balkans and the former Soviet Republics.

With regard to these areas, the report again mentions the objective of 'prevention and settlement of conflicts', and the EC policy towards these countries might thus include peacebuilding, peacemaking and even peacekeeping and enforcement measures. Second priority is given to the Maghreb and Middle East, where EC involvement seems to be restricted to peacebuilding and possibly peacemaking.

DECLARATORY PREVENTION

Declaratory prevention is an important factor in the Community's external policy. Indeed, an analysis of the declarations indicates that the Twelve consistently attempt to delineate and communicate both the type of behaviour that is desired or required and the type of behaviour that will not be tolerated.

First, there are the general declarations which emphasise the importance of human rights, democracy and the need to solve conflicts in a peaceful manner. Second, there are the many declarations which either encourage specific activities and political trends with peacemaking and peacebuilding implications (such as the efforts of the Contadora group, democratic reforms in Poland and Hungary in 1989 or the decisions to hold presidential elections in Lebanon) or denounce or warn against certain actions or developments (such as during the crises in Afghanistan, Poland or Yugoslavia).

The Community seems to be both more interested and more able than other international organisations, and even national governments, to delineate and communicate desired or unaccepted behaviour in advance. In contrast with the superpowers, the Community strongly emphasises the importance of moral persuasion. The Twelve in their declarations clearly opt more for a positive approach (emphasising the desired behaviour) than for the negative approach (delineating what it will not accept). Moreover, it is remarkable that, even in crises in which the negative approach and sanctions are seen as unavoidable, the Community usually takes more moderate stances than for instance the USA. In general, it tries to de-escalate a crisis and keep open possibilities of conciliation (as in the crises in Poland, Afghanistan and Kuwait).[7] Secondly, the EC is equipped quite well to issue declarations in view of the frequent meetings on all political and diplomatic levels and in view of its extensive early warning system.

This stream of innovation, these frequent meetings and this disposition to comment on events in the world result in a large number of declarations which can be issued by the European Council, the Council with the Ministers of Foreign Affairs or the Political Committee, as well as by the Presidency, the Commission on the EP (through its resolutions). Issuing declarations has often been considered as (and criticised for being) one of the main functions and instruments of EPC.[8]

DECISION-MAKING PROCEDURES

Different decision-making procedures apply for conflict management measures that fall under EC competence (based on the Treaty of Rome) or EPC competence (based on intergovernmental arrangements accepted within the EC framework through the Single European Act). This also implies that there are differences in the actors that can put a conflict on the agenda and in the possibility for timely and effective decision-making.

For measures falling under EC competence (e.g. economic assistance or sanctions), the European Commission has the responsibility to propose specific measures on its own initiative or at the request of the Council of Ministers. The latter implies that the Council, the Presidency and the member states can indirectly put a conflict on the EC agenda. The deliberations in the Council are prepared by the COREPER (the Committee of Permanent Representatives). Depending on the article of the Treaty of Rome which has to be used as a formal basis, the Council has to adopt a proposal by unanimity or by qualified majority. The latter option obviously increases the possibility for timely and effective decision-making.

Timely and effective decision-making is quite probable when it concerns conflict management measures which allow the European Commission to take the initiative. The Commission indeed disposes of a permanent and efficient infrastructure, and has considerable experience in such matters as sanctions or economic, financial and other kinds of assistance. However, the latter indicates that the range of possible decisions within the Commission's competence is rather limited. Its decisions in general also have to be confirmed by the Council. Nevertheless the Commission has frequently proved that it can react flexibly in new situations, proposing (and deciding on) new initiatives, and thus also trying to extend its competence. Furthermore, in the past, the Commission was often the only EC institution able to react quickly to an international crisis.[9]

The EP's ability to bring influence to bear on the Community's conflict management policy is rather limited. Nonetheless, it has some instruments at its disposal to influence specific issues. Firstly, being part of the EC's budgetary authority, the EP has the power to reject the budget, for instance if it considers that not enough credits are foreseen for certain items.[10] The EP can also use its budgetary powers to influence the EC's reaction to specific conflicts.[11]

Secondly, the Single European Act gave the EP two new powers to influence the Twelve's peacebuilding activities. Association agreements with third countries or groups of countries require the assent of the EP (Art. 9).[12] It can thus encourage or sanction certain developments in those countries, for instance through the rejection of protocols with third countries.[13] The EP's assent is also required for the accession of new countries to the EC (Art. 8). The EP can thus demand that certain economic, political and security requirements are satisfied before candidates are allowed to join, which can influence the potential candidate's attitude with regard to certain crises.

For measures that fall under EPC competence (SEA, Art. 30) unanimity is required among the Ministers for Foreign Affairs for each decision. However, there is a growing disposition to agree with the majority with regard to subjects that are not too sensitive.[14] The deliberations and decisions with regard to EPC matters are not prepared by COREPER but by the separate Political Committee (consisting of the Political Directors), which obviously complicates the decision-making process.[15] The Presidency as well as any member state can put a crisis on the agenda.

The Commission is 'fully associated' with the proceedings of EPC, but has not the same formal role as in EC matters (Art. 30(3b)). Nevertheless, as EPC does not have sufficient ad hoc instruments to lend weight to the Twelve's declarations (apart from the conventional methods of diplomacy) the Commission has very often been called upon to propose and implement Community measures to back EPC decisions.[16] The EP has no real impact on the EPC, but indirectly can bring conflicts onto the political agenda of the Community through its reports, debates and questions to the Council (and Commission).[17]

The different procedures and competences of the institutions for matters related to EC or EPC competences complicate and hamper the EC's conflict management efforts. The *Single European Act* states that the Presidency and the Commission are responsible for ensuring that EC and EPC policies are consistent. However, the formulation of a common response on a crisis is sometimes overshadowed by the internal power struggle between the Presidency, the Commission and member states on the question of who is competent to act (and on the question of whether the Twelve are competent to act at all).[18]

Since the Single European Act, though, the Ministers of Foreign Affairs and a member of the Commission can discuss foreign policy matters during both EPC and EC Council meetings, which implies that they can discuss foreign policy issues at least once a month (Art. 30.3(a)). The ability for timely decision-making is further increased through the development of a crisis management procedure adopted in the EPC's *London Report* of October 1981.[19] This procedure foresees that 'the Political Committee or, if necessary, the Ministerial Meeting, will convene within 48 hours at the request of three member states' and was very important for developing the Community's conflict management capabilities.[20]

These procedures and the frequent meetings formally allow timely decision-making in periods of crisis. However, two major structural constraints continue to hamper efficient and timely decision-making.

The first constraint is the unanimity rule in EPC matters, which is reinforced by the existing divergence among Member States on both the principle and the substance of EC actions. This explains why the reactions of the Twelve are in some cases merely vague declarations and why they were often unable to undertake more significant actions (especially when tough decisions were required). Seen from this perspective, it was normal that the EC at a certain point in the Yugoslav crisis was unable to take some more far-reaching measures (eg. with regard to the military protection of the observers), whereas the initiatives it had already taken (with regard to mediation and the sending of observers) were remarkable achievements, indicating the growing readiness of the member states to accept EC involvement in conflict management.

The second structural constraint is the lack of a single decision-making centre and a centralised political leadership which could induce member states to adopt and keep a common position and stick to a common action.[21] On the one hand, the President of the European Commission can only act in certain fields of conflict management and is not accepted by all member states as a legitimate leader in foreign policy fields. On the other, the country holding the EC Presidency can play a very active and influential part in conflict management issues, but can also be constrained in its actions and so can, on occasion, even be a hindrance to EC initiatives. The President-in-office cannot set out important new policy lines or pursue major initiatives without prior consultation with at least the major member states.[22] The EC Presidency is bound to follow the line of policy adopted by the twelve member states, with the larger states obviously having a greater freedom of action when holding the Presidency. Furthermore, because of the central role of the Presidency especially for EPC matters, the dynamism and quality of the EC's initiatives in a conflict depend largely on the interest and experience of the country that holds the presidency.[23] Finally, the EC Presidency changes every six months causing problems with regard to continuity and prompt and efficient reactions during periods of transition.[24]

The Treaty on European Union does not fundamentally alter the decision-making procedures with regard to conflict management nor does it solve the problems related to the lack of political leadership. With regard to the CFSP, the majority rule is introduced for implementing decisions but will, as a result of the severe conditions, only apply on very limited occasions (Art. J.3) and never apply for issues having defence implications (Art. J.4/3). Decision-making with regard to economic sanctions as part of a common position or action adopted within the CFSP is facilitated (Art. 228A). COREPER and the Political Committee are not merged. The position of the EP and the Commission is not substantially altered. The EP's influence on the conclusion of cooperation agreements is, however, increased (Art. 228), and the Commission is allowed to submit proposals (which already happens informally) (Art. J.9).[25] In this context it is interesting to note that the new European Commission which came into office from January 1993, for the first time also had a Commissioner who, besides his responsibility for external relations, is explicitly responsible for matters concerning the CFSP.

CONFLICT PREVENTION FACILITIES

Early warning and communications

The Community disposes of several major sources of information to provide those responsible with timely warning. First, the European Commission has a network of more than one hundred diplomatic missions abroad and the President of the Commission, as well as the Commission's Directorate General for External Relations, has close high-level contacts with a large number of states and international and regional organisations. The President of the Commission also participates in the meetings of the 'Group of 7'.

Secondly, the Community can draw on the experience and information of the twelve Ministries of Foreign Affairs and their diplomatic network. This is an important advantage as it enables the EC to rely on member states' specialised experience in diverse areas of the world. In view of their geographic position and traditional relationships, each member state, in fact has privileged relations with and deeper knowledge about certain areas in the world. The EC therefore is able to have a more comprehensive view on international developments than is possible for individual member states. The sensitivity of most member states to some particular area also results in the EC as a whole reacting rather quickly on the development of a crisis in a particular area, as the member state concerned wants its attitude or policy backed by the Community as a whole.

The Twelve have developed several methods by which to take advantage of the know-how of the different member states and to arrive at a common analysis and formulate common (re-)actions. First, there is permanently a close contact between the twelve European Correspondents in the Foreign Ministries of the member states.* They act as the central contact points and as assistants to the Political Directors for all EPC questions. Secondly, there are numerous meetings of the Ministers for Foreign Affairs, the EPC's Political Committee and the more than twenty Working Groups. The latter focuses on particular areas (such as the Middle East or Asia) or issues (such as non-proliferation, chemical weapons, arms exportation or the UN). After the European Council in Maastricht, a new high-level Ad Hoc Working Group on Security has been created to explore in what fields and how the EC could develop 'joint actions'. Ad Hoc Working Groups can be created to follow specific crises, as is now the case for Yugoslavia.

The Working Groups consist of the heads of sections or departments of Foreign Ministries and of a representative of the European Commission. Representatives of Ministries of Defence can be part of the Working Groups if the nature of the crisis requires it (as in the Yugoslavia crisis). One of the functions of the Working Groups is to analyse areas of potential crisis and to prepare a range of possible reactions.[26] However, as they do not meet continuously, they are not able to formulate an instant response to a sudden crisis.

Thirdly, an instant response is though made possible through the COREU (*Correspondance européenne*) telex network which is run by the twelve European Correspondents and which links each of the twelve Foreign Ministries, as well as the Commission and the EPC Secretariat.[27] The COREU network allows the member states to exchange confidential messages, to draft documents or declarations quickly and take decisions.

The Community also gains information through the network of consultative relations which it has developed with individual countries

* *European Correspondents:* Officials in EC foreign ministries responsible for the exchange of information on all matters relating to European Political Cooperation (EPC) and the evolving Common Foreign and Security Policy (CFSP).

and other regional organisations (such as ASEAN, the Contadora Group, the Gulf Co-operation Council).[28] Besides the regular meetings, these institutionalised contacts provide a basis to solicit the views of the leaders concerned when a crisis occurs in a particular region.

Two other methods to gain information about a crisis are the contacts with the Diplomatic Delegations to the EC of the countries concerned and the possibility of sending fact-finding missions abroad. The latter implies that the President-in-Office or the Troika[29] visits other countries or regions to gain more information from the partners involved and to play a more active role in finding a solution to a conflict.[30] A new method to gain information was recently adopted with the use of observer missions to be deployed on a permanent basis in a conflict area. Observer missions in Yugoslavia provide regular evaluations on the crisis as well as daily detailed information (though the COREU network) on the latest developments (such as new declarations of the fighting parties, compliance or non-compliance with cease-fires and human rights abuses).

Finally, the different sensitivities towards the outside world of each EC member state and political group explains why the EP, with its 518 MEP's from the twelve member states, fulfils a kind of early warning function. Its resolutions and the questions of MEP's to the Foreign Ministers concerning all kinds of developments or crises abroad indeed point to the rise and existence of particular crises in the world. The contacts with parliaments of third countries and other regions and the invitations of leaders of foreign countries, of opposition groups and of minority and ethnic groups also help to focus attention upon certain conflicts.[31]

The Community thus can draw on several major sources to enable it to be timely and thoroughly informed about incipient conflicts. However, this does not automatically imply that there is an effective 'intelligence unit' to provide those responsible with timely warning. Just as there is no single decision-making process and no centralised leadership, there is no central unit where the information on potential crises is centralised and where the formulation of a prompt reaction is guaranteed. This situation will perhaps partially be solved through the provision in the *Treaty on European Union* which requires the Political Committee to 'monitor the international situation in the areas covered by CFSP and contribute to the definition of policies ...' (Art. J.8(5)), if this articles implies that the Political Committee will assume a coordinating and leading role.

Conflict management methods

Peacekeeping and enforcement

The EC has no military means of its own to prevent or suppress violent conflicts. The constraints resulting from this lack of military instruments might in the future be reduced as a result of both formal and *de facto* developments.

The *Treaty of Maastricht* does not provide the EC with military instruments of its own. However, the objectives formulated in this Treaty and in the *Report on the likely developments of the CFSP* of June 1992 as well as the strengthened EC–WEU relationship foreseen in the *Maastricht Treaty* might in the future facilitate the possibility for the EC to rely on other organisations and possibly on forces of its member states for peacekeeping and enforcement purposes.

Recent developments also enhance the possibility for the EC to rely on 'external' peacekeeping and enforcement forces. New attempts to provide the EC indirectly with military instruments in contrast with earlier attempts, did partially succeed.[32]

First, during the Gulf crisis in 1990–91, there was a development in the EC–WEU relationship which would prove to be significant, in the light of the procedures and initiatives adopted during the Yugoslav crisis. As will be analysed later, the informal and indirect relationship between the EC and the WEU (through the largely overlapping membership) made it possible that EC decisions were partially implemented or further elaborated through WEU actions! This occurred from August 1990 in order to support the international embargo against Iraq and in April 1991 to coordinate the logistic support to the EC's humanitarian operations for the Kurds in Iraq.[33] These developments indicated that the EC might in the future be able to rely implicitly on the WEU (and thus on the EC/WEU member states) to provide military forces for peacemaking or peacekeeping purposes.

The Yugoslav crisis led to both a positive and negative development with regard to potential EC peacekeeping facilities.

A new step was the decision by the Council, with the backing of the CSCE, to send 50 observers to Slovenia and later on to Croatia (this number was later on increased to 200). This decision, which was accepted by the fighting parties in the *Brioni Agreement* of the 7th of July, 1991, implied that the observers would monitor (and thus not enforce) the implementation of the cease-fire.[34] The EC Monitoring Mission consisted of officials from the EC Commission and diplomats and unarmed military personnel from EC countries, who were later on joined by observers from other CSCE countries. The EC Monitoring Mission is coordinated by the Presidency and financed by the EC Commission and the member states. The Commission and some member states (in several cases through the involvement of their armed forces) provide the logistic support.

The observers played a useful role in Slovenia, but, especially from September 1991 on, were frustrated in their efforts in the escalating conflict in Croatia as a result of the repeated non-compliance with the cease-fires, their limited mandate and the lack of military instruments. Despite the failure of their main objective, their presence in many areas remained useful, containing, to some extent, excessive use of violence and providing the EC with detailed day-to-day information. The death of four EC observers in January 1992 resulted, for the first time, in lives being sacrificed for the EC flag. The EC decision to continue the observation mission nonetheless, indicated the growing commitment of member states towards the EC's involvement in military conflicts.

Despite the limitations and frustrations, the EC had achieved a new step forward towards increasing its involvement in military conflicts. The sending of observers also set some precedents that can be relevant for future peacekeeping operations.[35] Important too was the fact that it was the EC, and not military organisations like the WEU or NATO or such international organisations as CSCE or the UN, which assumed responsibility in the first stage of this military conflict and which took the leadership over the observers' mission.

Negative, however, was the failure to get a consensus within the EC to send – through WEU – any armed military forces to Yugoslavia. Some EC members understood that escalation of the EC commitment was necessary, in view of the deterioration of the crisis and of the fact that the EC monitor mission was no longer able to perform its task in full. France, Germany, Belgium, Italy and the Netherlands proposed that armed military personnel should augment the EC observer teams to provide some protection and to increase the credibility of the European commitment. In their view, WEU should envisage to lend military support to the EC actions. However, Portugal and especially the UK opposed even the least ambitious of four options proposed by a WEU ad hoc group (involving the logistic support of the EC observers by 2000 to 3000 soldiers).[36]

The negative attitude of some member states to increasing the EC commitment can partially be explained by the fact that this discussion occurred towards the end of the IGC on European Political Union. Some countries feared that accepting new measures in the Yugoslav crisis, implying the inclusion of military aspects in the EC framework or strengthening the EC–WEU relationship, would oblige them to put down these *de facto* achievements on paper at the IGC.

The repudiation of the use of armed force under almost any circumstances weakened the influence of the EC over the escalating crisis in Yugoslavia. The Community indeed placed self-imposed limits on the effectiveness of its mediation efforts in Yugoslavia.[37] The various indigenous armed forces and political leaders knew that they had no military consequences to fear when they ignored the ceasefire or other agreements which they concluded with the Twelve. Similarly the weaker parties in the conflict recognised that they could not count on the EC for protection. The logical consequence of the failure of the EC (and WEU) to agree on the use of military instruments was the decision by the EC to demand that the UN should take up responsibility in the military field.

Peacemaking

The EC endorsed the creation of the EPC peacemaking initiatives, which mostly took the form of diplomatic démarches outside the

Community to present the views of the EC on a given conflict and to suggest solutions. These initiatives are taken by diplomats or by the Minister of Foreign Affairs of the country holding the EC Presidency, by the Troika or by special representatives.[38]

In many cases, the importance of EC initiatives has rested more on the mere fact that there was such an initiative than on their preponderant influence. Nevertheless, especially in periods of East–West confrontation, the initiatives of the Twelve have not been insignificant as they have aimed at preventing a conflict from further escalation or negatively affecting other areas or policy fields (i.e. during the crises in Poland and Afghanistan in 1979–1983).[39]

The Gulf crisis in 1990–91 gave a new example of both the characteristics and limitations of the European endeavours. The Twelve (sometimes in contrast with the Americans) emphasised their preference for a peaceful solution, their awareness of the global dimension of the conflict, the need to avoid the complete isolation of Jordan and the need for economic support for the countries who had most suffered from the crisis.[40] However, on several occasions they failed to seize the opportunity to make a European contribution to the resolution of the conflict and, in general, conceded the lead to the United States.

The crisis in Yugoslavia forced the Twelve to recognise, in the summer of 1991, that the EC should do more than use such traditional methods as diplomatic missions and that new instruments had to be employed. This resulted in two new peacemaking methods and two new peacebuilding methods being adopted by the Twelve. The first of these was the active and sustained mediation in Yugoslavia between the warring factions by the Troika of foreign ministers to facilitate the dialogue between the conflicting parties and to bring about a cease-fire. The second measure was the appointment of a special representative to mediate permanently in the conflict (Lord Carrington, and later on David Owen).[42]

The successful use of these new peacemaking efforts was seriously hampered for two reasons. First, the EC was unprepared for such a peacemaking role, leading inevitably to ad hoc measures and improvisation. The need for a standing external policy apparatus to be established within the EC was thus again emphasised. Secondly, the complicated nature of the crisis in Yugoslavia and the apparent lack of interest in peace on the part of the warring factions, must often have made the efforts of the EC to appear as acts of desperation.[43]

The new peacemaking mechanisms can also be evaluated in a positive sense. First, the mediation led to positive results in Slovenia and ensured that the possibility of a negotiated solution was not immediately excluded. Second, it indicated that the Community could react creatively and quickly to newly developing peacemaking requirements. Third, and most important, a new precedent was set, new procedures and mechanisms were established and new experience was gained which can be useful in the future and form a basis for the development by the EC of a genuine peacemaking capacity (cf. the mediation in the Danube-barrage conflict[44]).

The establishment of such a capacity, however, requires that the new procedures and mechanisms used should be further elaborated and institutionalised and that a special task force should be created so as to ensure that the EC can rely on firm procedures, institutional structures and instruments when a new crisis occurs.

Peacebuilding

With regard to the avoidance or resolution of crises, the Community in its declarations consistently emphasises peacebuilding objectives by giving priority to dialogue and cooperation, advocating respect for human rights, supporting political democratisation and economic development and cooperation. This approach, and especially the emphasis on dialogue and cooperation, was often in contrast with the more confrontational attitude of the USA.[45] When compared with the superpowers, the EC de-emphasised the projection of power, ideological warfare, pressure and coercion in world affairs, and stressed moral persuasion, peaceful change and conflict regulation without force.[46] This emphasis on dialogue and cooperation can be explained by, first, the EC's own successful experience in solving in this way the traditional problems between the member states, and second, the EC's lack of military instruments of power.

The Community's emphasis on and support for peacebuilding had already appeared in the first years of EPC, when it took a leading role in the Helsinki CSCE-negotiations.[47] The efforts of the EC to prevent escalation of the East–West confrontation and to promote reconciliation and dialogue also appeared, *inter alia*, during the crises in Poland and Afghanistan and during arms control negotiations.[48]

The Community approach was also evident in relation to more 'limited' conflicts, such as in Central America or in Yugoslavia. In these crises, as well as in other areas of instability, the EC made use of attitudinal, socio-economic and political peacebuilding measures. The EC also supported regional cooperation initiatives (such as ASEAN or the Visegrad-group) and entered in to economic and political dialogue with them, as the EC viewed this inter- and intra-regional dialogue and cooperation as an instrument to strengthen peace and stability in the regions concerned.[49]

An example of such a peacebuilding effort was the EC policy in 1981–85 towards the conflict in Central America. In contrast to the Americans, who considered the problems with the Sandinista government in Nicaragua primarily as a facet of the East–West conflict, the EC supported the approach of the Contadora Group.[50] The latter viewed the origins of the problems in terms of economic, social and political inequalities, and called for multilateral negotiations and economic initiatives to help the countries involved. The EC promised economic and financial assistance for the region as well as the conclusion of a Cooperation Agreement. It also accepted to support the Contadora initiative through political dialogue between the EC and the Central American countries, but emphasised that this required the latter to act as a regional unit. This forced the Central American countries to enter into dialogue with each other before talking with the EC. The EC also conditioned inter-regional dialogue by progress in the Contadora process and with regard to free elections, pluralist democracy and respect for human rights.[51]

The *Cooperation Agreements* and the *Association Agreements* which have been concluded since 1988 with the countries in Central and Eastern Europe were similarly conceived as methods to support democratic and economic reforms, and respect for human rights and the rights of minorities. The readiness of the EC to negotiate on these agreements as well as the degree of cooperation and assistance promised by the EC in these agreements indeed depended on the compliance of these countries with these conditions. This element of conditionality also existed with regard to the financial, economic and food aid of the EC to these countries.[52]

The crisis in Yugoslavia led the EC to adopt two new peacebuilding methods.[53] The first method was the organisation of a peace conference attended by all the parties concerned, with the objective of agreeing on a long-term settlement of the Yugoslav problem.[54] Three working groups were set up which had to focus on the future institutional framework, the problems of the minorities and the future economic relations between the different republics. The sometimes contradictory and not always realistic attitude of the EC, the escalation of the conflict and the Serbian suspicion *vis-à-vis* the Community, however, made the working of the Conference impossible and led the EC to ask for the assistance of the UN.[55] The second new method was the creation of an arbitration board to examine and decide on disputes which could not be solved by the peace conference.[56] The arbitration board suffered from the same malaise as the peace conference.

The main and most positive conclusion to be drawn from the EC's peacebuilding efforts to date is that the EC decided to use new peacebuilding instruments and gained further experience. Those efforts were not able to stop the escalation of the Yugoslav civil war. Nevertheless, the EC is only partially to be blamed for this failure, in view of the fact that the conditions in Yugoslavia were so bad as to make the successful introduction of peacebuilding measures highly unlikely. Hence, the main future of the EC peacebuilding efforts did not occur during the military conflict, but during the years before the crisis took a military turn. It was in that period that the EC should have taken more comprehensive peacebuilding initiatives to prevent the escalation into an ethnic and military crisis. However, during that period the EC had been heavily preoccupied with events in the Eastern Bloc countries and so failed to recognise the dangers inherent in the developments in Yugoslavia.

Other measures dealing with the opportunity structure

The EC can back its declaratory prevention efforts and its

peacemaking and peacebuilding efforts with a whole range of non-military conflict management measures dealing with the opportunity structure. The promise, threat or decision to take a particular action if a particular attitude is adopted (or not adopted) by the conflicting parties can strengthen the impact of conflict management measures taken by the EC. These measures can be political–diplomatic, economic, or related to initiatives in other international organisations.

Firstly, with regard to political–diplomatic measures, a distinction can be made between the degree of formal relations between the EC and this country on the one hand and on the other the diplomatic recognition of a particular country. First, the desire of most European countries to conclude cooperation or association agreements with the EC and eventually become a member of the EC provides an excellent opportunity to influence effectively the behaviour of these countries (in particular in crises) by introducing certain elements of conditionality.[57] Second, the wish of new independent states in Europe to be recognised officially has provided a new instrument with which to influence their behaviour. In consequence in December 1991 the EC adopted *Guidelines on the Recognition of New States in Eastern Europe and in the Soviet Union* which also included rules which the new states had to follow in handling crises.[58] Other diplomatic instruments used by the EC are the threat or decision to close diplomatic posts or to propose the exclusion of a country from international organisations.[59]

Secondly, the credibility and effect of many declarations and other conflict management efforts of the EC are strengthened by the promise (or decision) to provide economic or other assistance and by the threat (or decision) to impose economic sanctions or an embargo.[60] The possibility of implementing economic measures quickly, and thus efficiently to lend strength to its political measures, depends, however, on the article of the Treaty of Rome which is used as a formal basis, as well as on the availability of funds in the EC budget.[61]

Finally, the EC can back its conflict management efforts by proposing or supporting moral, political-diplomatic or economic measures by other international organisations such as the CSCE and in particular the UN.[62] In recent years, the EC member states that are also members of the Security Council have proposed in several cases that the UN should take up the initiatives of the EC. Art. J.5(4) of the *Treaty on European Union* formally confirms this task of the EC states within the Security Council.

Cooperation with International Governmental Organisations (IGOs) and International Non-Governmental Organisations (INGOs)

In view of the EC's limited conflict management instruments as well as its limited mandate and limited experience, the EC was evidently forced to consider cooperation with other IGO's at the moment that real crises arose. This cooperation however suffered from the lack of institutionalised relations and procedures to negotiate and cooperate with the other organisations, from the incapacity of some of these IGO's, and from political motives which often undermined cooperation and relations with other organisations.

The coordination of the position of the EC countries within *the United Nations* since 1975 has been one of the objectives of EPC.[63] The EC has supported and financed actions of the specialised organisations of the UN (with regard to humanitarian aid, food aid, and support for refugees, for example), some of which have a conflict prevention or management dimension. The *Single European Act* and the *Treaty on European Union* referred to the UN Charter as a legitimising factor for the EC's involvement in preserving peace and strengthening international security. However, until recently, there was no real political cooperation between the EC as such and the UN Security Council or Assembly.

The EC–UN relationship assumed a new quality during the Yugoslav crisis (which is also due to the new role which the UN has assumed in recent years). First of all, the UN expressed its full support for the efforts of the EC and for the arrangements and measures which might result from these efforts, and thus gave the EC a kind of implicit mandate to try and solve the conflict. It also confirmed EC initiatives by adopting an embargo on the delivery of weapons and military equipment to Yugoslavia.[64]

In a second stage, at the request of the EC, which had recognized its limitations in conflict management, the UN cooperated with the EC to find a solution for the crisis. In October 1991 it appointed a special UN Representative for Yugoslavia (Cyrus Vance) who together with the special EC representative had to seek a solution for the crisis. The UN and the EC co-chaired the International Conference on the Former Yugoslavia, which replaced the Peace Conference initiated by the EC. In February 1992, the UN created a UN Protection Force (UNPROFOR) which had to act as a peacekeeping force in Yugoslavia.[65]

Consequently, the UN, being the only international organisition with serious experience in the field of peacekeeping, took over the peacekeeping role which the EC on its own could only fulfil in a very limited way. Nonetheless, the UN initiatives are still to a large extent based on the EC initiatives and proposals within the UN. Moreover, UNPROFOR consists for the largest part of soldiers from EC countries. It thus can be asserted that the EC is partially able to continue its actions in Yugoslavia through the larger legitimacy given by the UN and the support it gains in this way from other countries.

The CSCE is another organisation in which the EC, since the start of EPC, has coordinated its positions and adopted a very active role but with which the EC has, until recently, not cooperated intensively. This is due to the fact that, until recently, the CSCE could not be considered as an independent actor. Both the nature of the CSCE and of the EC–CSCE relationship changed with the adoption of the *Paris Charter* in November 1990 which foresaw the establishment of new mechanisms within the CSCE and created the Conflict Prevention Centre. The fact that an urgent meeting of the Committee of Senior Officials can be convened on the request of 13 CSCE-countries points to the influential position of the Twelve. The *Paris Charter* as well as the *Helsinki Final Act* have often been used by the EC as a point of reference and legitimation for its own positions or actions.

The Yugoslav crisis was also a significant test case for the EC–CSCE relationship. The CSCE largely renounced an active role of its own and left the initiative to the EC. However, the crisis pointed to the rather ambiguous nature of this relationship, with the two institutions both supporting and depending on each other. The CSCE, with the support of the EC, defined a formal framework for peace initiatives in Yugoslavia and strengthened the legitimacy of the EC actions. The EC, with the support of the CSCE, assumed the leadership of the European initiatives and ensured the practical implementation of the actions endorsed by the CSCE. In addition, the EC–CSCE relationship offered a useful framework for the participation of non-EC CSCE-countries to the observers' missions and for the transfer of information to them.[66]

It is recognised, however, that this division of labour between the EC and the CSCE in the Yugoslav crisis was closely related to the fact that Yugoslavia was considered as being a part of the EC's direct sphere of influence. This is not the case for the new republics in the former Soviet Union, and the CSCE is therefore considered as the best forum to handle crises in that region (especially as the USA is also a member of the CSCE). This would then imply that the CSCE is expected to take the initiative, with the EC supporting its actions (as is already the case with regard to the crisis in Nagorno–Karabakh).

Until now, there is no formalised and even barely an informal relationship or form of cooperation between the EC and NATO. As a result of the negative experience in 1954 over the plans for a European Defence Community, the EC always adopted an aloof attitude towards military issues and towards the Atlantic Alliance, which was responsible for the Western defence policy. Moreover, NATO, as well as several EC member states, was opposed to any action or position of the EC that might be interpreted as undermining the authority of NATO. The fact that not all EC countries were members of the EC also impeded cooperation but cannot, however, be considered as the main reason. The neutral position of Ireland has indeed often been used by other EC countries as an alibi to retain the strict separation between both organisations, whereas Ireland has often *de facto* adopted a very flexible attitude. The strict distinction between the EC and NATO can also be explained as a result of the attitude which the West adopted towards security and hence conflict management also, with a preponderance of the military dimension of security policy and with the non-military dimension being largely neglected.[67]

Nevertheless, there have been some cases wherein this strict division was at least indirectly overcome, as was for instance the case in the CSCE negotiations.[68] Moreover, it can be asserted that there was always a kind of coordination between both organisations, be it only as a result of most EC member states also being members of NATO.

During the last few years, the contacts between the EC and NATO have been enhanced on an *ad hoc* basis. This was unavoidable, as both organisations were involved in the management of the same international crises and their member states had to follow the policy formulated within both the EC and NATO.[69] The growing consultation and exchange of information, for instance through interventions of the EC Presidency in NATO meetings, as well as frequent informal contacts on lower levels were considered as an application of the commitments accepted in the *Copenhagen* and *Rome Declarations* by the NATO countries (and thus also by eleven EC member states) to ensure transparency between the Twelve, WEU and NATO.

However, these contacts are *ad hoc* arrangements, and the lack of formal institutional coordination prohibits efficient coordinated conflict management by the Western organisations. The *Treaty on European Union* does not provide a solution as it does not include measures to strengthen the EC–NATO relationship. The Alliance is only mentioned to confirm that 'The policy of the Union ... shall respect the obligations of certain Member States under the *North Atlantic Treaty* and be compatible with the common security and defence policy established within that framework' (Art. J.4(4)).[70]

The position of the EC is further complicated by the position of the USA as leading power within NATO. The USA pointed to the need for Western Europe increasingly to assume responsibility in ensuring peace and stability in Europe and the world in the post-1989 order.[71] However, in the period of the IGC on European Political Union, the USA (with the support of some EC countries) brought considerable pressure to bear on the Europeans not to accept any far-reaching provisions concerning defence and the EC–WEU relationship. In other words, the EC should do its duty, but it must not equip itself with the instruments needed for the purpose.[72]

A typical situation thus arose, with on the one hand the recognition of the need to change the division of labour and to increase the relations between NATO and the EC, and on the other the traditional constraints continuing to prevent such restructuring being carried through and contacts and methods of cooperation between both organisation being elaborated. As a direct link between both organisations remains difficult, the ineluctable linkage is increasingly ensured through WEU.

The EC–WEU relationship is characterised by a strong ambiguity. This results from the different opinions of EC member states on the status of the WEU. At one side of the spectrum, there is the opinion that the WEU should be considered as the future military arm of the EC and that in the long term an incorporation of the WEU within the EC or the European Union should be envisaged. From this point of view, the WEU could implement peacekeeping actions decided on within the EC. At the other end of the spectrum, the WEU is considered first and foremost as the European pillar of NATO, which implies that a stronger EC–WEU relationship is to be rejected. From this point of view, decisions on peacekeeping actions do not fall within the scope of the EC competences.

Until now, there is no formalised relationship or form of cooperation between the EC and the WEU. The interrelationship which nevertheless exists is based on three aspects. First, there is the fact that all WEU countries are members of the EC. This implies that the same Ministers of Foreign Affairs discuss the same crisis management issues in both organisations. This is often also true for the lower levels, with diplomats meeting each other within both the EC and WEU frameworks. For instance, a considerable number of the diplomats in the EOC's new Ad Hoc Working Group on Security also represent their country in the WEU committees. Such a double-hatting formula, which obviously strengthens the possibility of coordinating policy in both organisations, is not, however, adopted by all member states.

Secondly, since the Gulf crisis, a mechanism has been adopted to have WEU Presidency briefings in EC Councils and EC Presidency briefings in WEU Councils, which has facilitated the attempts to coordinate the conflict management efforts of both institutions.

Thirdly, some member states which favour a stronger EC–WEU relationship have tried, through *ad hoc* measures, to coordinate the policy of both organisations and to use WEU as an instrument to implement or further elaborate political decisions of the EC. The latter is a new pattern in the EC–WEU relationship which appeared since 1990: independently from the existence or non-existence of formal relations between the two organisations. The WEU in much of its activity has further elaborated the line of policy agreed on in the EC, the former not having the necessary procedures and institutions to define quickly a general common policy and the latter being unable to meet the military implications of its line of policy.

This pattern appeared on several occasions during the Gulf crises. Some weeks after the Iraqi invasion of Kuwait, it was decided to hold consecutive meetings of the WEU Council and of the EC Ministers of Foreign Affairs in Paris on August 21, 1990. The three EC countries that did not belong to WEU – Denmark, Greece and Ireland – were also invited to attend the WEU meeting, with only Ireland declining the invitation, setting a precedent for following WEU meetings.[73] The WEU Council largely repeated the points of view adopted in three foregoing EC declarations and deliberated on how to coordinate the naval operations with a view to enforcing the embargo against Iraq.[74]

Consecutive EC and WEU Council meetings were again held in Paris on January 17, 1991, the day that operation Desert Storm was launched,[75] and in Luxembourg on April 8. In Luxembourg, a special European Council meeting proposed the creation of a protection zone under UN supervision for the Kurds on Iraqi territory and decided to provide substantial humanitarian aid for the refugees, which was to be coordinated technically by the Commission. Immediately after this meeting, and to the discontent of several EC member states, the French (then holding the WEU presidency) convened an extraordinary meeting of the WEU foreign ministers to decide on the logistic support for the humanitarian operations decided on by the European Council.[76]

In September 1991, the EC's Dutch Presidency decided to convene on the 19th an extraordinary meeting of foreign ministers of the Twelve in The Hague, immediately followed by an extraordinary 'enlarged' WEU Council (with both foreign and defence ministers) which, at Dutch request, was convened by the WEU German Presidency. During the EC meeting, France and Germany defended their initiative to send an interposition force to Yugoslavia, with the Twelve discussing the possibility of sending military forces.[77] In their declaration, they 'welcome that WEU explores ways in which the activities of the monitors could be supported so as to make their work a more effective contribution to the peacekeeping effort' and added that 'the Community and its Member States would wish to have the opportunity to examine and endorse the conclusions of the study'.[78]

The WEU Council asked an *ad hoc* working group to explore possible actions, which were discussed eleven days later during new extraordinary WEU and EC Council meetings. WEU President-in-Office Genscher after the meeting of the 'enlarged' WEU Council (also attended by a representative of Ireland) mentioned that if both the EC and the President of the EC Conference on Yugoslavia at The Hague considered WEU action to be useful, a new extraordinary WEU Council would immediately be convened to take the decisions necessary. The subsequent EC Council decided to extend the mandate of the European monitors. However, both in the EC and in WEU, the opposition of the UK especially prevented any decision on a WEU action to support the EC observers.[79]

The discussions in September 1991 pointed to the nature of the EC–WEU relationship, with the EC taking the main political decisions and WEU possibly implementing or further elaborating on them, but also with both organisations referring to each other and so avoiding the need to take decisions. This revealed the remaining limitations of the EC to decide on military matters and of the WEU to act independently, forcing the European countries to transfer the responsibility partially to the UN. The WEU, from that moment on, together with NATO, became the organisation to implement UN decisions (and hence not EC decisions) on military matters.

The experience with the Yugoslav crisis also seems to confirm the views expressed in a reply of the WEU's Permanent Council in April 1990: 'Coordination of the action of armed forces of WEU countries can certainly be envisaged under the auspices of WEU ... Nevertheless, the provision of contingents for humanitarian or peacekeeping operations is a matter to be decided nationally – Any national decisions to commit forces should be taken with due regard for the overall political context which is in fact a matter for EPC'.[80] This statement not only points to the political preponderance of the EC over WEU, but also to the overall preponderance of the national states with regard to security and defence, which continues to be the main constraint to defining an efficient conflict management policy in both the EC and WEU.

The consecutive meetings were useful innovations in the EC–WEU relationship which made it easier to get a formal linkage accepted in the *Treaty on European Union*. However, these meetings remained exceptional *ad hoc* arrangements which had become possible only because of special circumstances or because of the attitude of member states holding the EC or WEU Presidency, who wanted to use (or abuse) these circumstances and apply in practice what they wanted to get accepted in the IGC on European Political Union.

The Treaty on European Union and the *WEU Declaration* added to it formalise the EC–WEU relationship. Article J.4(2) of the Treaty states that 'The Union requests the WEU, which is an integral part of the development of the Union, to elaborate and implement decisions and actions of the Union which have defence implications' and that 'The Council shall, in agreement with the institutions of the WEU, adopt the necessary practical arrangements'.[81] The related *WEU Declaration* proposes several measures to develop a close working relationship with the Union.[82]

However, the wording of Article J.4(2) as well as of the *WEU Declaration* is not at all unequivocal and points to disagreement among the member states. Moreover, the *WEU Declaration* also emphasises the objective 'to develop WEU as a means to strengthen the European pillar of the Atlantic Alliance' and formulates measures to strengthen the relationship between both.

Consequently, the *Treaty on European Union* and the *WEU Declaration* formalised the relationship between the EC and WEU, but did not solve the ambiguity which resulted from the disagreement about the role of WEU as the EC's military arm or as NATO's European pillar. Nevertheless, the new texts have at least increased the formal basis for a strengthened EC–WEU relationship, which can enhance the possibility for the EC or the EC–WEU tandem to set up and implement more comprehensive conflict management actions.

Finally, it is important to note that the EC established cooperation with *INGO's*, with the EC supporting and financing initiatives with a conflict prevention or conflict management dimension. These initiatives are related to support for democratisation and respect for human rights, food aid, humanitarian aid, support for refugees, etc. This occurs through INGO's such as the Red Cross or *Médecins Sans Frontières*, with which the European Commission elaborated clear procedures to allow a smooth collaboration in case swift action is needed.[83]

Funding

The conflict management efforts of the Community are funded by the EC budget and by contributions of the member states (there is no specific budget for EPC measures). Conflict management not being a formal objective of the Community and national contributions occurring on an *ad hoc* basis, it is difficult to get an exact idea of EC spending on conflict management.

First of all, there is the expenditure financed through the EC budget. Conflict management not being a formal objective of the Community, it is not a specific item on the budget. Nonetheless, several items are used for conflict management purposes, and new budget lines can be created as a response to a specific crisis (which happened, for instance, to finance the monitors in Yugoslavia). However, the effectiveness of turning to the EC budget for the implementation of EPC policies is often constrained by the preallocation of budget resources and the complicated procedures for increasing them, as was shown by the Twelve's attempts in 1990 to provide assistance to countries affected by the Iraqi invasion of Kuwait.[84]

Subdivision B7 ('Cooperation with developing countries and other third countries') of the 1992 EC budget adopted by the EP in December 1991 provides some interesting statistics.[85] In many cases it is hard to differentiate between expenditures for peacebuilding purposes or for development or other aid. Both objectives can indeed be considered as being closely related, especially if the prevention of conflict is emphasised. An example of this is the very considerable EC support for Central and Eastern Europe and the Commonwealth of Independent States (CIS), with the EC taking responsibility for nearly two-thirds of the credit guarantees and the technical and humanitarian aid given by the international community to the CIS.[86]

Whereas most funds are indeed assigned for economic, technical and financial support and cooperation, some funds, however, are aimed at specific peacebuilding measures. This includes, for instance, budget lines for 'measures to promote regional and subregional integration of developing countries' in the Mediterranean (64 m.*), Asia (2 m.) and Latin America (6 m.) the latter including support for the first direct elections of the Central American Parliament; 'support for refugees' in Latin INGO's and IGO's (such as UNRWA for Palestinian refugees, 28 m.); reconstruction projects in Lebanon (2 m.); humanitarian aid (43 m., besides the 300 m. in Title B0–5 'Reserves'); support (sometimes through NGO's and INGO's) of the process of democratisation and the respect of human rights in developing countries (10 m.), in Central and Eastern Europe (5 m.), and in Latin America, the latter including measures to reintegrate *guerrillero*'s in the society (10 m.); programmes of action to meet problems related to apartheid in South Africa and instability in the Frontline states (80 and 12 m.).

Some items on the EC budget are a translation of the international situation. For instance the 1991 budget provided for 587 m. for financial support to the countries most affected by the Gulf War (Egypt, Jordan, Turkey, Israel, as well as the Palestinians in the occupied territories). The 1990 and 1991 budget earmarked 18 m. and 10 m. to pay EC actions preparatory to the independence of Namibia.[87] In reality, the expenditure in 1992 was for some significantly higher budget items. Other new items are a translation of new priorities or new policies developed by the EC. In 1992, a new item 'External aspects of certain EC measures' was created (276 m.). In the preliminary draft of the 1993 budget, a new subdivision 'Common foreign and security policy' was created (no funds were yet

* All figures in millions of ECU.

inscribed in this new item).[85]

A remarkable decision was taken in December 1992, when the Council of Ministers agreed to finance three-quarters of the peacekeeping and enforcement actions of Belgian troops as part of the Provide Hope and UNOSOM operations in Somalia. This will be financed through budget lines which were foreseen for Somalia in the European Development Fund but could not be used as a result of the civil war.[89] This decision is considered as an 'exceptional' measure related to a crisis which is widely covered in the media. It can, however, also be interpreted as a precedent, and in any case shows the more flexible attitude adopted by all EC member states on conflict management.

The new financial structure proposed by the European Commission in the 'Delors-II Package' provided for a further significant increase of EC expenditure for external policy.[90] The proposals also foresaw the need for a faster procedure to decide on the use of funds from its Title VI ('Reserves': 1.4 billion) for unexpected special expenses related to external measures such as humanitarian aid, urgency aid and all kinds of incidental measures.[91] These increased funds would strengthen the financial resources available for conflict prevention and would strengthen the possibility of the EC to fulfil its external ambitions.

Secondly, there is the expenditure financed on an *ad hoc* basis through national contributions of the member states. This happens either through the member states themselves deciding how much they are willing to contribute to a certain conflict management initiative or through the contribution by member states being determined through one of the Community distribution codes. For instance, a part of the payment of the EC actions in and for Yugoslavia occurs through advances of the country holding the Presidency of the EC, with the other member states paying afterwards to that country the amount that they are due in accordance with the Community distributive code. As this method is not very efficient, it is expected that the EC budget will increasingly earmark funds for contingencies of this kind, as was partially the case in the 1993 budget.

Most Community initiatives consist of combined efforts by the EC and national budget authorities. The Yugoslav crisis is an example of this, as is the EC's support for the economic and political reforms in Central and Eastern Europe and in the CIS.

Evaluation and suggestions

An analysis of the EC's basic texts and of its conflict management facilities confirms that the EC was not created for external conflict management objectives, and was thus not given the instruments and decision-making procedures necessary for effective crisis management. During the last twenty years the Community has increasingly formulated its own policy towards external conflicts and gradually established procedures and instruments to handle them. Nevertheless, the experience of the EC has remained limited as it has generally been only one of the actors involved in conflict management and, above all, has merely been an actor of secondary importance. The reforms in Central and Eastern Europe and especially the Yugoslav crisis therefore constituted an important change, as, during certain periods of these crises, the EC was the main, or even the only, external actor involved.

These and other crises have shown that several interrelated factors contribute to the success or failure of the EC's conflict management efforts. These factors are related to the nature of the conflict, the nature of the relationship between the countries involved and the EC, and the nature of the EC's reaction. First, success is obviously more difficult to achieve when the crisis escalates into a military conflict, in which the parties involved have no real experience of (or, indeed, interest in) international relations, with the conflict focussing more on emotions than on any objective interests. Second, the EC's chances of success will be greatly enhanced when the warring factions regard their relationship with the EC as something fundamentally more important to them than the point at issue. Finally, those chances will always be greater when the EC's own declarations and subsequent actions are unambiguous, when there are no obvious areas of disagreement between member states and when any references to support or sanctions in those declarations are not only credible but capable of being implemented.

These interrelated factors show why the EC's efforts at conflict management in Yugoslavia have, in general, been unsuccessful. However, they also show that the burden of blame lies only partly with the EC. It is important to recognise that the Yugoslav crisis has led to some positive conclusions about the EC's conflict management capabilities. Not only did the Community prove willing to accept and shoulder its responsibilities in a military conflict (despite the fact that such a role was not properly within its competence) but, in a creative manner, it adopted new conflict management instruments to enable it to carry out its tasks, setting valuable precedents for the future.

This dynamic and creative approach to its involvement also made clear the limitations imposed on the EC by an *ad hoc* approach and the lack of the necessary instruments of policy and military resources. Three main areas of constraint existed:

- The lack of central political leadership, a centralised intelligence organisation and a single decision-making centre operating a standard, Community-wide, procedure.
- The limitations imposed upon the EC by the lack of a credible conflict management instrument including military resources.
- The lack of a common view on the nature of the EC and its role in conflict management and on specific conflict management issues.

In order to diminish the negative impact of the first area of constraint, it is essential that the distinction made between Community and EPC (or CFSP) affairs and procedures should disappear. The creation of a swift and efficient decision-making process covering all aspects of foreign affairs, security and defence requires the establishment of a single institutional framework. This points to a larger role for the Commission and the EP as well as to the increased use of majority voting in these policy fields. To make this use of majority voting acceptable to the member states, it can be foreseen that it may be necessary to accept that when quick decisions on crisis management are needed in an emergency, some member states will choose to abstain from participation in certain decisions whilst permitting the majority decision to be put into effect. The need for centralised leadership and centralised intelligence also points towards a larger role for the European Commission, and especially its

President, in all fields of foreign affairs, security and defence. In this context, the allocation of responsibility for CFSP to one of the Commissioners appointed in the current Commission may be seen as a first positive step.

The second area of constraint, the lack of a credible conflict management instrument and military resources, requires that the various methods and instruments created and used in recent years must be elaborated further and formalised if, in future crises, resort to improvisation and *ad hoc* solutions is to be avoided. Detailed procedures will have to be established with the member states and the WEU to allow a quick and efficient deployment of military forces if the need is decided by the EC. Just as the need of a single institutional framework points to the need to incorporate EPC or CSFP within it, so does it point to the need for the present separation between the EC and WEU to be eliminated as far as possible, with the EC holding political primacy. A further strengthening of the WEU's operational role and the establishment of military units, and information and planning facilities of its own are essential if the existing degree of dependency on other organisations and countries is to be reduced. Specific procedures have to be established with NATO, CSCE and the UN to permit a division of labour and efficient and close cooperation in conflict management.

The third constraint, the lack of a common view amongst member states on the nature and role of the EC, may be seen to be the most significant as its rectification determines the possibility of tackling the other two. The emotional discussions on the EC in 1992 and the consequent projection of a negative image did not offer very promising prospects in this context. The current debate on the degree of European integration that is acceptable to member states and the question of the loss of national sovereignty will determine whether the conclusion of the *Treaty on European Union* will lead to the adoption of the far-reaching measures necessary for the establishment of the conflict management capacity that has become so badly needed. In this respect, it is of the first importance that the general public within the EC should be educated to understand that an efficient conflict management capability is an essential ingredient of European security.

If the EC is to arrive at a common analysis amongst member states on the potential conflict areas and the measures that may be necessary for conflict management, a more pro-European attitude is needed throughout the Community. Only then will it be possible to do away with the present tensions between states which so often lead to different reactions amongst them towards external conflicts and so impede progress on the establishment of a Community conflict management capability.

NOTES

1. Karel De Gucht and Stephan Keukeleire, 'The European Security Architecture. The Role of the European Community in Shaping a New European Geopolitical Landscape', *Studia Diplomatica*, 44(6)1991, pp. 30 & 34.
2. The internal peacebuilding objectives appears, *inter alia*, in the statement that they wish 'to create, by establishing an economic community, the basis for a broader and deeper community among people long divided by bloody conflicts'.
3. 'Single European Act', *Bulletin – Supplement*, 2/86, p. 5. Its Title III ('Provisions on European cooperation in the sphere of foreign policy') gives further details on the commitment to formulate a European foreign policy but does not further elaborate on the peacebuilding and preservation objectives.
4. 'Treaty on European Union', *Europe – Documents*, No. 1759/60, 7/2/1992, pp. 31–33.
5. 'Declaration by the European Council on areas which could be the subject of joint action', *Europe – Documents*, No. 1750/1751, 13/12/1991, p. 29.
6. 'Report to the European Council in Lisbon on the likely development of the Common Foreign and Security Policy with a view to identifying areas open to joint action vis-à-vis particular countries or groups of countries', *Europe*, No. 5761, 29-30/6/1992, pp. 1–4.
7. Rheinhardt Rummel, 'Speaking with one voice – and beyond', in Alfred Pijpers, Elfriede Regelsberger and Wolfgang Wessels (eds.), *European Political Cooperation in the 1980's*. (Martinus Nijhoff, Dordrecht, 1988), pp. 130–133.
8. Reinhardt Rummel, *op. cit.*, pp. 120–121.
9. For instance, after the Soviet invasion of Afghanistan in December 1979, it suspended food aid to Afghanistan almost a week before the Council met to discuss the issue (Simon Nuttall, 'Interaction between EPC and the EC', *Yearbook of European Law*, Vol. 7, 1988, p. 235).
10. This happened in 1991 when the EP judged that not enough credits were foreseen in the budget to enable the Community to fulfill its promises for financial support for the former Soviet Union without compromising other financial commitments.

11. It did so, for example, when (against the opinion of the Council and Commission) it blocked the proposals for food aid and credits to the USSR in protest at the action taken by Soviet forces in the Baltic republics (K De Gucht and S Keukeleire, 'The European security architecture ...', *op. cit.*, p. 38).
12. L Planas Puchades, *Report drawn up on behalf of the Political Affairs Committee on the role of the EP in the field of foreign policy in the context of the Single European Act*, European Parliament, Doc. A2-0086/88, 26/5/1988, pp. 10–12.
13. The EP used this power to reject protocols with Syria and Morocco in 1992 (because of the violation of human rights) and with Israel in 1988 (because of discrimination against the Palestinians in the occupied territories). The concessions by Israel in favour of the Palestinian population showed the possible impact of this new power (EP, *Fact sheets on the EP and the activities of the EC*, PE 140.600, 1991, p. I/J; EP, *Proces-Verbaal van de zitting van 15/1/1992*, PE 158.853, pp. 17–18).
14. Geoffrey Edwards, 'European Political Cooperation put to the test', in Alfred Pijpers (ed.), *The European Community at the Crossroads. Major issues and priorities for the EC Presidency*. (Martinus Nijhoff, Dordrecht, 1992), p. 245.
15. See Elfriede Regelsberger, 'Gemeinsame Aussen- und Sicherheitspolitik nach Maastricht – Minimalreformen in neur Entwicklungsperspektive', *Integration*, 15(2)1992, p. 91.
16. This was true, for example, of the sanctions imposed on Poland in 1982, on Argentina during the Falklands crisis and recently on Yugoslavia, and of economic aid to the Central American countries (in support of the Contadora initiative) and, since 1988, to the Eastern European countries (Simon Nuttall, *op. cit.*, p. 235).
17. The Presidency shall ensure that the views of the EP are duly taken into consideration (SEA, Art. 30.4).
18. This also suggests that the Dutch Presidency was more inclined to cooperate closely with the Commission than the British Presidency, reflecting the UK's ability to rely on a stronger diplomatic structure and to act more readily as a regional power without much need of the Community in such circumstances.
19. 'Report on EPC issued by the Foreign Ministers of the Ten on 13 October 1981' (*London Report*) in Alfred Pijpers et. al., *op. cit.*, p. 326. Following its failure to respond adequately to the outbreak of the October War in 1973, the EC made a first attempt to establish a crisis management procedure and failed. This situation persisted until the Soviet invasion of Afghanistan, when the EC's response was again belated. In consequence of this second failure, the member states accepted the need for an effective procedure to be developed. (Simon Nuttall, *European Political Co-operation*, (Clarendon Press, Oxford, 1992), pp. 145–147 & 176–177.
20. This crisis management procedure enabled the Twelve to issue on the day of the Iraqi invasion in Kuwait a declaration condemning the invasion and to decide two days later on the freezing of Iraqi assets as well as on an embargo on oil and arms. During the Gulf crisis from

August 1990 to February 1991, there were 15 meetings of the Ministers of Foreign Affairs, and at least two meetings a month. In the same period there were four meetings within the WEU and three within NATO. ('Chronology' in Nicole Gnesotto and John Roper (eds.), *Western Europe and the Gulf*, (The Institute for Security Studies of the WEU, Paris, 1992), pp. 181–195.

21. Wolfgang Wessels, 'A mission as broker, guardian, and ambassador for a historic opportunity', in Alfred Pijpers (ed.), *The European Community at the Crossroads*, *op. cit.*, p. 17.
22. Alfted Pijpers, 'Between the Gulf War and a European Political Union', in Alfred Pijpers (ed.), *The European Community at the Crossroads, op. cit.*, pp. 278–280.
23. For instance, it is assumed that if France had held the EC Presidency in the second half of 1992 (instead of the UK, which took more of an attitude of desengagement) Paris would probably have attempted, as EC President-in-Office, to create, through a combined EC–WEU action, and with UN backing, 'save havens' under military protection in ex-Yugoslavia.
24. This was the case with the Soviet invasion of Afghanistan (26 December 1979), and during a crucial period of the Yugoslav crisis (June–July 1991).
25. See Karel De Gucht and Stephen Keukeleire, 'The European Security Architecture', *op. cit.*, pp. 76–79.
26. 'Report on EPC ...' *op. cit.*, pp. 326–327. Simon Nuttall, *European Political Co-operation, op. cit.*, pp. 17 & 22.
27. Most COREUs are copied to the diplomatic Missions of the Twelve in Geneva and New York as well as to the Permanent Representatives to the Community in Brussels.
28. These relations imply that meetings are organised on a regular basis between the twelve Ministers for Foreign Affairs, the Troika (*see Note 29*) or representatives of the Presidency with their homologues in the other organisation or country. Normally, a representative of the Commission is also present. (Reinhardt Rummel, *op. cit.*, p. 124).
29. The country holding the Presidency as well as the preceding and succeeding Presidency.
30. Fact-finding missions were sent, *inter alia*, to the Soviet-Union (during the Afghanistan crisis), the Middle East, Turkey, South Africa and its neighbouring states, and Yugoslavia (Elfriede Regelsberger, 'EPC in the 1980's: reaching a plateau?', in Alfred Pijpers, et. al., *op. cit., pp. 21–22).*
31. Gianno Bonvicini, *'Mechanisms and Procedures of EPC: more than Traditional Diplomacy?'*, in Alfred Pijpers *et. al.*, *op. cit.*, p. 63.
32. An example of such an unsuccessful attempt was the proposal in 1981 that EPC would provide political cover for participation of EC member states on behalf of the Ten in the Sinai Multinational Force and Observers. This was not accepted by all member states. In the later stages of the Iran–Iraq war, it was not the EC/EPC but only the WEU that was used to coordinate the participation of some EC members in the international effort to keep the sea lanes clear in the Gulf (Simon

Nuttall, *European Political Cooperation, op. cit.*, pp. 217–218).

33. See Karel De Gucht and Stephan Keukeleirè, *The European Security Architecture, op. cit.*, pp. 55–59.
34. 'Gemeinsame Erklärung der Ministertroika der Europaïschen Gemeinschaft und der jugoslawischen Konfliktparteien über einen Friedensplan für Jugoslawien, vereinbart in Brioni am 7. Juli 1991' and its 'Anlage II: Leitlinien für eine Beobachtermission in Jugoslawien' in *Europa-Archiv*, 42(21)1991, pp. 537–539.
35. James E Goodby, 'Peacekeeping in the New Europe', *The Washington Quarterly*, Spring 1992, p. 157.
36. 'Yugoslavia: Van Eekelen delineates limits of WEU action, which is backed by France, Germany and Italy, but not the U.K.', *Europe, No. 5571, Bruxelles, Agence Europe, 20/9/1991, p. 5; 'WEU Council/ Yugoslavia: WEU is ready to take on its responsibility', Europe*, No. 5578, (Agence Europe, Bruxelles, 30/9/1991), pp. 3–4.
37. James E Goodby, *op. cit.*, pp. 158 & 162.
38. There were, *inter alia*, a visit in 1981 of the then President-in-Office, Lord Carrington, to Moscow where he submitted the Ten's proposal for a neutral and non-aligned Afghanistan, several missions to the Middle East, fact-finding missions to South Africa of a ministerial Troika in 1985 and 1992 and by Sir Geoffrey Howe on behalf of the Twelve in 1986 (Elfriede Regelsberger, *op. cit.*, pp. 21–22 & 29–30). An other example is the two-day visit of Jacques Delors and Jacques Poos (President-in-office of the EC Council) to Yugoslavia less than a month before the conflict took a military turn. They mediated between the republics and promised considerable financial support and stronger relations if a political solution for the conflict was found (M Sebregts, 'EG blijft gekant tegen uiteenvallen Joegoslavië', *De Standaard*, 31/5/1991).
39. Rheinhardt Rumme, *op. cit.*, pp. 132–133.
40. Armand Clesse, 'Europe and the Gulf War as seen by the Luxembourg Presidency of the EC', in Nicole Gnesotto and John Roper (eds.), *op. cit*, pp. 91–94.
41. After the end of the Gulf War, the European idea to seek a fundamental solution for the problems in the Middle East through an international conference on the model of the CSCE was taken up, (Eric Remacle, *Les négociations sur la politique étrangère et de sécurity commune de la Communauté européenne*, Bruxelles, GRIP, Serie 'Notes et documents' No. 156, 1991, pp. 19 & 13; Lawrence Freedman, 'The Gulf War and the new world order', *Survival*, 33(3)1991, pp. 198–199).
42. EPS Declarations, 27/8/91 & 3/9/91.
43. John Zametica, 'The Yugoslav Conflict', *Adelphi Papers*, (270) 1992, pp. 61–63.
44. At the end of 1992, the EC successfully mediated in the escalating political conflict between Hungary and Slovakia on the highly sensitive problem of the barrage on the Danube (which in its turn threatened to enhance the problems with regard to the Hungarian minority in Slovakia). The countries concerned agreed with the proposal of the Commission to accept an investigation by a committee with specialists from the Commission and the countries concerned as well, if necessary, as the

judgement (with a binding character) of an international court. The pressure which the Commission could bring to bear on these countries, as a result of its strong economic and financial relationship with them and of their wish to join the EC, was obviously important in obtaining this result.

45. Such as in the crises in the Middle East or Central America. See Reinhardt Rummel, *op. cit.*, pp. 132–139.
46. *Ibid.*, pp. 130–131.
47. For instance, in its detailed proposals of January 1973, which were to become the basis of the Helsinki negotiations, the Community suggested that the Helsinki Conference would talk about several issues: political and military security, including CBM's and emphasis on human rights; cooperation in the field of economy, science, technology and environment; personal contacts, contacts in the field of education and culture, and a better flow of information. (H van der Velden and H A Visée, *Ontspanning in Europa; de Conferentie over Veiligheid en Samenwerking in Europa*, Baarn, Het Wereldvenster, 1976, pp. 113–114).
48. For instance, in 1986, the Twelve (despite American scepticism) emphasised the importance of the Stockholm Conference on Disarmament in Europe and in this way contributed to the success of this conference at which the Warsaw Pact for the first time accepted the principle of on-site inspection (Karel De Gucht and Stephan Keukeleire, *Time and Tide Wait for No Man. The Changing European Geopolitical Landscape*. (Praeger, New York, 1991), pp. 37 & 161).
49. Simon Nuttall, *European Political Cooperation, op. cit.*, pp. 288–289. See also Geoffrey Edwards and Elfriede Regelsberger (eds.), *Europe's Global Links: The EC and Inter-Regional Cooperation*, (Pinter Publishers, London, 1990).
50. Including Mexico, Venezuela, Panama and Colombia.
51. Simon Nuttall, *European Political Cooperation, op. cit.*, pp. 222–230. See also 'Joint political communiqué of the Luxembourg Ministerial Conference on political dialogue and economic cooperation between the countries of the EC, Spain and Portugal and the countries of Central America and of Contadora, held on 11 and 12 November 1985' in Alfred Pijpers et. al., *op. cit.*, pp. 356–360.
52. Karel De Gucht and Stephan Keukeleire, *The European Security Architecture …, op. cit.*, pp. 44–46.
53. EPS Declarations, 27/8/91& 3/9/91.
54. In addition to the Yugoslav parties, the President of the Council and representatives of the European Commission and of the member states also participated in the Conference.
55. Jean-Luc Pierson, La *Yugoslavie désintegrée, Les Dossiers du Grip*, Bruxelles, Fevrier 1992, pp. 58–60.
56. It had to consist of three jurists appointed by the EC and two by the conflicting parties. The latter could however not agree, and the EC therefore assigned two more jurists from EC countries.
57. For instance in April 1989, this policy resulted in the EC suspending the negotiations with Romania on a trade and cooperation agreement until

the Romanian government could prove that it respected human rights and other CSCE-commitments. The wish of Hungary and the two republics of the former Czechoslovakia to become a member of the EC gave greater weight to the EC mediation efforts in the conflicts between these states. (See K De Gucht and S Keukeleire, 'The European Security Architecture ...', *op. cit.*, pp. 45–47). For the Yugoslav crisis, see i.e. D Lopandic, 'Un example de sanctions économiques de la CEEL suspension/dénonciation de l'accord de cooperation', *Revue des Affaires Européennes*, 2/1992, pp. 67–72.

58. The new states were expected to respect UN and CSCE provisions on the rule of law, democracy and human rights, guarantee the rights of ethnic and national groups and minorities, respect the inviolability of all frontiers, accept the commitments with regard to disarmamemt and the commitment to settle by agreement all questions concerning state succession and regional disputes (*Declaration on the 'Guidelines on the recognition of new states in Eastern Europe and in the Soviet Union'*, EPC, Press release, p. 128/91).
59. For instance, in May 1992, the Twelve decided to call back their Ambassadors from Belgrade and to propose the exclusion of Yugoslavia from all activities of the CSCE ('Yougoslavia: Les Douze retirent leurs Ambassadeurs de Belgrade', *Europe*, No. 5752, (Agence Europe, 11/5/1992), p. 1).
60. See Simon Nuttall, *European Political Cooperation, op. cit.*, pp. 261–274.
61. For instance, the EC had sanctions in place within some days of the Iraqi invasion in Kuwait but, for budgetary reasons, could not implement quickly the decision to provide financial and economic aid to the countries in the region that were most hurt by the embargo against Iraq (C Cova, 'La CEE et la crise du Golfe', *Revue du Marché Commun*, No. 340, Octobre 1990, p. 563). For the Yugoslav crisis, see i.e. T C Salmon, 'Testing times for EPC: the Gulf and Yugoslavia', *International Affairs*, 68(2)1992, pp. 248–249, and C.-P. Lucron, 'L'Europe devant la crise yougoslave: mesures restrictives et mesures positives', *Revue du Marché Commun*, No. 354, January 1992, pp. 7–16.
62. This appeared i.e. in April 1991 when the European Council proposed and defended the idea that the UN would decide on the creation of 'protection zones' for the Kurds in Iraq (see *Nouvelles Atlantiques*, No. 2312, 10/4/91, p. 1).
63. See Philippe de Schoutheete, *La coopération politique européenne*, (Editions Labor, Bruxelles, 1986), pp. 208–211.
64. UN Security Council. Resolution 713, 25/9/1991.
65. UN Security Council. Resolution 743, 21/2/1992. See also Jean-Luc Pierson, *op. cit.*, pp. 69–72.
66. See Eric Remacle, 'La CSCE. Mutations et perspectives d'une institution paneuropéenne', *Courrier Hebdomadaire*, No. 1348–1349, (Crisp, Bruxelles, 1992), pp. 42–43; and Eric Remacle, *La politique étrangère ..., op. cit.*, pp. 35–37.
67. See also Karel De Gucht and Stephan Keukeleire, 'The European security architecture ...', *op. cit.*, p. 88.

68. During the very first negotiations in Helsinki, the EC countries first met to define a common viewpoint with regard to many issues to be backed by the EC Presidency at the subsequent NATO meeting. NATO experts from the EC member states took part in the EPC deliberations to facilitate coordination between EPC and NATO. (A Pijpers, 'EPC and the CSCE process', *Legal Issues of European Integration*, (1)1985, pp. 140–141).
69. For instance, both EC and NATO ministerial meetings were convened on 10 August 1990, to react to the invasion of Kuwait, which obviously allowed some coordination of their reactions through the partially overlapping membership. In September 1991, the North Atlantic Council was briefed on the results of the EC and WEU Councils of 19 September by Ambassador Wijnaendts, special envoy of the Dutch Presidency on the Yugoslav crisis. ('Crise du Golfe: le Conseil de l'OTAN insiste sur la consultation entre alliés', *Nouvelles Atlantiques*, No. 2247, p. 2; 'Consultation à l'OTAN sur la crise Yougoslave', *Nouvelles Atlantiques*, No. 2352, 21/9/1991, pp. 1–2).
70. On the other hand, the Atlantic Alliance, in its *Rome Declaration on Peace and Cooperation* of 7–8 November 1991, recognised 'that it is for the European Allies concerned to decide what arrangements are needed for the expression of a common European foreign and security policy and defence role' (NATO, Press Communique S-1(91)86, p. 3).
71. For instance, Washington repeatedly let it be known that the Yugoslav question was a European problem and thus not an issue for the USA or NATO.
72. Karel De Gucht and Stephan Keukeleire, 'The European security architecture ...', *op. cit.*, p. 70.
73. Turkey also participated in the meeting.
74. 'Crise du Golfe: les prises de position des Douze et de l'UEO', *Europe/Documents*, No. 1644, Agence Europe, 23/8/1990, pp. 1–5; 'UEO: le Conseil des Ministres decide de coordonner les activités militaires dans le Golfe', *Nouvelles Atlantiques*, No. 2247, Agence Europe, 24/8/1990, p. 1.
75. 'Chronology of the Gulf War' in Nicole Gnesotto and John Roper (eds.), *op. cit.*, p. 190.
76. 'Conseil Européen: A Luxembourg, les Douze proposent la creation de zone de protection pour les refugiés en Irak' and 'UEO: les Ministres des Affaires Etrangères discutent de la coordination de l'aide humanitaire aux civils irakiens', *Nouvelles Atlantiques*, No. 2312, (Agence Europe), pp. 1–2.
77. 'Yougoslavie: l'UEO pose des conditions très strictes à l'envoi d'une force de protection des observateurs européens', *Nouvelles Atlantiques*, No. 2352, (Agence Europe, 21/9/1991), p. 3.
78. 'Statement of the EEC Foreign Ministers', *Europe*, No. 5572, (Agence Europe(, 21/9/1991, p. 4.
79. 'WEU Council/Yugoslavia: WEU is ready to take on its responsibilities', *Europe*, No. 5578, (Agence Europe, 30/9/1991), pp. 3–4.
80. Arnaud Jacomet, 'The Role of WEU in the Gulf Crisis', in Nicole Gnesotto and John Roper (eds.), *op. cit.*, p. 162.

81. 'Treaty on European Union', *op. cit.*, p. 32.
82. Declaration of the countries which are members of WEU and also members of the European Union on the role of the WEU and its relations with the European Union and with the Atlantic Alliance', *Europe – Documents*, No. 1759–60, 7/2/1992, p. 56.
83. See for instance C P Lucron, 'Du devoir d'assistance á la tentation d'ingerence:l'aide humanitaire dans la crise du Golfe', *Revue du Marché Commun*, No. 349, Juillet 1991, pp. 502–503.
84. Simon Nuttall, *European Political Cooperation, op. cit.*, pp. 273–274.
85. 'Definitieve vaststelling van de algemene begroting van de EG voor het begroitingsjaar 1991', *Publicatieblad van de EG*, L 26, 3/2/1992, pp. 1107–1237.
86. 'Twee derde technische hulp aan GOS komt van EC', *Financieel Economische Tijd*, 6/11/1992.
87. 'Definitieve vaststelling van de algemene begroting ...', *op. cit.*, pp. 1210 & 1234–36.
88. Commissie van de EG, *Voorontwerp van algemene begroting van de EG voor het begrotinsjaar 1993: algemeen overzicht*, SEC(92)900, pp. 10–11 & 25.
89. 'EG financiert Somalische missie Belgische para's', *De Standaard*, 8/12/1992, p. 5.
90. This was 3.6 billion or slightly more than 5% in 1992, versus 1.4 billion or less than 3% in 1987 (Commission of the European Communities, *From the Single European Act to the Post-Maastricht Period: The Resources for our Ambitions*, COM(92)2000 def, 11/2/1992, p. 40).
91. Commission of the European Communities, *The Public Expenditure of the Community in 1997*, COM(92)2001, def, 12/3/1992, pp. 31–32 & 45.

6

Conflict Prevention: The Role of the Western European Union

*Eric Remacle**

The case of the Western European Union is a very signficant one for analysing what the transition from collective self-defence towards collective security means in the post-Cold War era. Indeed this organisation, initially conceived as an alliance, is presently transformed into a military instrument able to face different kinds of security challenges and military missions. This chapter will therefore not only rely on official documents but mainly on the analysis of the recent developments of this organisation.

PROVISIONS OF THE WEU TREATY REGARDING CONFLICT PREVENTION

The Preamble of the modified *Brussels Treaty* signed in Paris on 23 October 1954[1] defines very explicitly the main task of the Western European Union: 'to afford assistance to each other, in accordance

* Assistant Lecturer at the Free University Brussels (ULB) and Associate Researcher with the European Institute for Research and Information on Peace and Security (GRIP, Brussels).

with the Charter of the United Nations, in maintaining international peace and security and in resisting any policy of aggression'; furthermore it defines the treaty as 'a treaty for collaboration in economic, social and cultural matters and for collective self-defence'. Conflict prevention is thus not involved in this mandate. Nevertheless, Article X of the Treaty provides for an agreement regarding the peaceful settlement of disputes between the High Contracting Parties, which can be seen as a conflict prevention provision:

> (...) The High Contracting Parties will, while the present Treaty remains in force, settle all disputes falling within the scope of Article 36, paragraph 2 of the Statute of the International Court of Justice, by referring them to the Court, subject only, in the case of each of them, to any reservation already made by that Party when accepting this clause for compulsory jurisdiction to the extent that that Party may maintain the reservation.
>
> In addition, the High Contracting Parties will submit to conciliation all disputes outside the scope of Article 36, paragraph 2, of the Statute of the International Court of Justice.
>
> In the case of a mixed dispute involving both questions for which conciliation is appropriate and other questions for which judicial settlement is appropriate, any Party to the dispute shall have the right to insist that the judicial settlement of the legal questions shall precede conciliation.
>
> The preceding provisions of this Article in no way affect the application of relevant provisions or agreements prescribing some other method of pacific settlement.

The WEU was thus considered not only as an alliance against external threats but also as a tool for building confidence and co-operation among its member states, particularly France and Germany. Several provisions of the modified *Brussels Treaty* and its Protocols, providing for military constraints on Germany, fulfilled this aim.[2] But the history of the organisation shows that decisions regarding conflict prevention were really as few as the disputes among the member states.

THE EXPERIENCE OF THE WEU IN CONFLICT PREVENTION

The only meaningful case of the WEU's direct involvement in preventing conflicts and settling peacefully a dispute between two states is the settlement of the Saar question. The end of the Occupation régime in the FRG decided by the Western powers in 1954[3] implied an agreement between France and Germany on the creation of a European status under the WEU's authority for this territory, followed in a second stage by a referendum among its population about its final status. The WEU organised this referendum on 23 October 1955 and 423,000 inhabitants of the Saar territory against 200,000 refused the European status. Thereafter the WEU organised the elections for the creation of the Landtag of Saar which became then part of the Federal Republic of Germany.[4]

Such a mechanism of peaceful settlement of disputes was not used for other potential sources of conflict either between member states, such as the case of Gibraltar after the Spanish accession in 1988 or between member states and non-member states like the question of Northern Ireland.[5] On the other hand, the WEU never proposed its mediation in disputes among other European countries like the Greek–Turkish conflict, the partition of Cyprus, or more recently the Hungarian–Rumanian tensions, the breakup of Yugoslavia or the Slovak–Hungarian crisis. Its potential political role in conflict prevention seems to be limited to conflicts between its member states. The key statements of the WEU Council during the 80s, especially the *Rome Declaration* in 1984 and the *The Hague Platform on European Security Interests* in 1987, do not modify this interpretation.

CONFLICT PREVENTION CAPABILITIES AND FACILITIES

The end of the division of Europe and the risks of new armed conflicts in and outside Europe have nevertheless led the WEU, as well as NATO, to widen its tasks from a role of collective self-defence *stricto sensu* to collective security missions and out-of-area operations. In this respect, the two Gulf Wars and the Yugoslav crisis opened a new era for the WEU. The *Maastricht Treaty* and the annexed statement adopted by the WEU member states on 10 December 1991, followed by the *Petersberg Declaration* on 19 June 1992, translated this new reality in the institutional field. As far as operational capabilities for conflict prevention are concerned, the

WEU Council has specially decided during its Petersberg meeting to support the implementation of decisions taken by the CSCE or the UN Security Council in the field of conflict prevention and crisis management, including peacekeeping activities.[6] This declaration paves the way to an operational interlocking co-operation between these organisations. It has been confirmed by the Helsinki Summit of the CSCE in July 1992 which stated that the CSCE could rely on the resources and experience of the EC, NATO, WEU or the CIS for supporting its peacekeeping activities.[7] It could also mean that the WEU considers that its contribution to conflict prevention is limited to a participation in peacekeeping operations under the political authority of the CSCE and the UN Security Council. But another section of the *Petersberg Declaration* defines the missions of the military units of the WEU member states not only as peacekeeping operations but also as fighting forces missions for crisis management, including peacemaking operations[8] and refers only to the authority of the WEU itself. This ambiguity raises the question of whether the WEU accepts the subordination of its capabilities in conflict prevention to the political authority of the CSCE and the UN or prefers to keep the right to act autonomously under the terms of Article VIII, paragraph 3 of the modified *Brussels Treaty*.[9]

The capabilities and facilities of the WEU regarding peacekeeping and peace-enforcement are presently shaped by the organisation in the framework of its operational revival decided in Maastricht and Petersberg. This focus on the military and operational aspects of European security explains that there exists no political mechanism in the WEU for the peaceful settlement of disputes or for peacebuilding, which are tasks left to the CSCE. For the same reason, there is no difference between the global military missions of the organisation and specific conflict prevention missions. The analysis of the WEU's facilities in the field of conflict prevention must therefore be merged into the analysis of all its new operational capabilities. These can be divided into three categories.

The first category covers the *early warning and intelligence facilities*. Since its meeting at Vianden on 27 June 1991, the WEU Council has decided to create a Centre for the interpretation of satellite data as well as an *ad hoc* group in charge of the definition of

European needs in space co-operation. The Centre for the interpretation of satellite data is located in Torrejon (Spain) and is intended to train European experts in the interpretation of photos provided by satellites, to collect the available information and to communicate them to all the WEU member states, for arms control verification, crisis management or environmental monitoring purposes. France, which initiated the proposal to create the Torrejon centre and which is the best-equipped country of the WEU in this field, also suggested on 6 November 1991 to launch by 2005 a European project of a WEU military satellite system called EUMILSATCOM which would embrace all the former West-European systems.[10] The French government has already accepted to share the data of its observation satellite *Helios* with the other WEU member states. On the other hand a 4.6 million Ecu contract has been signed between the WEU and a consortium of about 30 European companies led by the Deutsche Aerospace AG in order to study the feasibility of a European satellite project for the monitoring of disarmament and environment and for crisis control. All these efforts to create a WEU capability in the field of intelligence would be directly useful for conflict prevention purposes, especially in the framework of CSCE and UN missions. Until 1995, the spatial activities of the WEU will be limited to the member states,[11] but the association of EC member states, European NATO countries and Central and Eastern European countries to the WEU decided in Maastricht and Petersberg is a sign that co-operation with non-WEU states could be envisaged in the context of a step-by-step enlargement of the European Union and the WEU.

A second dimension of the WEU facilities regarding conflict prevention is the existence of an effective *telecommunication system* between the member states. The WEUCOM system was indeed created after the decision to revive the organisation in 1984 and has been enlarged since the Petersberg Declaration of 1992 to accommodate the associate members of the WEU (i.e. Iceland, Norway and Turkey). The decision taken in Petersberg to create a consultative forum between the WEU Permanent Council and the Ambassadors of eight Central and Eastern European countries[12] is another way to improve the communications between the WEU and those regions of Europe where conflicts may occur. The work of the WEU Institute for Security Studies located in Paris and the network of experts it has created with institutes throughout Europe fulfils the same aim.

Last but not least, the emergence of *armed forces* available for WEU missions, including humanitarian, peacekeeping and peacemaking missions, prepared by a WEU military planning cell located in Brussels, could give the WEU an operational capability in peacekeeping and peace-enforcement.[13] Three types of armed forces could be created for these roles. First, France, Spain and Italy will examine the opportunity to build a European maritime force, consisting of warships and aircraft of the member states, to be called on for any mission decided on by the WEU. Secondly, the idea of a European Rapid Reaction Force for out-of-area operations, including peacekeeping, was raised in 1991 by the WEU Assembly[14] and by the Italian–British joint statement regarding the Political Union.[15] Thirdly, France and Germany decided in October 1991 to reinforce the existing Franco–German brigade in order to develop a bi-national corps of 35,000 troops including the present joint brigade deployed in Boblingen, one German mechanised division based in Sigmaringen and one of the two French divisions still based in Germany.[16] For President Mitterrand and Chancellor Kohl, 'the reinforced Franco–German units could serve as the core of a European corps, including the forces of other WEU member states'.[17] In order to convince their allies of their good faith regarding the relations between this Eurocorps and NATO, they stated in La Rochelle in May 1992 that the Eurocorps would not be the core of the WEU forces but one of its components, that there would be a structural link between the Strasbourg-based staff of the Eurocorps and the WEU military and political structures and that European forces would also be available for defensive missions under NATO control in case of an aggression.[18] They fulfilled thereby the conditions raised by Belgium and Spain for agreeing to send liaison officers to Strasbourg in order to prepare their likely participation in the Eurocorps. On the other hand, peacekeeping, peacemaking and humanitarian missions are explicitly defined as missions of the Eurocorps, but 'provided that it respects the constraints imposed by the national Constitutions and the rules of the UN Charter'. This last reserve is important with respect to the debate about the German Constitution which is not yet finished. It means that, even if the Eurocorps is the most concrete project for the development of WEU forces (it will be operational in 1995 at the latest), its exact role in conflict prevention has still to be defined in accordance with the German Constitution and with the evolution of NATO itself.

CO-OPERATION WITH OTHER INTERLOCKING INSTITUTIONS

The analysis of the WEU's role in conflict prevention also requires an assessment of its co-operation with the other international institutions. As has already been underlined, the non-constraining peacemaking mechanisms, like fact-finding, good offices, mediation and arbitration, are not seen by the WEU as one of its priorities. The CSCE seems to be conceived as the best responsible authority for such missions, with the help of the EC if necessary, as was the case during the Yugoslav war.[19] Nevertheless, in July 1992 the President of the WEU Assembly proposed to create a 'diplomatic planning cell' of the WEU, consisting of a hundred national diplomats, designed to send missions into tension zones in order to prevent conflicts. However, this proposal has not yet been accepted. The risk of a competition with CSCE and EC missions in the same field is the main reason for the reluctance to adopt this proposal.

In the field of military missions for peacekeeping and peace-enforcement, close co-operation with all the other institutions will be necessary. First, the participation of the WEU in such operations would require a previous call from the UN Security Council and/or the Committee of Senior Officials of the CSCE. Secondly, it must be approved by the Council of the EC, due to the political link between both institutions created by Article J.4 of the *Maastricht Treaty*. Thirdly, an agreement with NATO regarding the sharing of operational tasks will be needed.

The Yugoslav war provides a meaningful case study about this co-operation. WEU has been involved in four debates regarding the settlement of the crisis:

- the Franco–German proposal for the deployment of peacekeeping troops on the Croatian–Serbian border in August 1991;
- the plans for a Western European military intervention against the Serbian aggression against Croatia in the Autumn of 1991;
- the monitoring of sea operations in the Adriatic since July 1992;
- the proposal to send 5,000 troops of the WEU to Bosnia–Herzegovina for the protection of humanitarian corridors in September 1992.

The only case where these plans or proposals were implemented was the deployment of ships in the Adriatic Sea for the monitoring of the embargo against Serbia and Montenegro. The decision was taken by the Council of Ministers of the WEU in Helsinki on 10 July 1992, in order to implement UNSC resolution 757 of 30 May 1992, and the operations were led in co-operation with NATO, which monitored the northern part of the Adriatic Sea while the WEU monitored the southern Part (Otranto Channel and the Montenegro coast). The rules of engagement and operational coordination of the WEU operations have been established by the competent naval authorities at the initiative of the Italian presidency. An *ad hoc* group on Yugoslavia had prepared the decision and updated the options throughout the crisis. It is probably significant that, until now, the WEU had only had the opportunity to carry on naval operations: in the Gulf[20] in 1987–1988, and 1990–91, and in the Adriatic Sea in 1992. Air- and ground-operations seem to raise more reluctance from some member states either concerned by the risks inherent in such operations or preferring to act within the framework of NATO or to limit the joint actions to the participation of UN Blue Helmets.

In any case, the three other opportunities for a WEU intervention in the Yugoslav war failed, partly for internal political disagreements and partly for problems of coordination with the other interlocking institutions. The French–German proposal of August 1991 and the military options prepared by the *ad hoc* group on Yugoslavia in September 1991, which included four scenarios from the logistic support of the EC monitors to a peace-keeping force of 20,000 troops,[21] were refused by the United Kingdom, Portugal and the Netherlands for three reasons. First, these so-called 'atlanticist' countries did not want to give any impetus to a European defence capability during the negotiations of the *Maastricht Treaty* in which they refused any suspicious anti-NATO development. Secondly, the British experience in Cyprus and in Northern Ireland was raised by John Major as examples of the risk of getting bogged down in such conflicts. Finally, the political appraisal of the conflict by the member states of the EC was still very divergent: the moratorium on the unilateral Slovenian and Croatian declarations of independence was still in force and The Hague Peace Conference began only on 7 September 1991. After this failure of the EC to use the WEU as its military arm in the conflict, France, Britain and Belgium sought the intervention of the UN Security Council. The failed attempt to build a European peacekeeping capability through the WEU, in parallel with peacemaking intiatives of the EC, without any control of the UN Security Council, even for European crises, meant the end of the dream of an EC–WEU monopoly on conflict prevention issues in Europe.

The WEU has therefore to conceive its role as a European operational body in charge of missions decided by the UN Security Council, the CSCE or the European Community. These missions have to be coordinated with NATO which tries, since its Oslo meeting of May 1992, to find a new legitimacy for becoming another peacekeeper of the greater Europe.[22] This coordination seems to be also partly a competition between the transatlantic alliance and the WEU on West European security issues, in parallel with the Euro–American economic and political competition. Very significantly, both organisations proposed in July 1992 to monitor at sea the implementation of the embargo decided by UNSC Resolution 757 and in September 1992 to protect humanitarian corridors in Bosnia–Herzegovina after UNSC Resolution 770 asking for such a protection.[23] One should hope that this emulation between NATO and WEU does not undermine the aims of conflict prevention and crisis management, specially the need for early warning and quick reaction.

EVALUATION AND SUGGESTIONS FOR IMPROVEMENT

We can conclude that the role of the Western European Union in conflict prevention is limited for three reasons: its political subordination to the European Union, which confines the WEU to military affairs; its emulation with NATO, which implies a division of labour with this experienced, powerful and better equipped organisation; the geographical constraint of its membership which makes it less legitimate than the UN or the CSCE for taking decisions in the field of peacekeeping or peace-enforcement. The role of the WEU in conflict prevention will therefore exclude political peacemaking or peacebuilding initiatives which must remain a field of competence for the European Union within the framework of its Common Foreign and Security Policy, for the CSCE and for the UN Security Council. The absence of the WEU in such a field since the settlement of the Saar question in 1955 confirms this analysis. The decisions taken in Maastricht about the transfer of the WEU Council and Secretariat to Brussels, the harmonisation of the presidencies of the WEU and the European Union and the strengthening of the co-operation between the political bodies of the WEU and the Union (Council, Assembly, Secretariat) show that the primacy in political decisions will belong to the European Union. The hypothesis of a merging of the political bodies of the WEU into the European Union by 1998 could be imagined in this respect.[24]

The WEU has a more interesting role to play in the three fields where it is developing a real operational dimension: its telecommunications network WEUCOM; its satellite centre at Torrejon and the projects for space co-operation by the next century; the development of its naval and ground forces dedicated to peacekeeping and peace-enforcement missions. Some dimensions of the studies of the Institute for Security Studies could also be oriented in the direction of conflict prevention and crisis management. In this way, the WEU could be transformed from its original function of a collective self-defensive alliance into an operational tool for collective security, ruled politically by the European Union's bodies.

This would probably require four other changes in the European security architecture. First, the transformation of NATO and the WEU into operational instruments for collective security must not leave a *vacuum* as far as collective self-defence of the Western European countries is concerned. The next Treaty on European Union must therefore contain a commitment of assistance between the member states similar to Article 5 of the *Washington* and the modified *Brussels Treaties*. Secondly, the collective security needs for the greater Europe imply the transformation of the CSCE into an effective and efficient organisation, which means the end of the rule of consensus. Thirdly, the WEU cannot exclude the other European states from the benefits of its experience and its operational resources: some kind of association of the other EC, NATO and CSCE European states to the WEUCOM system, the satellite co-operation, the Eurocorps and other armed forces must be shaped for the late '90s. Finally, if the Europeans accept the principle of a new world order led by the UN Security Council, they have to renounce the use of military force on their own initiative (except for self-defence). The WEU should state that its peacekeeping and peace-enforcement missions will be subordinated to the decisions of the UN Security Council. A permanent seat for the European Union in this Council should be the counterpart for this statement.

NOTES

1. The texts of the Treaty, the Protocols and other Documents concerning Western European Union have been published by the Office of the Clerk of the Assembly of Western European Union in Paris. I use the edition of 1982.
2. Among the few analyses of the history of the WEU, see especially Alfred Cahen, *The Western European Union and NATO. Building a European Defence Identity Within the Context of Atlantic Solidarity*, Brassey's, London, 1989 (Brassey's Atlantic Commentary No. 2); Armand Imbert, *L'Union de l'Europe occidentale*, Librairie générale de Droit et de Jurisprudence, Paris, 1968.
3. See *inter alia The Final Act of the Nine-Power Conference*, London, 28 September–3 October 1954.
4. Marcel Merle, 'L'accord franco-allemand du 23 octobre 1954 sur le statut de la Sarre', *Annuaire français de droit international*, Paris, 1955, pp. 128–134.
5. The Northern Ireland question remains the only point which explains the Republic of Ireland's refusal to accede to NATO and the WEU and its

reluctance towards any defence policy in the framework of the European Community (Patrick Keatinge, 'Irish Neutrality in the European Community', in Bo Huldt and Atis Lejins (eds), *Neutrals in Europe: Ireland* (The Swedish Institute of International Affairs, Stockholm, 1990); Denis J. Maher, *The Tortuous Path: The Course of Ireland's Entry into the EEC 1948–73*, (Institute of Public Administration, Dublin, 1986).

6. *Petersberg Declaration. I. WEU and European Security*, paragraph 2, (Bonn, 19 June 1992).
7. *Helsinki Decisions. III. Rapid Alert, Conflict Prevention and Crisis Management (Including Missions of Inquiry and Missions of Rapporteurs and Peacekeeping Operations), Peaceful Settlement of Disputes*, paragraph 52, (Helsinki, 10 July 1992).
8. *Petersberg Declaration. II. Strengthening the Operational Role of the WEU*, paragraph 4, (Bonn, 19 June 1992). Two other missions – not linked to conflict prevention – are also quoted: the contribution to the common defence and humanitarian missions.
9. 'At the request of any of the High Contracting Parties the Council shall be immediately convened in order to permit them to consult with regard to any situation which may constitute a threat to peace, in whatever area this threat should arise, or a danger to economic stability'.
10. The French possess two generations of communications *Syracuse* satellites and will prepare the third one for the end of the century while the British use the *Skynet* system and the Spanish have had the first generation of *Hispasat* since 1992. The Italian *Sicral* system is not yet operational.
11. *Petersberg Declaration. III. On Relations Between the WEU and Other European States Members of the European Union or the Atlantic Alliance*.
12. Bulgaria, Estonia, Hungary, Latvia, Lithuania, Poland, Rumania and Czechoslovakia.
13. André Dumoulin, 'Enjeux et perspectives des forces multinationales', *Memento défense-désarmement 1992*, (GRIP, Brussels, July 1992), pp. 165–181.
14. See inter alia Sir Dudley Smith's report about *Armaments and Equipments for a European Rapid Reaction Force*, (WEU Assembly, Document 1292, 37th Ordinary Session (2nd Part), Paris, 27 November 1991).
15. *Declaration on European Security and Defence*, (London–Rome, 4 October 1991).
16. 'Arms and Equipment for a European Rapid Reaction Force', (*Military Technology–MILTECH*, London, March 1992), p. 14.
17. *Political Union: French–German Initiative on Foreign, Security and Defence Policy*, (Paris–Bonn, 16 October 1991).
18. Henri de Bresson, 'Paris et Bonn définissent les missions du corps franco-allemand', (*Le Monde*, Paris, 13 May 1992).
19. See my article 'La CSCE et la Communauté européenne face au conflit yougoslave', *Le Trimestre du Monde*, Paris, 1er trimestre 1992, pp. 219–233.

20. Willem Van Eekelen. 'WEU and the Gulf Crisis', *Survival*, Vol. XXXII, No. 6, (London, November/December 1990), pp. 233–247.
21. These scenarios are detailed in M De Hoop Scheffer's report *An Operational Organisation for the WEU–The Yugoslav Crisis*, (WEU Assembly, Document 1294, 37th Ordinary Session (2nd Part), Paris, 27 November 1991), p. 11.
22. See Chapter 5.
23. The WEU proposed 5,000 troops and NATO 6,000 troops but the Security Council decided finally to deploy more Blue Helmets of the UNPROFOR for fulfilling this task (Charles Goerens, *The European Security Policy – Answer to the 37th Annual Report of the Council*, WEU Assembly, Document 1342, 2nd Part, 38th Ordinary Session (2nd Part), 6 November 1992, p. 11).
24. See Karel De Gucht and Stephan Keukeleire's proposals in 'The European Security Architecture. The Role of the European Community in Shaping a New European Geopolitical Landscape', *Studia Diplomatica*, Vol. XLIV, No. 6, Brussels, 1991, pp. 29–90.

7

The International Organisation of Conflict Prevention

Luc Reychler and Werner Bauwens

The West seems to be losing the battle for the future. What is missing is a lack of foresight, a conceptual adaptation to the rapidly changing strategic landscape and a well-orchestrated international structure for dealing with the flood of turmoil around the world. The chance to prevent anarchy and violence in many parts of the globe may already have passed us by. And there may be worse to come: the next phase could involve the disintegration of the existing security community of the major Northern democracies (North America, Western Europe and Japan).

POLITICAL MYOPIA

We saw in Chapter 1 how many of the recent alterations to the international landscape had taken us all by surprise, due not only to lack of foresight but also to an air of complacency amongst the professionals: the diplomats, diplomatic correspondents and academics.

This has been shown to be an unacceptable state of affairs in the light of the very real possibility of some much less attractive scenarios arising in the future and the adverse effect that such attitudes must have upon the development of preventive diplomacy and more effective conflict prevention.

The old lesson of 'A stitch in time ...' has yet to be learned.

One of the authors addressing the lack of foresight in international relations is Robert Jervis.[1] According to him this is caused by the simple fact that prediction in international relations is difficult and he gives eight reasons why this is so. The first two refer to the state of the art of the science of international relations. The scientists have only a limited stock of knowledge to rely on and there are few laws whose validity is uncontested. Besides, the best propositions are couched in terms of conditions and probabilities. The third reason is that learning international politics can act as a self-denying prophecy. Practitioners who are, for example, acquainted with the literature about 'groupthink' could take measures to prevent it from happening. The fourth reason is that national behaviour and international outcomes are not entirely determined by the external environment, and that there is significant room for choice by publics and statesmen. To the extent that the latter are strongly affected by values, preferences and beliefs, the task is all the more difficult. The fifth obstacle to prediction is the unprecedented state of the current world situation. 'World politics has rarely been reordered without a major war. In fact, from looking at the behaviour and the condition of the Soviet Union, one could infer that it had just lost a war. And the enormous domestic failure is equivalent to a major military defeat. But this is a war without another country or a coalition that acts like a winner, ready to move into the power vacuum and structure a new set of rules to guide international behaviour'.[2] The sixth difficulty in making predictions, is the complex interdependence in international relations. 'With complex interaction and feedback, not only can small causes have large effects, but prediction is inherently problematic as the multiple pathways through which the system will respond to a stimulus are difficult to trace after the fact, let alone ahead of time'.[3] The seventh argument as to why prediction is so difficult is that in international politics, history matters; in other words, particular events can send world politics down quite different paths. For example, the United States might have joined the League of Nations had Wilson's personality been different or had his judgment not been impaired by his stroke. The final reason why prediction is difficult relates to the question of how different the new world will be, or in other words, the future validity of what we have learned in the past. 'Statesmen presumably will continue to be guided primarily by considerations of national security, but their behaviour will be different if there are changes in the problems they face and the solutions they see'.[4]

Another set of explanations for the lack of foresight refers to the difficult access to information. Both sets of explanations, about the state of the art of the study of international politics and the lack of good intelligence are valid but old arguments. They are frequently used as an excuse for intellectual complacency.

A comprehensive explanation for the underdeveloped prognostication in international politics should also include: a lack of interest; cognitive biases; societal epistemic pressure and the neglect of real public opinion.

A lack of interest

In many cases, a revolution or a war is necessary to trigger the attention of the media, the policymakers and the political scientists. Investigative reporting seems to require a threatening event or a portion of blood. The latter tend to attract cameras and a majority of think tanks awake when policy-makers and journalists appeal to the 'instant' expertise of 'ad hoc' specialists.

Cognitive biases

The historically exceptional Cold War stability in the northern part of the world enhanced the propensity to treat variables as constants. During the Cold War period it was relatively easy to teach international relations. The world system was dominated by the two superpowers; security was based on a balance of power between the NATO-16 and the Warsaw Pact-7. Eastern Europe was treated as a bloc. At the beginning of the eighties, people were predominantly concerned with the existence of nuclear weapons. The CSCE-35 tried to build detente between East and West on the basis of three pillars: security, cooperation and respect for human rights. Since then the world has changed drastically. Most constants are again variables. The speed and the complexity of the continuing changes are mind boggling.

A second cognitive bias is the propensity to treat the future as an extension of the past and as a gradual process. This is psychologically more comforting than living with uncertain futures. During a summercourse about European security, in June 1991, American students were asked to assess the probability of four scenarios of the Soviet-Union: (a) the future would be a continuation of Gorbachev's zigzag policy; (b) there would be a *coup d'état*; (c) chaos; (d) or everything would turn out positively; the democratisation process would continue; the economic reconversion would succeed and the arms control process would enhance further security. Of the 21 students attending the course, a great majority[15] opted for the first scenario; three expected further disintegration and chaos and 'one' a *coup d'état*. Two months later the latter scenario claimed a place in history.

Societal and epistemic community pressures

Under this heading one can distinguish (1) the existence of myths and taboos within the community of political scientists; (2) the short-term attention span of democracies and; (3) the role of interest groups.

Myths and taboos

First of all there was the belief in the 'irreversibility of communism'. Jeane Kirkpatrick preached that Western style authoritarianism could be reformed and even be removed but that communist totalitarianism could not.[5] In 1984 Samuel Huntington wrote in a study of the global prospects of democracy, that the likelihood of democratic development in Eastern Europe was virtually nil.[6] Secondly, there was the domino-theory in which democracies were threatened and were expected to tumble one after another if the advance of communism was not effectively contained. Third, there was also the myth that the indoctrination of several generations of peoples in Eastern Europe would have weakened ethnic and nationalist ties and created new loyalties towards the communist world. Finally, there were also a set of taboos which inhibited an open-minded discussion of the developments in Eastern Europe. Hawks and doves were not only unaware of the biased nature of their worldview, but also intolerant of alternative opinions. Hawks tended to focus mainly on the military dimension of the Warsaw Pact countries. The doves were predominantly NATO starers and considered any negative comment about Eastern Europe as reactionary and reinforcing the odious 'enemy image'.

The short-term attention span of democracies

Most diplomats are bureaucrats, who prefer to respond to real events rather than to reflect on probable developments. As we saw in Chapter 1, few Ministries of Foreign Affairs in Europe have a well functioning planning office or a 'Center for analysis and prognosis'. Characteristic of most politicians in democratic countries is a short-term thinking. Their time-span normally does not seem to go beyond the next elections.

The role played by interest groups

Interest groups aim at shaping the worldview of their audience, in order to promote their own interests. Representatives of military industrial complexes (MIC's) presented the world as insecure, full of threats and preferably with an enemy, who needed to be contained or deterred with a huge military force. Those and other interest groups have used disinformation to manipulate the worldview of the decision-makers and people of their own country and of other countries. In the case of the Soviet nomenclatura this finally led to self-deception. At the end of the eighties, nomenclaturas, who had been hiding behind their superior worldview had no choice but to face their self-distorted perception of reality and as failures rapidly accumulated, cognitive arrogance turned into cognitive defeat.[7]

An underestimation of the power of public opinion

One of the major causes of the many surprises in international affairs is the relative neglect of the mood of the people.[8] A majority of analysts focussed only on the governing and dissident élites in Eastern Europe; they were the Kremlin and dissident watchers. Not enough attention was given to the development of the post-totalitarian mind.[9] The changes in Eastern Europe were not only the consequence of a profound wish for change by many people. According to Jeffrey Goldfarb, the development of these changes in public opinion preceded the political and institutional changes. Long before Gorbachev, many people freed themselves from the state-sanctioned doctrine and developed a lively underground opposition culture. However, the spread was not very visible, because of its repression and the related 'preference falsification' and 'pluralistic ignorance'.[10] The term 'preference falsification' refers to the divergence between the preference that an individual expresses in public and the ones he or she holds in private. 'Pluralistic ignorance' refers to situations in which people cannot publicly express their real opinions, they tend to feel alone in their disapproval. (Poland needed 10 years; Hungary 10 months; East Germany 10 weeks; Czechoslovakia 10 days; and Romania 10 hours to have a successful revolution). A better understanding of the distribution of the 'revolutionary thresholds' of the people would give us a better insight into the revolutionary dynamics. If the world does not like to be caught off guard, greater efforts will be needed to track the changes in the private opinions of the world public.

AN ADEQUATE ADAPTATION OF INTERNATIONAL ORGANISATION

During the past few years, at various levels, serious efforts have been made by the UN, CSCE, NATO, EC and WEU to evaluate and adapt their respective security strategies and organisations to the new international environment. These efforts have not been translated into a successful handling of some of the new challenges. The historic opportunity to replace the old bipolar security organisation by a

Pan-European Security Community is slipping through our fingers. Several ethnic and nationalist conflicts have turned into bloody civil wars. Yugoslavia is a nagging reminder. A comparative analysis of the main organisations in our multilayered security arrangement provides some insight into the organisational problems with which we are confronted.[11]

MANDATE (*see Table 7.1*)

The UN and CSCE have a broad mandate and NATO, the EC and WEU more specialised ones. The geographic extension of the mandates of most organisations, formally or *de facto*, applies to sub-areas of the world; only the UN has a worldwide mandate. Problematic, especially for NATO, remain the so called 'out of area' problems or the geographic limitations of its mandate. Equally constraining are the constitutional restrictions of some important countries such as Germany and Japan to send their military forces beyond their own territory or territorial waters. A third problem is overburdening, caused by charging the UN, the Conference on Security and Cooperation in Europe (CSCE) or other international organisations, with tasks – without giving them the means to carry them out properly. The result has been a rapid frustration of the peace machinery at a crucial time.

UN:
The policy framework for the UN's preventive diplomacy is based on the UN Charter, especially Article 1, which stipulates that the purposes of the UN are to maintain international peace and security. Article 24 specifies the functions and powers of the Security Council and Article 25 spells out that the Member States agree to carry out the Security Council decisions, which are mandatory, especially if taken under Chapter VII. Chapter VI refers to peaceful settlement of conflicts and Chapter VII foresees that the Security Council may call upon states to comply with measures agreed as necessary.

CSCE:
Broad agenda, covering security, cooperation in the field of economics, of science and technology and of environment, and cooperation in the humanitarian field; objectives: promotion of better relations among participating states for true and lasting peace free

from any threat to security; peace, security and justice (*Final Act of Helsinki, 1975*) to build, consolidate and strengthen democracy (Paris Charter, 1990); to foster and manage change in Europe (*Helsinki Decisions, 1992*).

NATO:
The policy framework governing NATO's approach to preventive diplomacy and crisis management is composed of: (a) the commitment to a transformation of the Alliance; (b) the new Alliance Strategic Concept; and (c) the commitment to a concept of 'mutually reinforcing' institutions. Cf. the 1991 Rome Summit Declaration and NATO communiques since then.

The relevant documents include the main elements of the 1949 Washington Treaty, specifically: Article I, to refrain from the threat or use of force for purposes inconsistent with the objectives of the UN charter; Article IV, the commitment to consult together; and Article V, collective defence in the event of armed attack.

European Community:
A clear mandate for peacebuilding activities in the Treaty on European Union. A clear mandate for peacemaking and an implicit mandate for peacekeeping (and possibly enforcing) in a Report approved by the European Council in June 1992. Geographic area of application not specified.

WEU:
Mutual assistance between the member states in maintaining international peace and security and in resisting any policy of aggression; collective self-defence; peaceful settlement of disputes (by conciliation or judicial settlement) between the member states (Article X of the modified Brussels Treaty). Geographic area of application not specified.

Table 7.1: Mandate

DECLARATORY PREVENTION (*see Table 7.2*)

The most experienced organisations in declaratory prevention are the United Nations, the CSCE and NATO. The UN Charter and the CSCE Charter of Paris both indicate how their member states ought to behave *vis-à-vis* each other. They define what is acceptable and unacceptable international behaviour. The UN and CSCE are cooperative and collective security organisations, and differ from the collective defence systems, such as NATO. During the Cold War,

NATO was very effective in preventing conflict through its defensive posture, deterrence and reassuring initiatives. Several factors limit the effectiveness of declaratory conflict prevention. First, many principles or concepts guiding international behaviour are still very abstract and have no clear operational definitions. Second, there are several conflicting principles. Think of the competition between the traditional principles of national sovereignty, non-intervention, inviolability of borders and the new principles about humanitarian intervention, self-determination of the people, and human and minority rights. A third factor undermining declaratory prevention is the selective or inconsistent application of these principles. A fourth problem is the fact that the CSCE principles are politically, and not legally, binding. Finally, the impotence of the organisations to cope with Yugoslavia and other conflicts in Europe has considerably reduced their credibility.

UN:
General Assembly Resolution 47/120 '*An Agenda for Peace: Preventive Diplomacy and Related Matters*' of December 1992, which foresees measures on peaceful settlement of conflicts, early warning, fact-finding, confidence-building measures, resources and logistical aspects of preventive diplomacy and states that the General Assembly, together with the Security Council and the Secretary-General, have an important role in this regard.

Statements of the Presidency of the Security Council, such as that following the summit of the Security Council of January 1992, S/23500, as well as communiques and resolutions on an *ad hoc* basis (e.g. the crisis in Iraq, ex-Yugoslavia or Somalia).

The '*Handbook on the Peaceful Settlement of Disputes Between States*', 46/58 of 1991 and the '*Declaration on Fact-finding in the field of maintenance of International Peace and Security*' 46/59 of 1991 provide a new reference for activities of conflict prevention.

Agreed terms of reference concerning, for instance, disarmament régimes also provide means by which the UN can take measures in the prevention of conflicts or responding to crises.

The '*Universal Declaration on Human Rights*' of 1948 remains the basic document providing guidelines on human rights world-wide.

CSCE:
Declaration of 10 principles in the *Helsinki Final Act* (sovereign equality; refraining from threat or use of force, inviolability of frontiers; territorial integrity; peaceful settlement of disputes; non-intervention in internal affairs; respect for human rights and

fundamental freedoms; equal rights and self-determination of peoples; cooperation among States; fulfilment in good faith of obligations under international law).

NATO:
The Washington Treaty can be regarded as a statement of conflict prevention, because it declares the political willingness and legal obligation to defend collectively against armed attack.

Additional political statements are made on a semi-annual basis through communiqués of the North Atlantic Council, as well as through statements of an *ad hoc* nature (e.g. the situation in the USSR, August 1991) or on a specific topic (e.g. on the ongoing Yugoslav crisis). There is also an internal inventory of preventive measures which the Alliance could adopt on a case-by-case basis if required or appropriate.

Various agreed documents establishing arms control and disarmament régimes also provide the means by which Allies can take steps in the prevention of conflict or responding to crisis (e.g. the *Vienna Document 1992*; the *Open Skies Treaty* and the *CFE Treaty*).

European Community:
Indirectly, the EC plays an important role in conflict prevention through general declarations which emphasise human rights, democracy and the need to solve conflicts peacefully, and more directly through more specific declarations encouraging or inhibiting specific developments.

WEU:
Not mentioned.

Table 7.2: Declaratory prevention

DECISION-MAKING PROCEDURES (*see Table 7.3*)

In all the organisations except the UN (and the EC in certain cases), decisions are made on the basis of consensus. In the CSCE, NATO, EC and the WEU this means the approval of respectively 53, 16, 12 and 10 member states. The CSCE decision-making process is the most cumbersome one and in its effectiveness it is comparable to the League of Nations. To function more effectively not only as a cooperative security system but also as a collective security system, many suggestions, such as the creation of the function of Secretary-General, the acceptance of 'unanimity-minus one' rule for security related decisions and the establishment of a European Security

Council, have been offered. Although an obstacle, the impact of the decision-making system should not be exaggerated. More important is the lack of consensus among the major powers. If a consensus among the major powers could be reached, the smaller countries would find it difficult to obstruct.

UN:
UN Resolutions under the UN Charter Chapter VII are adopted under the political authority of the Security Council composed of representatives of the five permanent and the 10 non-permanent member states. UN decisions are reached by a majority vote with the possibility of veto by the permanent members. During the Cold War period, the decision-making procedure was weak and the veto power was used as an instrument of ideological confrontation.

CSCE:
Consensus principle among all participating states; bodies: follow-up meetings of the (original) CSCE; Council of Foreign Ministers; Committee of Senior Officials (CSO); and several *ad hoc* groups. Some procedural and specific arrangements no longer require a full consensus decision.

NATO:
All decisions within the Alliance are taken by and under the political authority of the North Atlantic Council, composed of representatives of the governments of the 16 Alliance members. The Defence Planning Committee (DPC) , composed of defence ministers, is responsible for activities of the Alliance's integrated military force structure in responding to crises. Alliance decisions are reached by consensus.

European Community:
Different decision-making procedures for EC matters (unanimity or majority vote; roles for the Council, Commission and European Parliament) and for EPC matters (unanimity and main role for Council). Lack of a single decision-making centre and a centralised leadership.

WEU:
Unanimity principle among 10 member states; consultative status of associate membership for the other European NATO countries (plus a voting power for them in matters transferred to the WEU from the IEPG or EUROGroup); observer status for the other EC countries. Bodies: located in Brussels: Council of Ministers (Foreign and Defence Ministers); located in Paris: Parliamentary Assembly; Institute for Security Studies.

Table 7.3: Decision-making procedures

CONFLICT PREVENTION FACILITIES: EARLY WARNING

(*see Table 7.4a*)

The whole point of early warning is not to predict, but to anticipate potential problems sufficiently far ahead so that corrective measures can be taken. Most of the early warning systems are not measuring up to expectations. They are still in an embryonic stage and rely heavily on national intelligence. In addition, all the organisations, with the exception of NATO and WEU, lack an adequate infrastructure for security related planning. The reason for this state of affairs lies in the reluctance of states to pool their intelligence and also in the short-term thinking and the reactive, rather than proactive, mindset of national and international decision-shapers and makers.

UN:
The Office for Research and the Collection of Information (ORCI) existed from March 1987–March 1992 in the UN Secretariat and had a mandate for early-warning. Since April 1992, this function has been integrated into the Department of Humanitarian Affairs (humanitarian early-warning) and the regional political services in the Secretariat (political early-warning).

In 1992, the Administrative Coordinating Committee (ACC) had set up an inter-agency early warning system in the humanitarian field regarding new flows of refugees and displaced persons. The ACC early warning system is comprised of a core group including UNHCR, UNICEF, UNDP and WPF.

UNHCR had established an internal early warning working group in 1990 for emergency preparedness (Refugee Emergency Alert System – REAS) and for preventive action.

CSCE:
With CSO ('as the Council's agent'), but also with the High Commissioner on National Minorities; with Consultative Committee (CC) of the Conflict Prevention Centre.

NATO:
Main sources of early warning are the national intelligence-gathering and assessment systems of individual Allies. Other sources would be available to Allies on a national basis through activities carried out in connection with various arms control and disarmament régimes.

European Community:
More than 100 diplomatic missions of the EC, information of the

member states, permanent close contacts through the 'European Correspondents' of the twelve member states, the COREU telex network consultative relationships with third countries and other regional organisations, diplomatic delegations of third countries to the EC, fact-finding missions. However, no centralised 'intelligence unit'.

WEU:
Torrejon Centre for the interpretation of satellite data; projects and feasibility studies for WEU military satellite system by 2005.

Table 7.4a: Conflict prevention facilities: early warning

CONFLICT PREVENTION FACILITIES: COMMUNICATION (*see Table 7.4b*)

The facilities for communication have improved considerably. Most organisations can now rely on effective communications systems. The problem however seems not to be the communication but its translation into effective action. Contributing to this problem are overloaded agendas, the lack of 'credible analysts' and the definition of a conflict situation as strategically insignificant.

UN:
Transmitting of information on potential crisis situations is carried out by advanced technologies (radio and satellite) especially between Headquarters in New York and other important UN offices around the world to provide speedy information and analyses to the Secretary-General.

CSCE:
Communications network among Capitals.

NATO:
Monitoring of potential crisis developments is carried out by the NATO Situation Centre with NATO-wide communications, supported by the automatic data processing resources of the NATO Integrated Communications system.

European Community:
COREU telex network.

WEU:
WEUCOM telecommunications system among the governments of the member states and of the associate members.

Table 7.4b: Conflict prevention facilities: Communications

CONFLICT MANAGEMENT METHODS: PEACEKEEPING / ENFORCEMENT (*See Table 7.4c-1*)

Recent experience has made decision-makers more aware of the limits and possibilities of peacekeeping and peace-enforcement. The increased use of peacekeepers to perform all kinds of old and new roles in conflicts is attended by a growing awareness that peacekeepers are at their best in conflicts where the conflicting parties desire peace. If not, they will be ineffective or, after having been installed for a long time, even reduce the incentives to resolve the conflict. The popularity of peacekeeping, however, has remained high because it is considered to imply not too risky military operations; because it could be used for alleviating human suffering and because it helps to legitimise the military forces in the Post-Cold War era. In Boutros Boutros-Ghali's *Agenda for Peace* several recommendations have been made to improve the organisation of peacekeeping operations. The decision to deploy peace-enforcement troops is comparatively much more difficult. It requires more leadership, a joint perception of a strategic interest, the availability of sufficient military forces and preferably a peace plan to be reinforced.

UN:
Actions taken by the UN in this regard can be grouped into two main categories:

- Conflict resolution/management with preventive potential with a military component (peacekeeping, peacemaking, peacebuilding, peace-enforcement);
- Conflict resolution/management with preventive potential with a non-military component (good offices, fact-finding, enquiry, negotiation, mediation and conciliation, arbitration and judicial settlement).

Peacekeeping. Traditional peacekeeping serves to create conditions in which negotiations can go on (e.g. Cyprus, Lebanon, ex-Yugoslavia, Somalia).

Newer type of peacekeeping forms a part of political settlement which has already been negotiated but requires an impartial third party to monitor its implementation (e.g. Namibia, El Salvador, Mozambique).

Of thirteen current United Nations peacekeeping operations, two are funded from the UN regular budget (UNTSO and UNMOGIP), one is funded through voluntary contribution (UNFICYP) and ten are financed from their own separate accounts on the basis of legally binding assessments on all member states. Since the mandates of most forces are renewed periodically, starting from different dates, annual cost estimates for comparative purposes are approximate. The figures provided for operational strength, some of which include both military and civilian personnel, vary slightly from month to month due to rotation (PS/DPI/15/Ref. 5 – January 1991).

Number of United Nations peacekeeping operations 1948–1993: 27 – UNTSO, UNMOGIP, UNEF I, UNOGIL, ONUC, UNSF, UNYOM, UNFICYP, DIMREP, UNIPOM, UNEF II, UNDOF, UNIFIL, UNGOMAP, UMNIIMOG, UNAVEM I, UNTAG, ONUCA, UNIKON, UNAVEM II, ONUSAL, MINURSO, UNAMIC, UNPROFOR, UNTACM, UNOSOM, ONUMOZ.

Numbers of military personnel served 1948 to January 1993: over 600,000.

- Total fatalities (1948–January 1993): 859.
- Missions currently underway: 13 Military and civilian police personnel serving in January 1993: over 52,000 (UNTSO – 248, UNMOGIP – 38, UNFICYP – 1,539, UNDOF – 1,119, UNIFIL – 5,251, UMNIKOM – 343, UNAVEM II – 224, ONUSAL – 425, MINURSO – 329, UNPROFOR – 22,639, UNTAC – 19, 253, UNOSOM – 696, ONUMOZ – 23.
- Countries currently contributing military/civilian police personnel: 67
- Peace-enforcement: The UN enforcement measures under Chapter VII include: 1961 when the Security Council authorised use of force in the Congo operation. 1990 to evict Iraqi forces from Kuwait.

CSCE:
Peacekeeping mandated in Helsinki decisions; decision-making with CSO. No mandate for peace-enforcement (which would contradict self-definition as 'regional security arrangement' according to Chapter VIII, UN Charter).

NATO:
Actions taken by the Alliance recently can be grouped under the headings: peacekeeping; peacemaking (including peace-enforcement); and peacebuilding (including preventive diplomacy).

Peacekeeping: various activities through which support is given to the implementation of UN Security Council Resolutions concerning the conflict in the former Yugoslavia; doctrinal development for conduct of peacekeeping operations; training and education programmes for peacekeeping; establishment of a Rapid Reaction Force.

European Community:
Some precedents with the EC being provided indirectly (through the WEU) with military instruments to implement an EC decision (Humanitarian aid for the Kurds in Iraq) and with the EC sending unarmed EC observers to monitor the implementation of cease-fire agreements in Yugoslavia.

Discussions, but no consensus, on sending armed military forces to Yugoslavia.

WEU:
Peacekeeping mandated in the *Petersberg Declaration*. Not yet concretely implemented. Peace-enforcement in the modified *Brussels Treaty* and confirmed in the *Petersberg Declaration*. Some experience with naval operations during the Gulf Wars and the Yugoslav War. Three projects for common WEU forces: air–naval French–Italian–Spanish force; Rapid Reaction Force of the WEU; French–German Corps to be transformed in a Eurocorps with participation of Belgium (and likely participation of Luxembourg and Spain).

Table 7.4c-1: Conflict management methods: peacekeeping and peace-enforcement

CONFLICT MANAGEMENT METHODS: PEACEMAKING (*see Table 7.4c-2*)

Most organisations have experience with the traditional peacemaking approaches. Characterising 'traditional' peacemakers are: their legal mindset; the predominance given to the principles of national sovereignty, non-intervention and inviolability of boundaries; the preference given to professional diplomats for handling negotiations and their limited definition of conflict prevention. For them, conflict prevention refers to traditional negotiation and the use of peacekeeping and peace-enforcement. Practically no attention is given to the use of alternative negotiation methods, peacebuilding measures and the development of comprehensive peace plans. Considerably more attention should be given to the involvement of non-governmental specialists in peacemaking and peacebuilding. Without serious peacebuilding efforts involving the people, the chief negotiators, parties to conflict, could experience reentry problems and have a difficult time convincing their constituency in the field that the agreements are fair and should be respected. Efforts should be made to develop alternative ways and means to manage conflicts. There is also a need for the development of a 'diplomacy without borders' involving non-governmental organisations and paying much more attention to the internal and the transnational dimensions of conflict dynamics.[12]

UN:
Instruments for peaceful settlement of conflicts abound. Practice and results are less impressive. In most cases, peacemaking efforts start only once conflicts have arisen. Experience of the UN shows that implementation combining methods of good offices, fact-finding and negotiation have often been successful.

CSCE:
Fact-finding and rapporteur missions; good offices, mediation or conciliation; peaceful settlement of disputes, consultations (bilateral; or in Consultative Committee, in Committee of Senior Officials or among all CSCE participating states).

NATO:
Provisions of political and logistical support for the coalition operation 'Desert Storm', under the auspices of the UN, demonstrated flexibility and adaptability to accommodate participation of non-NATO nations in crisis management operations on behalf of the UN Security Council; involvement in contributing to the UN's efforts to end the Yugoslav crisis.

European Community:
Diplomatic démarches. New methods and experience gained during the Yugoslav crisis: mediation between the warring factions and the appointment of a special permanent representative to mediate.

Table 7.4c-2: Conflict prevention facilities: peacemaking

CONFLICT MANAGEMENT METHODS: PEACEBUILDING (*see Table 7.4c-3*)

Peacebuilding is the most recent addition to the battery of conflict management methods. In contrast to the other methods, which target the politicians and the warriors, peacebuilding addresses itself to the people. Peacebuilding efforts aim at constructing an environment that is politically, economically and socio-psychologically reassuring. It could involve the media in order to prevent the development of stereotypes and to counter war propaganda; it could also involve efforts to prevent a further deterioration of the economic fabric; and efforts to reinforce democratic practices – such as the rule of law and transparency in decision-making – and the achievement of an effective and stable political system. At least as important as post-conflict peacebuilding promoted by Boutros Boutros-Ghali to prevent a recurrence of the hostilities, are peacebuilding efforts before and during the outbreak of violence. The mutual expectation of a new environment characterized by good governance and socio-economic welfare could considerably reinforce the other peace efforts.

UN:
Methods include economic and social developments, as well as technical assistance to be given to protagonists of a dispute once peace has been reached.

Political conflicts (e.g. former Yugoslavia, Somalia, Angola).

Verification and implementation of disarmament. The location and destruction of weapons of massive destruction.

Cooperative activities with regional bodies (e.g. the European Community (former Yugoslavia), Organisation of African Unity (somalia), ASEAN (Cambodia), Organisation of American States (Central America and others).

Coordination with the EC in humanitarian aid efforts, particularly in former Yugoslavia but also in major humanitarian crisis in the developing world and Eastern and Central Europe.

CSCE:
No explicit mandate but in conformity with the basic philosophy of 'cooperative security policy' (and could be decided ad hoc by Council/CSO within their mandate).

NATO:
Methods include political statements in support of activities to resolve the conflict in the former Yugoslavia; cooperation in verification and implementation of arms control and disarmament measures; cooperative activities under the aegis of the NACC; contribution to humanitarian aid efforts.

European Community:
Major peacebuilding efforts, promoting reconciliation and dialogue. New methods and experience gained during the Yugoslav crisis peace conference to define a long term settlement and arbitration board. Use of other (diplomatic political and economic) measures dealing with the opportunity structure.

Table 7.4c-3: Conflict prevention facilities, peacebuilding

CONFLICT PREVENTION FACILITIES: COOPERATION
(*see Table 7.4d*)

The application of the subsidiarity principle to the organisation of Europe's security implies a multilayered security system consisting of national, EC–WEU, NATO, CSCE and UN levels of security. The engagement of one or more levels would depend on the specific security task with which one is dealing. In most foreseable conflicts all the so-called interlocking institutions are expected to be involved. Smooth cooperation however is slow in forthcoming. Several factors, such as the post-Maastricht European identity crisis, the competition between the WEU and NATO, the ideological instead of cost-benefit assessment of security, and the lack of a fair responsibility and burden-sharing among the participating countries inhibit the development of effective cooperation.

UN:
Cooperation with other regional organisations includes:

EC:
In peacemaking (e.g. former Yugoslavia). NATO: operational support for implementation of peace-plan and sanctions. WEU: operational support for implementation of sanctions. CSCE: in a context of 'regional security arrangements'. ECOWAS: peacekeeping and enforcement in Western Africa. OAU: consultations at the political level. OAS: consultations at the political level; at the humanitarian level (e.g. Haiti) and on human rights (e.g. El Salvador).

CSCE:
With the UN: self-definition as regional security arrangement, but no experience so far with EC; endorsement/enlargement of participation by non-EC members in monitoring missions in former Yugoslavia; with NATO/WEU: possible cooperation/support in peacekeeping explicitly mentioned.

NATO:
Development of a supportive role which contributes to efforts undertaken by collective security institutions such as the UN and the CSCE in the area of conflict prevention and crisis management (cf. Oslo Declaration June 1992, Brussels Declaration December 1992). Relations between the Alliance and the UN/CSCE are in the midst of development and elaboration on the political level. At present, the Alliance has provided operational support of UN UNPROFOR

activities in the former Yugoslavia, as well as military contingency planning with WEU, NATO maintaining military command in the latter case.

European Community:
UN support for EC actions in Yugoslavia. CSCE legitimation of and participation in EC actions in Yugoslavia. NATO: some ad hoc contacts.

WEU:
Political link with the future European Union (Article J.4 of the *Maastricht Treaty*). Operational link and division of labour with NATO (annex statement to the *Maastricht Treaty*). Availability for action under UN or CSCE mandate (*Petersberg Declaration*).

Table 7.4d: Cooperation

CONFLICT PREVENTION FACILITIES: FUNDING (*see Table 7.4e*)

Although conflict prevention is generally considered a cost-effective investment in security, its funding has been inadequate. For peacekeeping, for example, countries give the UN's blue helmets only $1.40 for every $1,000 spent on their own forces. Most countries still seem to prefer to commit their money to the national or collective defence of their security interests. A stronger financial support for international conflict prevention seems also to be obstructed by the general 'peace-dividend movement'.[13]

UN:
The total cost to the United Nations of 27 operations (1948–1992) was about $8.3 billion. Rough annual cost to the UN of current missions is about $2.8 billion. Outstanding contributions to peacekeeping operations amount to about $1.1 billion.

CSCE:
Separate budgets for negotiations/meetings and for the three subsidiary institutions; Budget for the Conflict Prevention Centre (exclusive meetings): 1.3 mill US $/year (1992–1993).

NATO:
Funding for 'internal' Alliance crisis management procedures and operations are through the financial contributions that each member makes to the Alliance. In support of other organisations, the individual Allies would likely seek standard UN and CSCE cost assessment formulae.

European Community:
Funding by the EC budget and by national and ad hoc contributions. The number of specific 'conflict management' items in the budget is growing slightly.

WEU:
Difficult to identify the part of the budget dedicated to conflict prevention.

Table 7.4e: Conflict prevention facilities: funding

EXPERIENCE (*see Table 7.5*)

Although all organisations have experience with some or all of the conflict prevention tools, the involvement in internal conflicts is relatively new. This accounts for part of the relatively low success scores.

UN:
The UN has almost 50 years of experience. During the 40 years of the Cold-War, conflict prevention was difficult and, only in some cases, possible. In the new international climate, where cooperation is possible, almost world-wide, recent experience shows an increasing demand and confidence in UN activities for conflict prevention and crisis management.

CSCE:
Experience with emergency meetings (since 1991) is positive; other instruments as agreed in the Helsinki decisions (1992) are too new to evaluate.

NATO:
Persian Gulf provided a recent example of how NATO can indirectly support a crisis management operation sponsored by another international organisation. Current Alliance support of UNPROFOR in Yugoslavia is also providing experience in this type of support. More broadly, the contributions of the Alliance to stability and security in Europe and to East–West relations in general, during the difficult period of the Cold War, suggest four decades of successful conflict prevention and crisis management experience.

European Community:
Experience with declaratory prevention, peacebuilding and non-

military measures since the 1970s. Limited experience with peacekeeping and peacemaking since recently.

WEU
Peaceful settlement of disputes by conciliation: European status and referendum on self-determination for the Saar territory. Military involvement in peacekeeping or peace-enforcement: some experience with naval operations during Gulf Wars and the Yugoslav conflict.

Table 7.5: Experience

EVALUATION (*see Table 7.6*)

The minimalist, dilatory and not always coherent handling of internal conflicts by the international community clearly indicates that we still have a long way to go before being able to prevent destructive conflict escalation successfully.

UN:
The UN's collective efforts world-wide towards peace and security during and after the Cold War suggest successful conflict management and, sometimes and more recently, conflict prevention.

CSCE:
CSCE is a framework for cooperative rather than 'collective' security; its institutions are instruments rather than actors in international relations; the CSCE cannot act by itself but requires initiatives by States; it remains a forum, not an international organisation.

NATO:
The use of NATO resources, assets and experience, in conflict prevention and crisis management cannot prejudice or preclude the involvement of other, non-NATO states. This means that the political dimension of Alliance activities in this area will become of paramount importance; this implies that relations with international organisations such as the UN and the CSCE will have to be developed to a high level. This process seems underway.

European Community:
Major constraints: the EC was not created for external conflict management objectives and was not given the instruments and decision-making procedures needed for efficient crisis management. The EC nevertheless took conflict management initiatives, developed

new methods and gained experience which can be useful in the future, but its impact remains limited as long as the structure constraints remain.

WEU:
WEU was created more for collective self-defence of the member states than for conflict prevention purposes. The end of the Cold War transformed it into a military instrument under political control of the future European Union which can also be used for conflict prevention and crisis management in cooperation with NATO and under the mandate of the UN or the CSCE.

Table 7.6: Evaluation

SUGGESTIONS FOR IMPROVEMENT (*See Table* 7.7)

Crucial for the improvement of the international organisation of conflict prevention is the cultivation of a strategic culture among the public opinion leaders. This implies increasing their awareness of international security interdependence and of the limits of national or even collective defence arrangements. It would also involve stimulating long-term thinking and a proactive approach to conflicts. What is also missing is determined international leadership for bringing together the necessary coalitions of countries to cope with the flood of turmoil around the world. Finally we need a better international régime for the coordination of conflict prevention efforts. This requires not only a significantly greater transfer of funds, but also a more effective cooperation between the existing international organisations.

UN:
- Early identification and management of potential conflict areas with UN ambassadors and/or political officers in UN field posts.
- Operational linkage between political and humanitarian affairs and peacekeeping operations, early warning at UN Headquarters and through a core group of concerned UN agencies and offices.
- Strengthening of the Security Council's collective leadership through efforts to include monitoring, and where necessary, applying existing instruments of disarmament, arms control and non-proliferation through use of warnings and, if necessary, followed by sanctions.

- Integration of refugee protection and voluntary repatriation into the framework of political affairs, peacekeeping and peacemaking efforts.

CSCE:
In cooperative security policy, it is the States' approach which has to be improved towards a higher degree of cooperation. If the CSCE should acquire qualities beyond cooperative security policy (e.g. collective peace-enforcement), its institutional features would have to change drastically.

NATO:
The development of political consensus, not just within the North Atlantic Council but also within the CSCE and the UN, for using NATO's resources and assets for conflict prevention and crisis management. This implies acceptance of a political role for NATO in international security issues that may be unfolding outside the national territories of the Alliance member States.

European Community:
A single decision-making centre through the disappearance of the EC–EPC/CFSP division. Use of majority voting (and opting-out possibility). Provide military instruments through detailed procedures with national States and WEU to use military forces. Development of a common analysis of potential crises and of actions required.

WEU:
Pursue the self-defence purpose of the WEU by including a commitment to mutual assistance in the next Treaty on European Union. Associate the non-WEU European countries to its operational shaping. Peacekeeping or peace-enforcement should be carried out with a UN or CSCE mandate.

Table 7.7: Suggestions for improvement

CONCEPTUAL PROBLEMS

The Cold War was conceptually easy.[14] The new international environment is confronting the security community with a set of very complex problems. To cope with them more effectively, serious efforts will have to be made to increase our understanding of conflict-dynamics. The current tools for diagnosis and prognosis are not up to the task. The development of an international research network of conflict analysts should therefore be a major priority.

Better cooperation between the national intelligence services and the building of a conflict data bank for practitioners is also important. Most document centres on data banks provide analysts and information about national and international politics in general; some are specialised in collecting information about conflicts; a few process conflict data; but there are no data banks with up to date, reliable and processed information ready for diagnosis and prognosis. Finally, efforts should be made to develop new effective conflict prevention strategies and to train governmental and non-governmental conflict managers in using new conflict management techniques: for example as developed by R Fisher, J Burton, E Azar and H Kelman. International law also needs to be adapted to the new international realities. Concepts such as internal and external conflicts are too simple to grasp the complex reality; definitions of peoples (nations) and minorities are too vague to be useful; the predominance of traditional principles such as national sovereignty, non-intervention or inviolability of borders is being challenged by human and minority rights, the greater acceptance of humanitarian intervention and the principle of self-determination of peoples. Yugoslavia has demonstrated that all the sacred cows of international conduct were slaughtered on the altar of *Realpolitik*: self-determination, inviolability of frontiers, and non-use of force. None of those principles was upheld with great consistency by the international community, nor was there any systematic attempt to reconcile them with each other, a role which the CSCE could have undertaken as Europe's standard-setting organisation.[15] Serious efforts should be undertaken to resolve the fundamental tensions between the earlier mentioned international principles. They could be classified, or guidelines should be provided, at least, on how to reconcile them with each other. This would reduce the chances of destructive improvisation that so characterised the international community's involvement in the Yugoslav crisis.

NOTES

1. Robert Jervis, The Future of World Politics: Will It Resemble the Past? *International Security*, Winter 1991/92, Vol. 16, No. 3.
2. Jervis, *op. cit.*, p. 41.
3. *Ibid.*, p. 42.

4. *Ibid.*, pp. 45–6.
5. J Kirkpatrick, Dictatorships and Double Standards, *Commentary*, November 1979, pp. 34–6.
6. S Huntington, Will More Countries Become Democratic? *Political Science Quarterly*, Summer 1984, pp. 193–218.
7. Di Palma, Legitimation From the Top to Civil Society: Politico–Cultural Change in Eastern Europe, *World Politics*, October 1991, pp. 49–80.
8. Luc Reychler, The Power of Public Opinion, *Veiligheid en Strategie*, Nr 16, May 1991.
9. Jeffrey Goldfarb, *Beyond Glasnost: The Post Totalitarian Mind*, (University of Chicago Press, 1989).
10. Timur Kuran.
11. The data in the comparative tables are provided by the authors.
12. Term coined by R Moreels.
13. Term coined by W Bauwens.
14. Quote Jamie Shea.
15. John Zametica, The Yugoslav Conflict, *Adelphi Paper* Nr. 270 Summer 1992 (IISS/Brassey's (UK)).